Learn Microsoft® Visual Basic® Scripting Edition Now

Gary Cornell

Learn Microsoft Visual Basic Scripting Edition Now

Published by **Microsoft Press**
A Division of Microsoft Corporation
One Microsoft Way
Redmond, Washington 98052-6399

Library of Congress Cataloging-in-Publication Data
Cornell, Gary.
    Learn Microsoft Visual Basic Scripting Edition Now : teach
  yourself Microsoft Visual Basic scripting edition the quick and easy
  way / Gary Cornell.
      p.   cm.
  Includes index.
  ISBN 1-57231-347-1
  1. Microsoft Visual BASIC.   2. BASIC (Computer program language)
I. Title.
QA76.76.B3C67 1998
005.2'76 2--dc21   97-43136
                                                   CIP

Printed and bound in the United States of America.

1 2 3 4 5 6 7 8 9 WCWC 3 2 1 0 9 8

Distributed to the book trade in Canada by Macmillan of Canada, a division of Canada Publishing Corporation.

A CIP catalogue record for this book is available from the British Library.

Microsoft Press books are available through booksellers and distributors worldwide. For further information about international editions, contact your local Microsoft Corporation office. Or contact Microsoft Press International directly at fax (425) 936-7329. Visit our Web site at mspress.microsoft.com.

Acquisitions Editor: **David Clark**
Project Editor: **Patricia N. Wagner**
Technical Editor: **Linda Rose Ebenstein**

For my nieces

CONTENTS *at a Glance*

TABLE OF CONTENTS

Acknowledgments

One of the best parts of writing a book is when the author gets to thank the people who helped him or her, for rarely (and certainly not in this case) is a book produced by the author or authors alone. First and foremost, I have to thank these people at Microsoft Press: David Clark, Patricia Wagner, and Linda Rose Ebenstein. They went far beyond what an author can expect— or even hope for—in handling acquisitions, development, and technical editing for this book. Although, like many authors, I know many words, none truly suffice in expressing my thanks to these three people.

Next, Andrew Clinick and Cathy Banks (product managers for VBScript and Script Debugger, respectively) were always there to cheerfully lift my veil of ignorance by patiently answering questions. Kurt Meyer proved invaluable at helping me with the difficult issues involved with working with beta software. The rest of the production team at Microsoft Press, notably Teri Kieffer in Proof and Paul Vautier in Composition, did a fabulous job of producing a beautiful-looking book under immense time pressure.

Finally, I want to thank my friends and family who put up with my strange ways and occasional impatience: no visits and a short temper were all they got for so many, many months.

Introduction

This book is for people who want to make Web pages come alive using Microsoft Visual Basic Scripting Edition or simply learn VBScript for use in more general Microsoft Windows programming. (Visual Basic Scripting Edition is certainly a mouthful; from now on, I'll just call it VBScript—that's how most people refer to it anyway!) However, this book isn't for experts. I am not assuming you have *ever programmed before.* Moreover, I won't expect that you have done much with fancy interactive Web pages either.

However, I do expect you to know a bit about the Internet. I will be assuming you have spent some time cruising the Web and know that an ISP (Internet Service Provider) supplies you with the software to connect to the Web via your phone line and that a Web browser application, such as Microsoft Internet Explorer, allows you to read documents on line.

I also assume that you know a little about creating Web pages. On the other hand, don't worry if you have never worked with "raw" HTML (Hypertext Markup Language) but have instead used tools like Microsoft FrontPage to build your Web pages. Chapters 2 and 3 explain how to create Web pages as well as discuss how to use HTML to do what FrontPage does automatically.

It's not that tools such as FrontPage (or even its sibling, Microsoft Front-Page Express) aren't great—I use my copy of FrontPage all the time for VBScript programming. It's just that even a powerful tool like FrontPage can't do everything for a VBScript programmer. As you will soon see, someone who programs in VBScript often needs to work directly with the underlying HTML tags. For example, that is the only way to create custom Web pages with VBScript.

You can't go to the store and buy a copy of VBScript; it's not a shrink-wrapped product like Microsoft Office 97 or Visual Basic. As I write this, VBScript usually runs inside a version of Internet Explorer, and so comes with any version of Internet Explorer after version 3. The companion CD for this book contains Internet Explorer 4 and therefore an up-to-date version of VBScript. It's not essential to purchase tools like FrontPage because everything you need to work with VBScript for Internet Explorer is on the companion CD.

Organization of This Book

This book is divided into three parts: *Part I: The Basics, Part II: Beyond the Basics,* and *Part III: Advanced Topics.*

Chapter 1, *A Little History,* is an introduction to VBScript.

Chapter 2, *HTML and VBScript,* gives you a quick survey of what you need to know about HTML tags in order to be a successful VBScript programmer. I show you how to write basic scripts and how to work with ActiveX controls.

Chapters 3 through 6, *Fundamentals of VBScript Programming, Controlling Program Flow, Functions and Arrays,* and *Writing Your Own Procedures,* discuss the ins and outs of VBScript the *language.* I not only explain the commands but also teach you how to program. And make no mistake about it—learning VBScript is an excellent way to start programming.

No serious program gets written without some errors, so Chapter 7, *Testing, Debugging, and Error Trapping,* explains the basics of debugging your scripts. I introduce you to Microsoft Script Debugger, which, for the first time, gives VBScript programmers debugging tools like those provided by the full version of Visual Basic.

Chapters 8 and 9, *The Internet Explorer Object Model* and *Dynamic HTML,* introduce you to the exciting new world of Dynamic HTML including the latest technology (only a couple of months old as I write this) called *Scriptlets.* These two chapters should serve as a firm foundation for working through books dedicated to Dynamic HTML. You'll see everything from validating user input to controlling the internal workings of Internet Explorer.

The Companion CD

The companion CD includes the following items:

- An online version of the book
- Sample files for the book
- Microsoft Internet Explorer version 4
- Microsoft ActiveX Control Pad
- Microsoft Script Debugger
- VBScript documentation
- Microsoft Visual Basic Control Creation Edition
- Microsoft Internet Client SDK

Instructions for installing these components are included in the Readme.txt file in the root directory of the companion CD.

Support

Every effort has been made to ensure the accuracy of this book and the contents of the companion CD. Microsoft Press provides corrections for books through the World Wide Web at:

http://mspress.microsoft.com/mspress/support/

If you have comments, questions, or ideas regarding this book or the companion CD, please send them to Microsoft Press via e-mail to:

MSPINPUT@MICROSOFT.COM

or via postal mail to:

Microsoft Press
Attn: Learn Microsoft Visual Basic Scripting Edition Now Editor
One Microsoft Way
Redmond, WA 98052-6399

Please note that product support is not offered through these addresses. For support information regarding Internet Explorer, you can connect to Microsoft Technical Support on the Web at:

http://www.microsoft.com/support/

In the United States, you can also call Internet Explorer technical support at 425-635-7123 weekdays between 6 a.m. and 6 p.m. Pacific time. Outside the United States, please contact your local Microsoft subsidiary for support information. Microsoft also provides information about Internet Explorer at:

http://www.microsoft.com/ie

The Basics

A Little History

If you're reading this book, you're probably working on one of these:

- Your own personal Web page
- A page of your company's external Web site
- A page on an intranet
- A page that you are building for a third party

No matter which of these situations you find yourself in, VBScript is the easiest way to *activate* that Web page. But what does activate really mean? To answer this question, first I need to tell you a little history about the way things used to be.

The Way We Were

The World Wide Web was originally developed by scientists for their own use—the general public was not invited. I won't go so far as to say the Web was boring in those days, but it certainly couldn't be used for commerce or for anything fun. Web pages were downloaded from very big, very expensive computers (*servers*) to the scientists' personal desktop computers (*client machines*).

For the first few years of its existence, the World Wide Web was simply a way to use *hypertext,* as shown in Figure 1-1.

 NOTE Hypertext refers to the type of point-and-click system used in Microsoft Windows Help files. When you click a *hyperlink*, you are taken to the correct Help page. As you know from cruising the Web, you do the same thing: you click a hyperlink and your browser takes you to a new Web page.

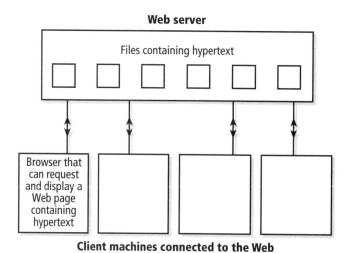

Figure 1-1. *How hypertext works on the World Wide Web.*

In those days, there were no images either—*everything* was text together with hyperlinks. There were other significant differences, too. Early Web pages were certainly not interactive like the order-taking Web pages that are so common today. It was also impossible to do calculations, such as the ones performed by the mortgage calculators that many financial institutions have put on their Web pages. By no stretch of the imagination could the early Web have been described as "alive." Figures 1-2 and 1-3 show a simple Web page and a more complex one. Notice how Figure 1-3 also has a more sophisticated look and feel than Figure 1-2.

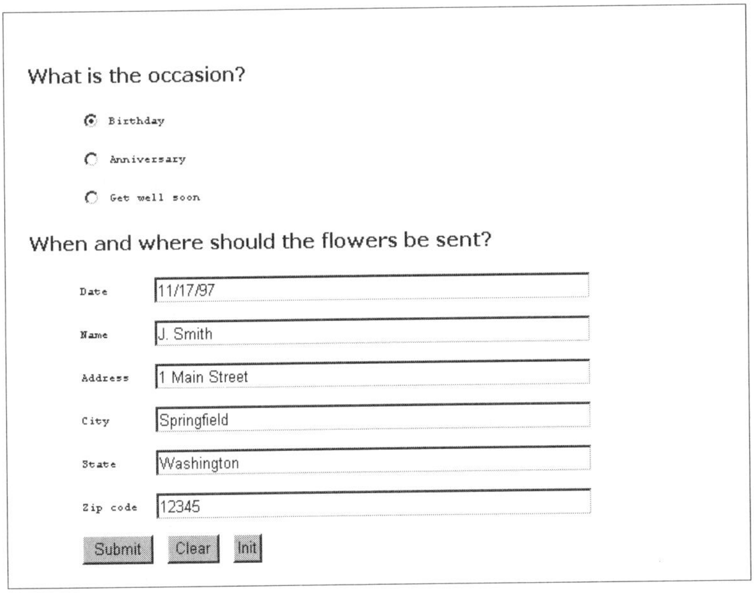

Figure 1-2.   *A simple order-taking Web page.*

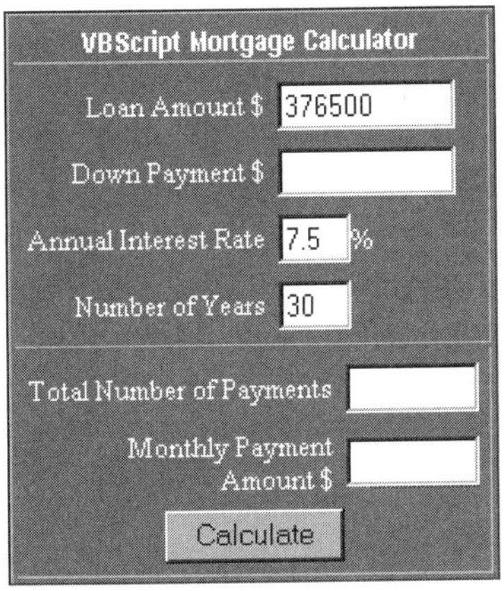

Figure 1-3.   *A mortgage calculator.*

Originally, a Web page was created by writing instructions in a special language called HTML (Hypertext Markup Language). The instructions simply told the browser where to display the text and hyperlinks on the page.

Over time, HTML was extended to allow browsers to do more. For example, you could finally see images. Also, a method was developed to have the server do calculations and other kinds of data processing. This method was called *CGI scripting.* (CGI stands for Common Gateway Interface, and CGI scripts are special kinds of programs that reside on the server, as you can see in Figure 1-4.)

CGI scripts enabled all Web browsers to send information to the server for eventual processing. The results that the server generated were then sent back to the client machine. This was often in the form of new Web pages that were generated "on the fly." Clicking a hyperlink, for example, might have caused a new Web page to be created and then displayed. Interactivity on the Web was finally possible.

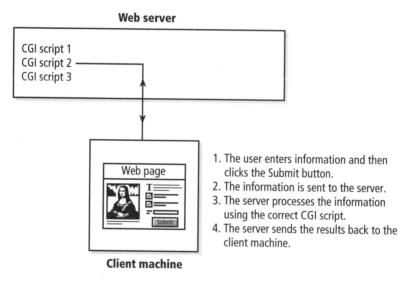

Figure 1-4.   *CGI scripting at work.*

However, there are drawbacks to using CGI scripts to provide interactive Web pages. The most important one is that CGI isn't easy to set up. Originally, CGI required a lot of expensive technical help to install the necessary programs on the server. Even though it has become a little simpler, CGI installation is still time-consuming and work-intensive.

Another drawback is that CGI scripts are stored on the server. There are two problems associated with this. First, the server hosting the Web page has to do a lot of work. (Imagine how many people were trying to go to pages with interactive tax forms on April 14th!) Since computers are getting more powerful, it seems natural to reduce your waiting time by moving as much of the work as possible from the server to the client machine. After all, although your computer might not be as powerful as the one being used as a Web server, you probably have 100 percent of its attention. A Web server might be trying to perform hundreds, if not thousands, of tasks simultaneously.

Second, CGI scripts can be a security risk. For this reason, many Webmasters prohibit anyone other than themselves, or someone they authorize, from placing CGI scripts on the server.

Using CGI scripts for interactive Web pages leads us to examine the following issues:

- How can you transfer work to the client machine?

- How can you eliminate the security risks associated with CGI scripts?

Let's start with the first issue. Initially, the solution to moving work to the client machine was to extend the browser. For example, if a browser had the ability to play audio files, then when someone downloaded a Web page containing a sound, the part of the browser that knew how to play sound took over and played it for the user.

This kind of solution is still useful in specialized situations, but imagine you are trying to create a Web page that takes an order. (Figure 1-2 shows such a page.) You could use CGI scripting for this, but here's what would happen:

1. You send the order information to the server by clicking the Submit button.

2. The CGI script takes over. (The server might be busy, so be prepared to wait.)

3. The CGI script totals your order.

4. A new Web page is created that contains the same order information you sent plus the total cost of your purchases.

5. The CGI script sends the new Web page back to you.

Rather a lot of work to total a few numbers (which your computer can do instantly), isn't it? If you're not convinced, read on. Suppose you forget to fill in one of the lines. You'd have to wait for the round trip to the server only to find that the server has sent back a message saying, "Sorry, try again—please fill in your zip code." Wouldn't it be better if you could check that all the lines were filled in correctly *before* you spent the time sending the information over the net?

At this point, you might be wondering why you can't do this with some sort of browser extension like the one that played audio files. Keep in mind, however, that an extension would have to work for each and every order form you might encounter. Because order forms are not all the same, this situation is nothing like the one for playing sound in which there are only a few common formats for audio files. But you're correct in thinking that the answer lies somewhere in the browser.

The Way We Are Now

The obvious solution is to have the browser do calculations *based on information already on the Web page.* (Remember, both the browser and the Web page are on the client machine.) You can do this by embedding within the Web page a *script* that instructs the browser how to do the necessary work. For example, the browser could total an order, warn the user that 50 dozen roses were ordered, and ask the user if this was a mistake. The idea is that the order will be sent to the order processing server only after a check has been done on what the user entered. To make this possible, the browser needs a means to interpret the directions given in the script.

By building a VBScript interpreter into Internet Explorer version 4, Microsoft has accomplished just that. The directions in the script are added to the HTML instructions for the page. Just as any browser can interpret HTML to make a page look right, a browser such as Internet Explorer can also interpret scripts. The scripts can contain commands like *add this, multiply that, is this a number?* and so on. By enabling the browser to understand simple directions, there's no longer a need to have special-purpose CGI scripts for all the different tasks that need to be done.

The first way to have the client machine do some of the work came in early 1996 with the introduction of the Java programming language. Companies like Microsoft quickly added Java interpreters to their browsers. These interpreters could understand the *code* that Java created.

 OTE   Unlike Java, VBScript is embedded in a human-readable form on your Web page.

Let's be up front about it—Java can do all that VBScript can do and far more. So why use VBScript instead of Java? Because using Java for simple tasks is like swatting flies with a sledge hammer.

Here's why:

- Java is not an easy language to use. Even displaying a short message like *Hello World* on the screen requires 10 or 20 lines of code (versus one line in VBScript). Using Java for simple tasks such as order taking or calculating loan payments would be too much work.

- To use Java effectively, you need to be familiar with high-powered programming language concepts like object-oriented programming.

I think the majority of programmers would agree that Java is difficult for most people to learn. Most comprehensive treatments of Java start by assuming you are an experienced programmer and then spend hundreds of pages teaching you the ins and outs of the Java language. Many colleges are now devoting a significant part of the first year of their computer science sequence to teaching Java.

 OTE   On a personal note, I like Java a lot; I even helped write a book about it. But that book, which covers only the core features of Java, started at about 700 pages in its first edition and is now more than 1000 pages in its third. For me, even though I know it pretty well, Java is too much of a good thing for most of what I need to do on a Web page.

Visual Basic and the Component Approach to Programming

Microsoft Visual Basic is, by most accounts, the most popular programming language in the world today—estimates are that more than 3 million people use it. There are many reasons for Visual Basic's success, but the most important is that Visual Basic changed how we program. *Visual Basic allowed the component approach to programming to take off.*

The idea behind the component approach to programming is simple—it's no more than the programming equivalent of "why bother reinventing the wheel?" For example, how many applications accept your name and address in a little form like the one shown in Figure 1-5?

First Name:	MI:	Last Name:
Street Address:		
City:	ST:	Zip Code:
	Finished	

Figure 1-5. *A form for accepting a name and address.*

In this example, we want the user to enter exactly five digits in the Zip Code box. Can you imagine how many hundreds of people have created the same form for accepting a name and address? Or how many people have written a program to check that the user enters five digits for the zip code? Wouldn't it be great if someone could program all this once and for all and then you could reuse it effortlessly?

Visual Basic uses the term control *rather than* component.

That is the magic of Visual Basic—it is easy to reuse a component that another person has built. Visual Basic's success is based on people coming up with lots of ideas for great reusable components that can be used easily and efficiently. In fact, many people have become rich by writing really nifty reusable components—after all, they needed to sell them to only a fraction of the millions of Visual Basic programmers out there.

The current versions of these reusable components are called *ActiveX controls.*

How Is VBScript Related to Visual Basic?

VBScript is essentially a subset of the Visual Basic programming language. The result of this slimming down process is a very small language that is easy to use. Appendix A shows the differences between VBScript and Visual Basic.

 OTE Because VBScript is a subset of Visual Basic, correct VBScript code will almost always be correct Visual Basic code but not vice versa. VBScript does have a few unique features—for example, those that make working with text easier—that are not yet part of Visual Basic.

I can't stress enough that while it is true that Microsoft slimmed Visual Basic to its essentials to make VBScript, *the essentials are there.* As you read further, you will see that you can use VBScript to do any calculations you would ever need on a Web page. You can analyze what the user enters, total a group of numbers, make Web pages on the fly, and much, much more.

 OTE VBScript is a great first programming language. After you master VBScript, it is easy to move on to mastering Visual Basic. You should also be able to customize the products in Office 97, and to automate any tasks you do repetitively in those products, by using their versions of Visual Basic. (These versions are part of the Visual Basic for Applications, or VBA, family. They are named VBA for Word, VBA for Excel, and so on.) It is a little harder to make the transition from VBScript to Java, but this will also be well within your reach after you finish this book.

ActiveX Controls and VBScript

A key point about VBScript is that it is easy to use ActiveX controls to do many of the tasks you want. There is now a seemingly inexhaustible supply of reusable ActiveX controls that you can use in VBScript (and in Visual Basic). Microsoft estimates there are more than 4000 commercial controls, and there are probably tens of thousands of free and shareware controls. (A free control is exactly that—free. A shareware control relies on the honor system; if you like it, you are asked to send a payment to its creator.) This means if you need a particular functionality on your Web page, just look around for the control that does it. To start you off, the companion CD has

ActiveX controls, including ones for playing videos, making marquee banners on your Web page, doing financial calculations, and a whole lot more. The companion CD also includes a free version of Visual Basic version 5 called the "Visual Basic Control Creation Edition" that you can use to make your own ActiveX controls.

 OTE Interested in the most up-to-date list of the many commercial ActiveX controls? The best one I know is found by pointing your browser to http://204.203.124.10//activexisv/direct.htm

Using Objects with VBScript

In addition to ActiveX controls, VBScript allows you to use other objects that people have already created. For example, if someone writes a Java program that does something you want, you can use it with your VBScript program. You can even think of Microsoft Internet Explorer as the ultimate object for the Web. You can create a script that tells Internet Explorer to go to a new Web page or a script that tells Internet Explorer to visit all the hyperlinks on the current Web page, one by one. You can make Internet Explorer display a new Web page that you compose using VBScript, and much, much more.

Security

VBScript itself is secure. Microsoft removed all the features of the Visual Basic language that were risky, such as the ability to wipe out your hard disk. If you are only using VBScript to do order validation or calculations, you don't have to worry about security; VBScript alone can never harm the machine on which it is run. But what about the combination of VBScript with ActiveX controls? Here you have to be careful.

As I discussed earlier in this chapter, ActiveX controls bring both ease of use and power to a Web page. However, once you add an ActiveX control to your Web page, the security of using VBScript alone is gone. You shouldn't be surprised—power is always associated with risks. You need to keep in mind that ActiveX controls can do anything that ordinary programs can do. This is why these controls are so powerful and so useful. But this also means that a malicious ActiveX control could take over your hard disk and wipe it out.

Does this scare you? Good, I want you to be scared—scared enough to practice *safe computing*. What does safe computing mean? It means that you use ActiveX controls only from sources you trust. (I hope you are not using programs that come from untrusted sources either. Virus checkers are very, very good, but they are not perfect.)

How can you know where an ActiveX control comes from? The idea is that designers of ActiveX controls can embed a *signing certificate* into a control that tells you who they are. This is based on a technology called *Authenticode* that is built into Internet Explorer. The default setting allows you to download an ActiveX control only if it contains a signing certificate. The first time you try to download a new ActiveX control, you'll see a dialog box like the one shown in Figure 1-6.

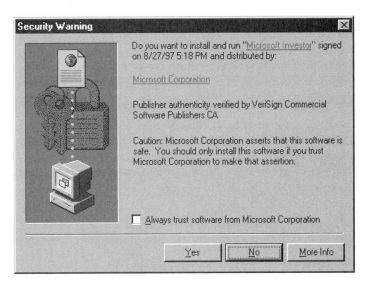

Figure 1-6.   *A signing certificate.*

The signing certificate is embedded in the ActiveX control and cannot be forged without breaking a security system—the same kind of security system used by banks to transmit money or by governments to keep their most confidential transmissions secret. Various companies such as VeriSign (www.verisign.com) issue certificates. If an Authenticode certificate says that a piece of software comes from a specific company, you can rely on this. Usually, absolute statements are false or dangerous, but everybody in the computer industry today is sure about this one: *nobody can forge an Authenticode certificate.*

However, Authenticode doesn't guarantee that the ActiveX control has no bugs in its code. These bugs could very well cause you some problems down the road. Authenticode guarantees only where the code came from.

That an ActiveX control might have bugs should come as no surprise—all powerful programs have bugs. The more powerful an ActiveX control is, the more likely it is to have bugs. That's the nature of the beast. Reputable vendors don't ship programs that have dangerous bugs, however, and Authenticode guarantees that you know where a control came from.

Alternatives to Authenticode certificates

A Java applet is the technical name for a Java program that a Web browser can understand.

Are there alternatives to Authenticode certificates? Yes. Java applets use something called the *sandbox model.* Like a child playing in a sandbox, a Java applet is restricted in what it can do. A Java applet downloaded from the net can't affect files on your machine, for example. The trouble is that most of the time the sandbox model is too limited in what it allows applets to do. A sandbox model for security is particularly silly on a corporate intranet, which, after all, might not be connected to any other computers. In this case, all information comes from a trusted source. For example, suppose your company consolidates its financial projections via a browser page. You want to use this information in your own files. You need the ability to save this information in a local file.

 OTE For situations in which the sandbox model is appropriate, you can use VBScript to control prewritten Java applets.

More on Internet Explorer Security

Internet Explorer security is controlled from the Security tab in the Internet Options dialog box, which is shown in Figure 1-7. (Select Internet Options from the View menu.)

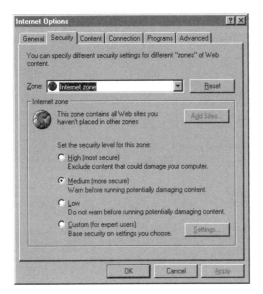

Figure 1-7. *The Security tab.*

As you can see, Internet Explorer uses *zones* to describe its security model. Each zone can be assigned a different security level—depending on the actions you want authorized. Within each zone, you can choose from three preset levels of security and one customized level. The preset levels of security are as follows:

- The *High* security level prohibits Internet Explorer from downloading any ActiveX controls.

- The *Medium* security level prohibits Internet Explorer from downloading any ActiveX control without a signing certificate. For a control with a signing certificate, the certificate is displayed so that you can make an informed decision about whether or not to download the control. (This is the level I use, and it is the default level for the Internet. It is the one I recommend for most people, although your company might, for perfectly good reasons, choose the High setting.)

- The *Low* security level allows any ActiveX control with a signing certificate to be downloaded. Although certificates are not easy to obtain, it is certainly possible for a malicious hacker to get one. I strongly recommend against choosing this level for the "Internet Zone."

■ The *Custom* security level is designed for expert users. Choosing this level and then clicking the Settings button displays the dialog box shown in Figure 1-8. This lets you control all aspects of security. For example, if you scroll through the dialog box, you will see that you can even control what kind of scripting is allowed. (See Figure 1-9.) Active Scripting is the jargon for allowing scripts to run on your machine and it is the default.

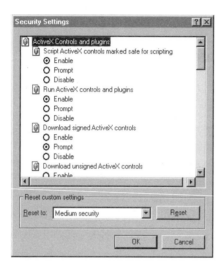

Figure 1-8. *The dialog box in which you can customize security settings.*

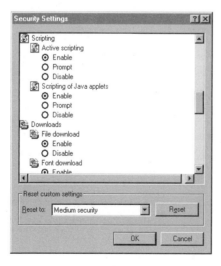

Figure 1-9. *The Scripting section of the Security Settings dialog box.*

Zones

As you can see in Figure 1-10, there are four zones of Web content:

- Local intranet zone

- Trusted sites zone

- Internet zone

- Restricted sites zone

Each zone can have a separate level of security.

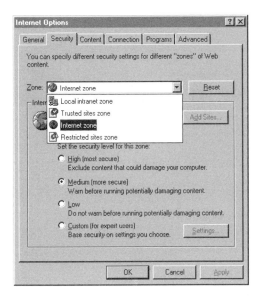

Figure 1-10.   *The zones in Internet Explorer.*

The default security level is High for restricted sites, Medium for the Internet and local intranets, and Low for trusted sites. If you want to add a trusted site (such as the part of your company's Web site that only employees have access to), do the following:

1. Select Trusted Sites Zone from the drop-down list shown in Figure 1-10.

2. Click the Add Sites button to display the dialog box shown in Figure 1-11 on the following page. You can add any sites you want from this dialog box.

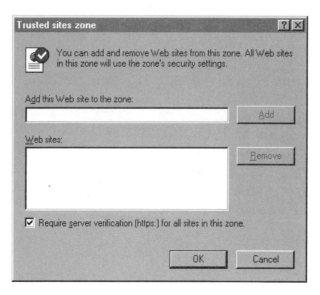

Figure 1-11.   *The dialog box for adding a trusted site.*

HTML and VBScript

As I explained in Chapter 1, a Web page is created by writing instructions in a language called HTML (Hypertext Markup Language). Originally, a markup language was a way to give a typesetting program directions for printing a page. What HTML does is give the browser directions on how to *display* a page.

In a book about VBScript, it might seem strange to devote most of a chapter to HTML. After all, for most people, knowing HTML is becoming less and less important. This is because great inexpensive Web page creation tools like Microsoft FrontPage 98 and good *free* tools like Microsoft FrontPage Express (which comes with Microsoft Internet Explorer version 4) are easily available.

Tools such as these are simple to use, and they create the HTML instructions for you. So why am I explaining (or reviewing) HTML? The reason is that VBScript lives on a Web page, and you can't write a script unless you understand how your script instructions will work with the HTML instruction for that page. Also, you need to understand the structure of a Web page and how HTML works if you want to use VBScript to create Web pages on the fly. This ability, which is one of the most important features that VBScript offers, *requires* you to be able to write HTML instructions.

Basics of HTML

Figure 2-1 shows part of the set of HTML instructions for Microsoft's VBScript home page (www.microsoft.com/vbscript)—a good page to visit periodically! You can display the instructions for any Web page by going to that page and choosing Source from Internet Explorer's View menu. (*Source* is the term for a set of instructions written in any computer language, such as HTML. Source is also referred to as *source code* or just plain *code*.)

 IP Looking at the source code for your favorite Web pages is a great way to get ideas on how to write the code for your own Web pages.

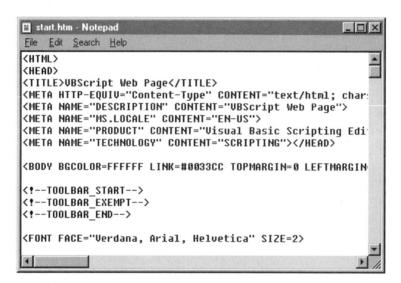

Figure 2-1. *The HTML source for www.microsoft.com/vbscript.*

As you can see above, the HTML source is in an ordinary, if complicated-looking, text file. After all, Figure 2-1 is showing you the HTML source in Notepad—a text file editor! (Compare this to the garbage you would see if you tried to open a Microsoft Word file in Notepad.) An obvious difference between an HTML file and an ordinary text file is in the file-naming convention. The standard extension for a text file is .txt; for an HTML file it is .htm (or sometimes .html).

The important thing to notice in Figure 2-1 is that it includes items surrounded by directions, which are contained in angle brackets (<>). For example, the following line tells Internet Explorer what the title of the Web page should be:

```
<TITLE>VBScript Web Page</TITLE>
```

The directions with their angle brackets are called *HTML tags*. HTML tags usually give directions to the browser. They usually tell it what to do with the information between the tags. In addition to displaying the title, you can give other directions about how to display the text between the tags. For example, the following line tells the browser to display in boldface the text that is surrounded by the pair of tags:

```
<B>This will appear in boldface</B>
```

As the two above examples show, the closing tag usually uses a slash (/) to indicate to the browser to stop doing whatever it was that the previous tag told it to start. The general framework for a pair of HTML tags is this:

```
<WHAT TO DO>What to do it to</WHAT TO DO>
```

The convention is that tags are uppercase, although case doesn't matter to the browser.

The only exceptions to this framework are the tags that don't work on any text. For example, the <BR> tag inserts a carriage return. It wouldn't make any sense to have a </BR> tag!

The Structure of the HTML Source for a Web Page

Figure 2-2 on the following page shows the framework for any HTML source. You put the various HTML tags, with their associated text, inside this framework.

```
<HTML>
<HEAD>


</HEAD>
<BODY>


</BODY>
</HTML>
```

Figure 2-2.   *The framework for any HTML source.*

As you might expect, the pair of <HTML></HTML> tags enclose all the instructions for the actual Web page. Everything you want to be displayed or processed by the browser must be placed between these two tags. The HTML source is usually divided into two parts. The first part is called the head section, and the other is called the body. The head section starts after the <HEAD> tag; this is where you place information about the Web page that you don't want the browser to display. It is also where you put the tags needed to give your Web page a title.

For VBScript programmers, however, the head section is also where most of the VBScript code is placed; it is unusual to place a script in the body.

Traditionally, the body is where all the important stuff is found. It is still the place where you put the HTML tags that describe the page. For example, Figure 2-3 shows just about the simplest Web page you can build. Here's the HTML source:

```
<HTML>

  <HEAD>
    <TITLE>Just about the simplest Web page</TITLE>
  </HEAD>
```

```
<BODY>
  <B>Hello World</B>
</BODY>

</HTML>
```

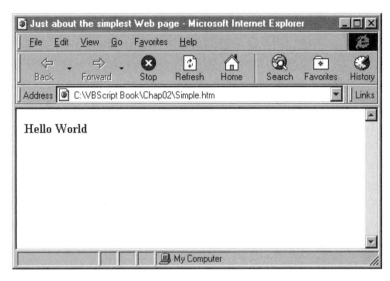

Figure 2-3. *Just about the simplest Web page.*

I actually created this Web page the old-fashioned way by doing the following:

1. Opening Notepad (by clicking the Start button, selecting Programs, selecting Accessories, and then selecting Notepad)

2. Typing the HTML source

3. Saving the source to a file named Simple.htm

4. Selecting Open from Internet Explorer's File menu, and browsing for the file

 OTE Using FrontPage 98 or FrontPage Express is sometimes overkill. Anyway, most VBScript programmers get very comfortable with Notepad since that is what selecting Source from Internet Explorer's View menu brings up.

White space consists of spaces, carriage returns, and tabs—everything that creates white areas on a printed page.

One of the most confusing things about writing HTML source code is that white space almost never matters. For example, I inserted blank lines around the head section and body. This was to clearly indicate the different parts of the HTML source. In fact, white space generally doesn't affect what your Web page looks like. That's why you need to use a tag like <BR> to indicate a carriage return. This can be startling the first time you see it. A browser displays the following two lines of source code in exactly the same way:

```
<B>Hello World</B>

<B>Hello                    World</B>
```

This might seem strange, but browsers do this for a very good reason. Only the browser knows the resolution of the machine displaying the page, and only the browser knows the size of the page's window. By letting the browser do the formatting and space the text, you get the best possible look on your Web pages.

The Basic HTML Tags

This section discusses the simplest HTML tags. I'll leave the more sophisticated tags, such as the ones needed for making tables, until later in this book. I just want to give you enough tags so you can start programming.

Before I do that, I need to explain what *attributes* are. An attribute sits inside a tag to give the tag directions. For example, the <BODY> tag can take an attribute named BACKGROUND. This is how you set the "wallpaper" for your Web page. For example:

```
<HTML>

  <HEAD>
    <TITLE>Adding a background</TITLE>
  </HEAD>

  <BODY BACKGROUND="Somegif.gif">
    <B>Hello World</B>
  </BODY>

</HTML>
```

URL is the technical term for the address you type into a browser.

This would tile your Web page with the image stored in the file named Somegif.gif. Generally, you can use the URL (uniform resource locator) of the file as shown in the following example:

```
<BODY BACKGROUND="www.MyCompany.com/logo/CompanyLogo.gif>
```

Now I'll provide short descriptions of the basic tags.

Paragraph and text tags

I already said that a browser ignores white space such as carriage returns, so how do you tell it to break up your text? I've talked about using the <BR> tag to add a carriage return. While the <BR> tag certainly has its uses, a better way to tell the browser that you are starting a new paragraph is to surround each paragraph with a pair of <P></P> tags, as shown in the following example. To spice it up, I also use the two most common *text attribute tags*. In addition to the pair of <B></B> tags for bold, I throw in the pair of <I></I> tags, which indicate italics:

```
<HTML>

  <HEAD>
    <TITLE>Showing off the paragraph tags</TITLE>
  </HEAD>

  <BODY>

    <P>

      Hello. This is the first paragraph. Notice
      that I use carriage returns inside the tags
      because this information won't fit on one line.

    </P>

    <P>

      Hello. This is the second paragraph. Notice that
      I used carriage returns to separate the paragraphs.
      <B>This is for my convenience; the browser doesn't
      care.</B> Notice that the previous text was in bold
      and that the following text has a word in italics.
      This shows that you can <I>nest</I> tags.

    </P>

  </BODY>

</HTML>
```

Figure 2-4 on the following page shows you the Web page created by this HTML source.

OTE To *nest* tags is to embed one set of tags within another. But keep in mind that nesting works like the dolls that have one within another—you must insert the ending tags in the reverse order from the starting tags, like this:

    <P><B>Test</B></P>

Lines like this give erratic results at best:

    <P><B>Test</P></B>

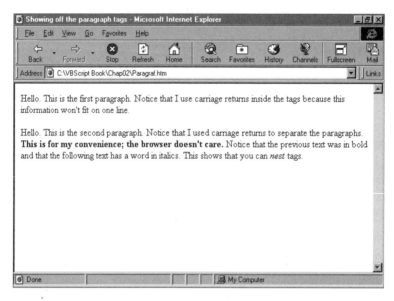

Figure 2-4.   *The effect of the <P>, <B>, and <I> tags.*

The <P> tag can have one attribute. This attribute controls how the paragraph is aligned. For example:

    <P ALIGN=CENTER>This will be centered</P>

There are three alignment attributes: CENTER, LEFT, and RIGHT. Figure 2-5 shows the effect of using these attributes. The HTML source for the page is this:

    <HTML>

      <HEAD>
        <TITLE>Showing off the paragraph alignment tags</TITLE>
      </HEAD>

```
<BODY>

  <P ALIGN=CENTER>
    This text is <B>centered.</B>
  </P>

  <BR><BR><BR>

  <P ALIGN=LEFT>
   This text is <B>left-aligned.</B>
  </P>

  <BR><BR><BR>

  <P ALIGN=RIGHT>
    This text is <B>right-aligned.</B>
  </P>

</BODY>

</HTML>
```

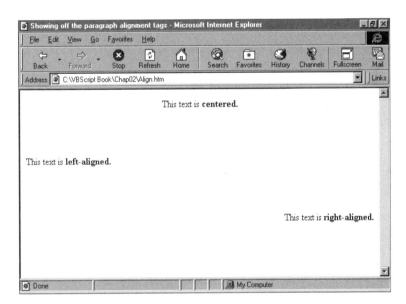

Figure 2-5. *The effect of the ALIGN attribute.*

Occasionally, you will want to format some text instead of letting the browser do it. This can be done by surrounding the text (exactly as you want it displayed) with the pair of <PRE></PRE> tags. (PRE stands for *preformatted text.*) Generally, this is not a good idea, as you have no way of knowing the resolution of a user's computer or the size of his or her browser window. However, you do have this option if you need it.

 OTE Resolution refers to the number of dots (or *pixels*) that your computer is set to display. People speak of 640x480 resolution, for example, and this means that the computer displays 640 dots across the screen and 480 dots down. On most PCs, resolution can be specified from 640x480 through 1280x1024. (You'll need a big monitor or exceptional eyes to see the latter comfortably.) Fifteen lines of text (in a standard font) in a maximized browser window on a machine set to 640x480 covers most of the screen; on a machine set to 1280x1024, it covers only a small portion. Therefore, if you use the <PRE> tag to display 20 lines on a user's screen, you have no way of knowing how much screen real estate you used up (or even whether all 20 lines will fit).

Heading level tags

A *heading level* is a descendent of what English teachers call an outline level. Heading levels are used to break up a document into coherent pieces and to indicate the importance of the various pieces. A level 1 head is the highest level, a level 2 head is the next highest, and so on. HTML supports up to six levels of heads. The heading level tags are simply <H1>, <H2>, <H3>, all the way up to and including <H6>. A heading level tag can use the same ALIGN attribute that the paragraph tag uses.

Figure 2-6 shows the six different heading levels produced by the following source:

```
<HTML>

  <HEAD>
    <TITLE>Showing off the heading level tags</TITLE>
  </HEAD>

  <BODY>

    <H1>
      This is a level 1 head.
    </H1>

    <H2>
      This is a level 2 head.
    </H2>
```

```
<H3>
  This is a level 3 head.
</H3>

<H4>
  This is a level 4 head.
</H4>

<H5>
  This is a level 5 head.
</H5>

<H6>
  This is a level 6 head.
</H6>

</BODY>

</HTML>
```

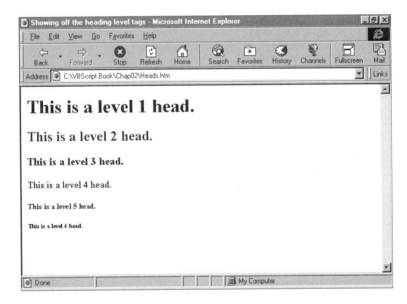

Figure 2-6. *The effect of the heading level tags.*

Links

Links are, of course, what the World Wide Web is all about. The idea of simply clicking some text and being taken to the correct place is what the term hypertext was coined to describe. (Ted Nelson originated this term in 1965. You might want to do a Web search on this fascinating man and explore his equally fascinating ideas!)

HREF stands for hypertext reference.

The tag to describe a link is called the *anchor* tag, and it is represented by <A>. The important point about an anchor tag is the HREF attribute.

For example, here are two ways to place a link to Microsoft's VBScript Web page on your site:

```
<A HREF="www.microsoft.com/vbscript">
  www.microsoft.com/vbscript
</A>

<A HREF="www.microsoft.com/vbscript">
  Click here to go to the VBScript site
</A>
```

The results are shown in Figure 2-7. Notice that the text surrounded by the pair of <A></A> tags is what is underlined in the browser. You won't see the URL for the Web page that you are linking to unless you put it in your source, as I did in the first example.

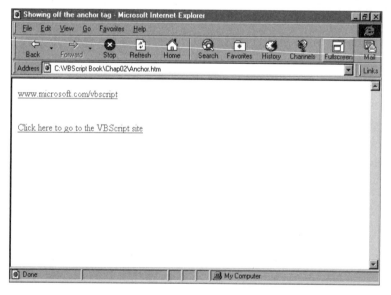

Figure 2-7. *Adding a link using the <A> tag.*

The anchor tag has one other attribute that can be very useful—NAME. The NAME attribute can be used to allow a user to move from one part of a Web page to another. For example, you have probably seen Web pages with a table of contents at the top. If you click the link called Chapter 2, it takes you to the part of the document where Chapter 2 starts. Creating this requires a two-step process. Let's assume the name of the document is InternalJumpingAround.htm.

1. Place an anchor tag at the beginning of the Chapter 2 section and name it using the NAME attribute:

```
<A NAME="Chapter 2">
  Chapter 2
</A>
```

2. Place the following version of the anchor tag at the beginning of the appropriate line of the table of contents:

```
<A HREF="InternalJumpingAround.htm#Chapter 2">
  Chapter 2
</A>
```

Be sure to place the # symbol inside the quotes and follow it by the same text that you used for the NAME attribute.

 OTE   These kinds of internal links were the most common ones in the early days of HTML; that's why the link tag is <A>. The A stands for anchor, and you used it with the NAME attribute to anchor parts of the document for future reference.

Comment tags

Normally, you use a comment tag only to document your code; the text you place inside the tag is ignored by the browser. A comment can describe what your HTML code does or it can include your name, the date, and so on. Actually, I think that *comment* is a bad name for what goes inside this tag because in HTML, as you will soon see, a script is also placed inside a comment tag! A better term would be nondisplayed text, rather than comment.

Anyway, the comment tag is a little different from other HTML tags in that you place the information you want inside a single tag. For example:

```
<!--This is a comment-->
```

A convention that many people adopt is to break up the pieces of the comment tag as follows:

```
<!--
  This is a comment
-->
```

This is closer to the <TAG></TAG> model. In any case, this style is necessary for multiple lines that you don't want displayed by the browser.

Starting to Program in VBScript

Now that you have seen the basics of HTML, it's time to start programming in VBScript. Figure 2-8 shows the framework for a page programmed in VBScript. Notice that the HTML comment tags surround the script. This is because some browsers can't understand VBScript without the comment tags. (Remember, they should really be named the nondisplayed tags; your script will not be displayed on the Web page.)

```
<HTML>

  <HEAD>

    <TITLE>Your title goes here</TITLE>

    <SCRIPT LANGUAGE="VBSCRIPT">
    <!--

      Your script goes here,
      inside the comment tag

    -->
    </SCRIPT>

  </HEAD>

  <BODY>

  </BODY>

</HTML>
```

The Framework for any HTML source that contains VBScript code.

Figure 2-8.

Our First Script

Now that we have the framework for VBScript code, let's write our first script. We'll start with the VBScript MsgBox command, which displays a message box containing whatever text you specify. The text for the message box must be surrounded by quotes, as you can see in the following script:

```
<HTML>

  <HEAD>

    <TITLE>Our first script</TITLE>

    <SCRIPT LANGUAGE="VBSCRIPT">
    <!--

      MsgBox "Hello World"

    -->
    </SCRIPT>

  </HEAD>

  <BODY>
  </BODY>

</HTML>
```

Figure 2-9 shows you what you will see. (Click OK to make the message box go away.)

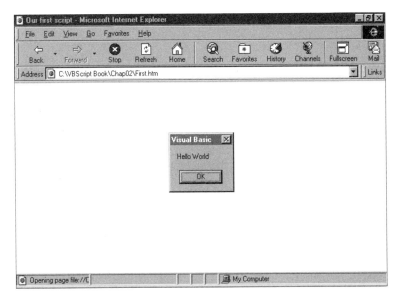

Figure 2-9.   *Creating a message box.*

Getting Information from the User

Although there are a lot of ways to get information from the user, I will cover the simplest way here. This is called an *input box*. An input box accepts information, as shown in Figure 2-10. The trick to using an input box is that you need to assign the information to a *variable*. I'll have a lot more to say about variables in the next chapter—for now, think of them as places to store information. The following script asks for a name and then stores it in a variable called YourName. After the name is entered, the script displays it in a message box.

 OTE When you use a variable with the MsgBox command, you don't use the quotes.

```
<HTML>

  <HEAD>

    <TITLE>Input box example</TITLE>

    <SCRIPT LANGUAGE="VBSCRIPT">
    <!--

      YourName = InputBox("What is your name?")
      MsgBox YourName

    -->
    </SCRIPT>

  </HEAD>

  <BODY>
  </BODY>

</HTML>
```

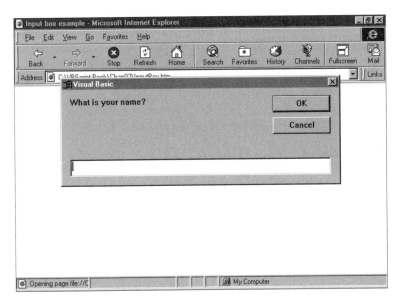

Figure 2-10. *An input box example.*

Building Web Pages on the Fly:
The Document.Write Command

In the two previous examples, our scripts displayed information in boxes. This technique is occasionally useful, but wouldn't it be more visually pleasing to display the information such that it seems to be an intrinsic part of the Web page? Instead of putting the user's name in a message box, we would display the user's name directly on the Web page—without putting any code in the body of our HTML source. Note that this is a *dynamic* process—the script will produce a unique Web page in response to the name that the user enters. (A *static* process, on the other hand, produces the same Web page every time. A script that is written to always display *Gary Cornell,* for example, is a static script.)

The key to dynamic Web page production using VBScript is the Document.Write command. For example, if VBScript processes a line of code like this:

```
Document.Write "<P>Hello World</P>"
```

it will actually display the "Hello World" text as a paragraph on the Web page. Here's the script. (Figure 2-11 on the following page gives you a sample of what it can do.) I'll explain what's happening in the key lines after you have had a chance to run it:

```
<HTML>

  <HEAD>

    <TITLE>Dynamic Web page creation example</TITLE>

    <SCRIPT LANGUAGE="VBSCRIPT">
    <!--

      YourName = InputBox("What is your name?")
      Document.Write "Your name is"
      Document.Write "<H1>"
      Document.Write YourName
      Document.Write "</H1>"

    -->
    </SCRIPT>

  </HEAD>

  <BODY>
  </BODY>

</HTML>
```

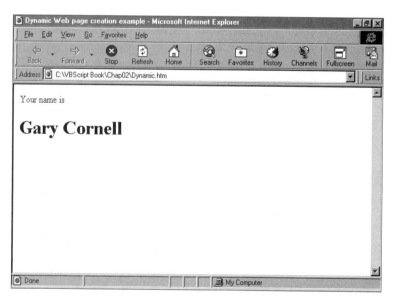

Figure 2-11. *A dynamic Web page.*

The key lines are:

```
Document.Write "Your name is"
Document.Write "<H1>"
Document.Write YourName
Document.Write "</H1>"
```

Notice that we are dynamically writing the <H1> heading level tag into the document. Since VBScript processes this code from top to bottom, VBScript will, in effect, tell Internet Explorer to:

1. Put the text *Your name is* at the top of the Web page

2. Start a level 1 head

3. Put the text that we stored in the variable *YourName* inside the level 1 head

4. End the level 1 head

Inserting ActiveX Controls

The previous section got you started on the road to serious VBScript programming, but as I mentioned in Chapter 1, much of the power of VBScript comes from its ability to control the thousands of ActiveX controls that are out there. In this chapter, I want to show you how to use Microsoft ActiveX Control Pad (which is included on the companion CD) to add ActiveX controls to your Web pages.

 OTE The best tool for working with ActiveX controls is FrontPage 98, with FrontPage 97 and FrontPage Express both being significantly less powerful. (FrontPage Express, which comes free with Internet Explorer, is a slimmed down version of FrontPage 97.) Still, in my opinion, ActiveX Control Pad is the best of the *free* tools available to VBScript programmers for working with ActiveX controls.

Why do you need a tool to insert an ActiveX control?

Before I show you how to use ActiveX Control Pad to insert an ActiveX control, you might be wondering why it's best to use a special tool for this. You might even still be creating your Web pages by using a text editor, such as Notepad, to write all the HTML source code by hand. You have avoided tools like FrontPage for a long time and might be reluctant to start using them now. I sympathize. I certainly use a text editor to write simple

HTML files and to modify existing files, but when it comes to inserting ActiveX controls, trust me—you don't want to do this by hand. Why? Well, to make ActiveX controls usable on different machines, each type of control needs to have a special id named a CLSID (for class id). You might think the name of a text box is "text box", but to your PC *and to every other PC on the planet now and in the future,* its name is really:

```
8BD21D10-EC42-11CE-9E0D-00AA006002F3
```

The idea behind these absurdly long identification numbers is that if the person displaying your Web page speaks a language other than English, that person's computer displays everything in the other language. In this case, "text box" is meaningless to the computer but the CLSID is understandable. Also, one operating system might use text boxes that look different from the text boxes of another operating system. The CLSID will always identify a text box regardless of what it looks like, and the appropriate one for the operating system will be displayed.

 OTE   Because a CLSID is a type of GUID (globally unique identifier), you will sometimes see the CLSID referred to as a GUID.

Of course, nobody in their right mind wants to work with raw class ids! For example, as you will see in the next section, if you wanted to insert a text box ActiveX control on your Web page, you would need to type something like this in your HTML source:

```
<OBJECT WIDTH=96 HEIGHT=24
  CLASSID="CLSID:8BD21D10-EC42-11CE-9E0D-00AA006002F3">
</OBJECT>
```

Obviously, if this is what it took to get an ActiveX control on a Web page, nobody would bother—but tools like ActiveX Control Pad or any version of FrontPage (including FrontPage Express) make entering information, such as the CLSID, a snap.

Using ActiveX Control Pad

ActiveX Control Pad combines a simple HTML editor (not much better than Notepad, in my opinion) with some very powerful features for working with ActiveX controls. The key is that ActiveX Control Pad will let you do the following:

- Specify the type of ActiveX control, such as a command button or text box, that you want to insert

- Set the control's initial *properties*

Properties include the background color of the control, the height of the control, the font in which text will be displayed, and so on.

Figure 2-12 shows you the initial window of ActiveX Control Pad.

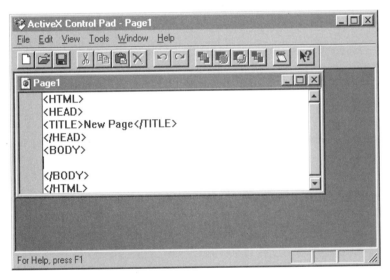

Figure 2-12. *The initial window of ActiveX Control Pad.*

Inserting an ActiveX Control

ActiveX controls should be inserted in the body of your HTML source, so make sure that the cursor is in the body. (Conveniently, ActiveX Control Pad opens with the cursor on a blank line in the body.) Next select Insert

ActiveX Control from the Edit menu. This opens a dialog box like the one shown in Figure 2-13. (The control types you'll see listed depend on which ActiveX controls you have installed on your system.) For the sake of illustration, I'll work with the Microsoft Forms 2.0 CommandButton control, so scroll down until you see it.

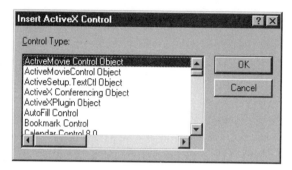

Figure 2-13. *The Insert ActiveX Control dialog box.*

ARNING   Do not select New HTML Layout from the File Menu or Insert HTML Layout from the Edit Menu. They work in Internet Explorer version 3, not in Internet Explorer version 4.

Setting Properties with ActiveX Control Pad

Notice that when you insert an ActiveX control, two different windows appear, as shown in Figure 2-14. The Edit ActiveX Control window shows the command button (surrounded by small white squares known as *sizing handles*) as part of a page layout; the Properties window shows a table of all the properties you can set. It's easy to set a property. You can work in the Edit ActiveX Control window to shrink or expand the control. To do this, drag one of the eight sizing handles that are on the boundary of the control; this automatically changes the Height and Width properties in the Properties window. (Note that dragging the control itself to a different place on the page layout doesn't change its ultimate position on the Web page. This position is determined by where the control's <OBJECT> tag is placed in the HTML source. Initially, this will be where the cursor was located; later, you can move the tag by cutting and pasting it.)

The Properties window lets you change any of the properties, including Height and Width, so it is more flexible than the Edit ActiveX Control window. To use the Properties window to change the properties of an ActiveX control, follow these steps, using Figure 2-14 as a guide:

1. Select the property you want to set or change.

2. Type the new value in the text box next to the Apply button.

3. Click the Apply button.

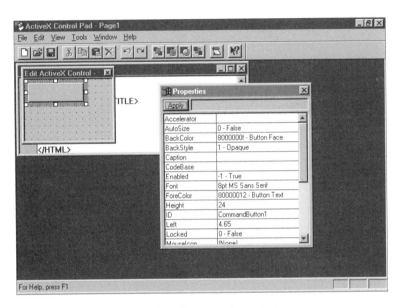

Figure 2-14. *The Edit ActiveX Control and Properties windows.*

For example, if you follow the above steps to change the Caption property of the command button to read "Click Me," then you will see a preview of the change reflected immediately in the Edit ActiveX Control window. (See Figure 2-15 on the following page.)

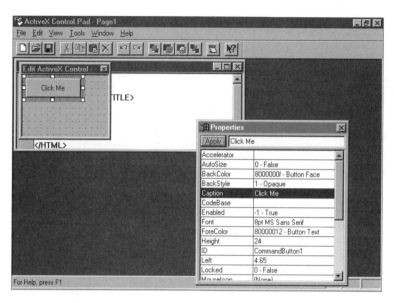

Figure 2-15.   *Setting a property.*

 OTE   Not all properties are supported by all browsers. You might have to experiment to see what properties your browser supports.

After you close the Edit ActiveX Control window and the Properties window, ActiveX Control Pad will automatically place the needed code (including the CLSID) in your HTML source. (See Figure 2-16.) Notice that there's a little blue box in the left margin. If you want to change the properties of the control, you can click this box to reopen the Edit ActiveX Control window and the Properties window.

Next let's change a more sophisticated property—the one that controls the background color of the button. To do this, select the BackColor property in the Properties window. Notice that it has a totally inscrutable value of *8000000f - Button Face.* There are two ways to change this value. The first way is to open the drop-down list box next to the Apply button, and then choose from one of the standard types. (See Figure 2-17.)

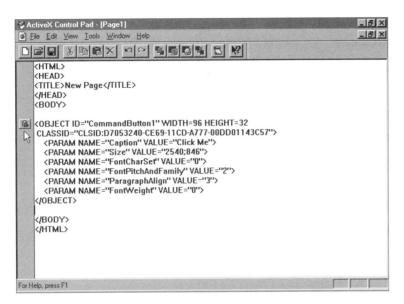

Figure 2-16. *The HTML source after an ActiveX control has been inserted.*

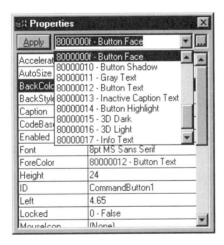

Figure 2-17. *Choosing a background color.*

The second way is to click the ellipsis button to the right of the drop-down list box. This opens a standard Microsoft Windows color palette. You can select one of the colors from this palette or even define a custom color.

IP   To cycle through the complete list of options for a property, double-click the right column for that property in the Properties window. Each time you double-click, you will see the next available option. (Of course, this works only for properties that have a list of options. It will not work for the Caption property, for example, because in this case you must type the text you want. Furthermore, the ellipsis button appears only for some properties. Double-clicking the right column of one of these properties is equivalent to clicking the ellipsis button.)

The Most Useful Properties of Command Buttons

Even as simple a control as a command button has 24 properties you can set from the Properties window. With 24 properties for a command button alone, I won't go over all of them in detail—some are self-explanatory—but I will discuss the most commonly used ones.

 OTE   One of the ways ActiveX controls become more manageable is that each property has essentially the same function for many different controls. For example, many controls have a Caption property, and all visible controls have Height and Width properties.

AutoSize

AutoSize makes the command button shrink or expand to fit the caption. It is an example of a *Boolean* property. (Boolean means that a value is either True or False.) You can double-click the right column to cycle through the two options.

BackStyle

There are two possibilities: Opaque (the default) and Transparent, which allows the wallpaper you are using on your Web page to show through.

CodeBase

What if a user is displaying your Web page but the command button ActiveX control is not installed on that user's system? You can use the CodeBase property to specify the URL where the user's browser might find the control on the Web, if necessary.

Enabled

The Enabled property specifies whether anything will happen if a user clicks the command button. Normally, you set Enabled to True because you want something to happen! You do not want to change the Enabled property casually. If you set Enabled to False, the command button no longer functions, which might confuse your users.

Height and Width

These properties specify the height and width in points. A point is a measurement for typesetting; this book is set in 10.5-point type.

ID

ID is the name you give the command button so that you can refer to it in your VBScript code. As you will see in the section on event procedures that follows, choosing a meaningful name for a control can make your code easier to read. The ID must begin with a letter. After that, you can use any combination of letters and digits (but no spaces). The ID cannot exceed 128 characters.

 OTE   The convention that many programmers like to use is that the ID of a command button begins with the lowercase letters cmd (for example, cmdClickMe). I won't be using this convention in this chapter but will often use it in later chapters.

MousePointer and MouseIcon

MousePointer specifies what the mouse pointer will look like when a user moves it over the command button. Setting MousePointer to something other than the usual arrow is a good way to give the user feedback that he or she can now click the button. If you want to use a custom mouse pointer, set this value to *99 - Custom* and then change the MouseIcon property. After selecting MouseIcon, click the ellipsis button to display the Load Picture dialog box where you can browse for an icon (.ico) or cursor (.cur) file.

Picture and PicturePosition

On a command button, you can display a picture instead of the caption text. Select the Picture property, and then click the ellipsis button to display the

Load Picture dialog box, where you can browse for a picture file. Use the PicturePosition property to determine where the picture will be displayed on the button face.

WordWrap

If you set WordWrap to True, the caption text will be displayed on as many lines as necessary on the button face. A value of False means that only one line will be used; the text will be cut off if it doesn't fit.

The Effect in HTML of Setting Properties

After you finish setting the properties for an ActiveX control, close the Edit ActiveX Control window and the Properties window. You will then be able to see the HTML source with the code that ActiveX Control Pad added for the control. As an example, let's insert a command button ActiveX control and make the changes listed below:

■ Set the ID property to *ClickMe*

■ Set the AutoSize property to *True*

■ Set the Caption property to *Click Me*

Here's the HTML source:

```
<HTML>
<HEAD>
<TITLE>New Page</TITLE>
</HEAD>
<BODY>

<OBJECT ID="ClickMe" WIDTH=59 HEIGHT=29
 CLASSID="CLSID:D7053240-CE69-11CD-A777-00DD01143C57">
   <PARAM NAME="VariousPropertyBits" VALUE="268435483">
   <PARAM NAME="Caption" VALUE="Click Me">
   <PARAM NAME="Size" VALUE="1535;767">
   <PARAM NAME="FontCharSet" VALUE="0">
   <PARAM NAME="FontPitchAndFamily" VALUE="2">
   <PARAM NAME="ParagraphAlign" VALUE="3">
   <PARAM NAME="FontWeight" VALUE="0">
</OBJECT>

</BODY>
</HTML>
```

The information describing the command button is contained inside the pair of <OBJECT></OBJECT> tags. I want to go over this section in more detail. First we have:

```
<OBJECT ID="ClickMe" WIDTH=59 HEIGHT=29
```

This gives the name that we will use to identify the command button in our scripts, followed by the width and height in pixels. (In ordinary HTML, you cannot change the width and height once the Web page is displayed. In *dynamic HTML,* which is the subject of Chapter 9, you can do this.) Next comes the totally inscrutable CLSID line containing the globally unique identifier that I talked about before. Finally we see the object's properties. If you look at this example closely, you can see that the name of the property is determined by the PARAM NAME attribute, and the setting you gave it is determined by the VALUE attribute.

```
<PARAM NAME="Caption" VALUE="Click Me">
```

Once you get comfortable with what your HTML source looks like, you'll find that the following steps are a shortcut to putting multiple controls of the same type in your HTML source when the differences are minor (such as having only a different ID and caption):

1. Use ActiveX Control Pad to set the properties for the first control, having it insert the needed pair of <OBJECT></OBJECT> tags in your HTML source.

2. Type any <BR> tags that you need to separate the controls on the Web page.

3. Copy the section to the new location starting from the <OBJECT> tag and going to the closing </OBJECT> tag.

4. Using ActiveX Control Pad's editor, change by hand the value of the <PARAM> tags that correspond to the properties you want to change. Also, be sure to change the value of the ID.

This is often a lot faster than using ActiveX Control Pad to insert multiple controls of the same type. Finally, remember that after you build the Web page, you need to save it by choosing Save or Save As from the File menu.

To see the page in Internet Explorer, select Open from the File menu. You can then use the Browse button to find the file that you saved.

Event Procedures

If you save your Web page and then open it in Internet Explorer, you will see a command button with the caption Click Me. The trouble is that clicking the button doesn't do anything. In this section, I want to show you how to make the button active. The essence of most scripts is, after all, to make your Web pages respond to user actions.

Remember that each ActiveX control is programmed to respond to certain events. For example, as you might expect, the command button can respond to a user clicking it! The key is that although ActiveX controls can theoretically recognize many different events, your Web page will do nothing unless you've written code to tell it what to do when an event occurs.

The idea is that you must write an *event procedure* for every event that you want an ActiveX control to respond to. An event procedure is nothing more than the lines of programming code that tell a Web page how to respond to a given event.

 TIP   The ID property is very important when you start writing event procedures for ActiveX controls. This property determines the name that VBScript uses for the event procedures you will write. Picking a meaningful name for the ID of a control goes a long way toward making the programming process easier.

Writing an Event Procedure

We want to add an event procedure to the HTML source that displays the command button. Here's what you have to do. Move back into the head section, and add the following lines:

```
<SCRIPT LANGUAGE="VBSCRIPT">
<!--

  Sub ClickMe_Click
    MsgBox "Hello World"
  End Sub

-->
</SCRIPT>
```

You should also change the title. The entire HTML source then looks like this:

```
<HTML>
<HEAD>
<TITLE>A first event procedure</TITLE>

  <SCRIPT LANGUAGE="VBSCRIPT">
  <!--

    Sub ClickMe_Click
      MsgBox "Hello World"
    End Sub

  -->
  </SCRIPT>

</HEAD>
</BODY>

<OBJECT ID="ClickMe" WIDTH=59 HEIGHT=29
CLASSID="CLSID:D7053240-CE69-11CD-A777-00DD01143C57">
  <PARAM NAME="VariousPropertyBits" VALUE="268435483">
  <PARAM NAME="Caption" VALUE="Click Me">
  <PARAM NAME="Size" VALUE="1535;767">
  <PARAM NAME="FontCharSet" VALUE="0">
  <PARAM NAME="FontPitchAndFamily" VALUE="2">
  <PARAM NAME="ParagraphAlign" VALUE="3">
  <PARAM NAME="FontWeight" VALUE="0">
</OBJECT>

</BODY>
</HTML>
```

The indentations were just to make everything easier to read—VBScript doesn't care. Now if you save your Web page, open it in Internet Explorer, and click the button, you will see a message box saying "Hello World". (See Figure 2-18 on the following page.)

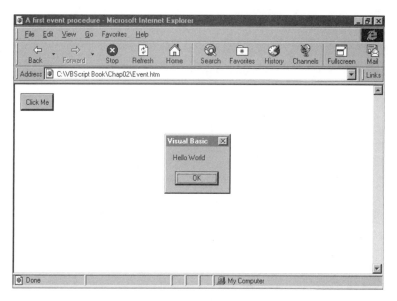

Figure 2-18.   *The effect of our first event procedure.*

The general form of an event procedure

It doesn't matter where you put the event procedure; it can go in the head section or in the body. I place all my code in the head section unless there is a specific reason to put it in the body. (I haven't found one yet.)

The general form of an event procedure is this:

```
Sub IDofControl_TypeOfEvent

End Sub
```

You substitute the value of the control's ID property for IDofControl, and you substitute the type of event for TypeOfEvent. You keep the underscore, as in ClickMe_Click, for example. You then place your code inside these two lines. (Even as simple a control as a command button can respond to ten events, but in most cases only the Click event really matters.)

Typos

Nobody types accurately all the time. If you make a mistake and then run the script (by clicking the command button), Internet Explorer will display an error message. For example, in the preceding event procedure, change the word *MsgBox* to *Msg,* so the line reads:

```
Msg "Hello World"
```

Save the Web page, open it in Internet Explorer, and try to click the button. You'll soon see a dialog box like the one shown in Figure 2-19. The simplest way to correct this kind of error is to do the following:

1. Click the No button in the dialog box.

2. Choose Source from Internet Explorer's View menu to open the HTML source file in Notepad.

3. Make the changes, save the file, and close Notepad.

4. Choose Refresh from Internet Explorer's View menu. (F5 is the shortcut.)

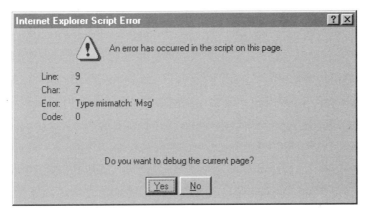

Figure 2-19.   *A dialog box resulting from a script error.*

Text Boxes and Labels

Before moving on, I want to discuss two more ActiveX controls—a text box and a label. The official names of these controls are Microsoft Forms 2.0 TextBox and Microsoft Forms 2.0 Label.

A text box is used to display text or to accept user input. Most event procedures for a text box process the information the user enters into the text box. All the ordinary editing tools, such as the Ctrl-X and Ctrl-V shortcuts for cutting and pasting, are available. The usual limit on the information that can be contained in a text box is 32,767 characters. A label, on the other hand, is for display purposes only. Most of the time, you place it next to an object like a text box to identify what the object is for. Occasionally, you use a label to display output.

Text Boxes

A text box has 39 properties available. Many of them are similar to those available for command buttons. For example, the AutoSize property causes a text box to automatically resize itself to fit the text it contains. One difference to keep in mind is that instead of having a Caption property, a text box has a Text property that controls what is displayed in the box. When you change the Font property, you reset the font for all the text—an ordinary text box can display only one font at a time. (Some systems have a control named RichTextBox that allows multiple fonts to be displayed simultaneously.)

A label has 26 properties. All the significant ones work in the same way as they do for a command button or a text box. For example, the Caption property controls what the user sees, just as it does for a command button. Here are short descriptions of some of the most commonly used properties of text boxes and labels.

BorderStyle (text boxes and labels)
There are two possible settings for the BorderStyle property. The default value is 1, which gives you a single-width border. If you change the value of this property to 0, the border disappears.

ScrollBars (text boxes only)
The ScrollBars property determines whether a text box has horizontal or vertical scroll bars. Without scroll bars, it becomes much harder for the

user to move through the data contained in the text box. There are four possible settings for the ScrollBars property:

Value	Meaning
0	The text box has neither vertical nor horizontal scroll bars. This is the default value.
1	The text box has horizontal scroll bars only.
2	The text box has vertical scroll bars only.
3	The text box has both horizontal and vertical scroll bars.

MultiLine (text boxes only)

MultiLine is a Boolean property that determines whether a text box can accept or display more than one line of text. If this property is True, more than one line is allowed. Text will automatically wrap to the next line when a user types more than one line of information—unless the text box has horizontal scroll bars. The user can also employ the standard keys to move through the text box: the arrows, Home, End, Ctrl-Home, and Ctrl-End.

MaxLength and AutoTab (text boxes only)

The MaxLength property determines the maximum number of characters the text box will accept. The default value is 0, which (somewhat counter-intuitively) means there is no maximum other than the 32,767-character limit for text boxes. Any setting other than 0 will limit the user's ability to enter data into that text box to that number of characters. The AutoTab property works with the MaxLength property. The idea is that after the user enters the maximum amount of text, VBScript will automatically move to the next control. As you can imagine, this can be very convenient—moving from the State field directly to the Zip code field after the user enters 2 characters in the State field!

PasswordChar (text boxes only)

The PasswordChar property lets you specify the character to be displayed when a user enters a password in the text box. (All characters that the user enters are stored internally, however.) The convention is to use an asterisk (*) for the password character.

Locked (text boxes only)

This Boolean property lets you prevent users from changing the contents of a text box. If Locked is set to True, users can still scroll and highlight text but they won't be able to change it. (Because users can highlight text, they will still be able to use standard techniques to copy information from the text box—they just won't be able to change the text in it.)

TextAlign (text boxes and labels)

This property determines whether the text inside the control is left-aligned, centered, or right-aligned.

Events for Text Boxes

A text box can respond to a maximum of 12 events. For example, the Click event is triggered when the user clicks inside the box. There's even a DblClick (double click) event that is triggered when the user double-clicks in the box. You could write the following event procedure for the DblClick event:

```
Sub IDofTextBox_DblClick
  MsgBox "Please click once, not twice!"
End Sub
```

Probably the most important events for a text box are the Change event, which is triggered whenever the user changes the contents of the box, and the KeyPress event, which is triggered whenever the user types a character in the box.

I want to give you some ideas of why you would use these event procedures. So imagine you want to do the following two things:

■ Make sure the user types only digits (0...9) in the text box

■ Make sure the user never pastes anything but numbers in the text box

The first would be controlled by code in the KeyPress event procedure. The second would be controlled by code in the Change event procedure. In Chapter 9, I will tell you more about the KeyPress event.

 OTE   Although labels can respond to a few events, it is uncommon to write an event procedure for one.

Script Wizard

ActiveX Control Pad comes with a tool named Script Wizard that was supposed to make programming skills for people who wanted to create scripts irrelevant. The idea was that Script Wizard would automatically generate your script when you gave it directions. In my opinion, Script Wizard isn't worth much. At best, it can't do much more than create the simplest scripts for you—and you can create those a lot faster yourself! For this reason, I rarely, if ever, use Script Wizard's automatic code-generation features. So why am I bothering with it? Because you will turn to it, time and time again, to see what events your ActiveX controls support.

 OTE FrontPage 98 has a much better Script Wizard too, but I still prefer to do things by hand—it is almost always faster once you get used to coding.

You activate Script Wizard by selecting Script Wizard from the Tools menu. This displays the window shown in Figure 2-20.

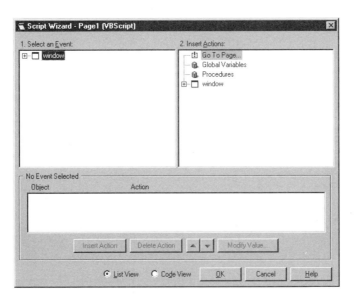

Figure 2-20. *The initial window of Script Wizard.*

The left pane displays the objects on your Web page and the right pane displays what you can do with the objects using the automatic code-generation features. Just like in Windows Explorer, you click the plus sign (+) to expand an item. If you click the plus sign next to the item marked "window" in the left pane, you will see the expanded item, as shown in Figure 2-21. Now you can see that there are two possible events that the window object supports.

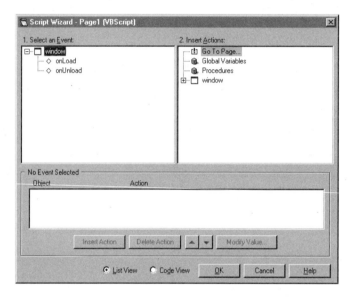

Figure 2-21.   *Window events in Script Wizard.*

While I will have a lot more to say about the window object in Chapter 8, here are brief descriptions of these two events.

The onLoad event is automatically triggered when a Web page is loaded onto a user's system. This means that every time the page is loaded or the Refresh button is clicked, Internet Explorer executes the code that you have placed in the onLoad event procedure. (There is not much difference between placing code in the onLoad event procedure and placing it at the beginning of the head section.) Here's an example of this event procedure:

```
Sub Window_onLoad
  Name = InputBox("What is your name?")
  MsgBox "Welcome " & Name
End Sub
```

The onUnload event is automatically triggered whenever the page is unloaded, which occurs whenever one of the following conditions are met:

■ You move to a different Web page

■ You click the Refresh button

■ You close Internet Explorer

I want to lead you through a session using Script Wizard to show you its powers. I'll have it generate some code, and then I'll show you how to use it as your "browser" to find the events that an ActiveX control supports.

A Sample Script Wizard Session

To follow along you might want to use ActiveX Control Pad to place a Microsoft Forms 2.0 CommandButton control (with a Caption of Click Me) and a Microsoft Forms 2.0 TextBox control in your HTML source as shown in Figure 2-22.

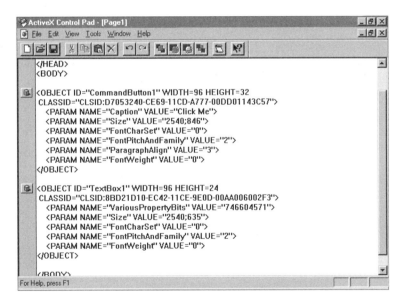

Figure 2-22. *The HTML source at the beginning of our Script Wizard session.*

Open Script Wizard. As you can see in Figure 2-23 on the following page, there are now three objects listed in the left pane.

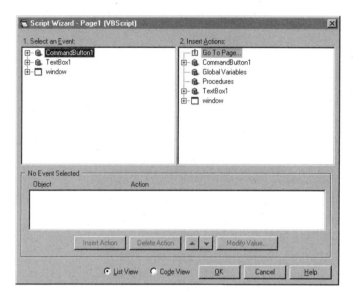

Figure 2-23.   *Script Wizard with multiple objects.*

Click the plus sign next to the item marked TextBox1 to reveal all the events that a text box can respond to. We want to write some code for the DblClick (double click) event. Notice that the right pane is entitled "Insert Actions." This is because clicking the plus sign next to an item in the right pane lists the actions that you can have Script Wizard insert into your HTML source. For example, suppose we want to make the text box say, "You double clicked me!" in response to a double click. Here is how to proceed if you want to use Script Wizard:

1. Make sure that DblClick is highlighted in the left pane.

2. Display the possible actions for the TextBox1 text box by clicking the plus sign in the right pane.

3. Scroll down to the Text property.

4. Double click it.

Your screen will look like Figure 2-24.

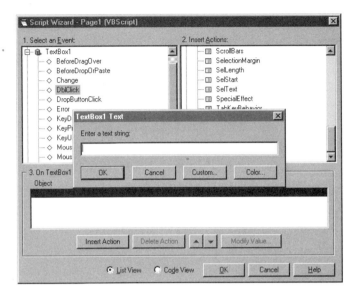

Figure 2-24.   *Inserting an action via Script Wizard.*

In this dialog box, remember not *to surround the text with quotes.*

Now you can type the string you want in the dialog box. When you click OK, Script Wizard will write the code for you. To see the code, switch to the Code View option by clicking the radio button at the bottom of the Script Wizard window. Your screen will look like Figure 2-25.

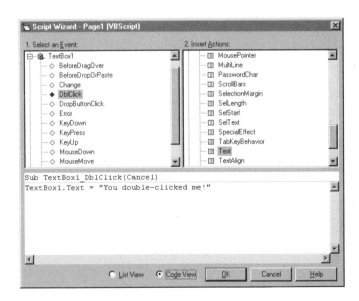

Figure 2-25.   *Code View option in the Script Wizard.*

Notice that it looks like Script Wizard forgot to add the "End Sub" that must end any event procedure. Well, it hasn't! If you close Script Wizard by clicking OK, you will see that an end sub is there. (See Figure 2-26.)

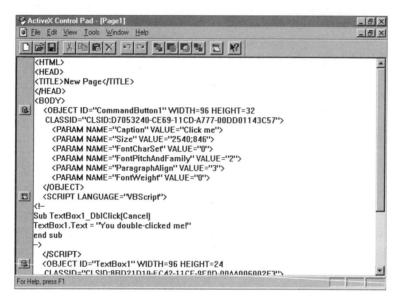

Figure 2-26.   *Results of using Script Wizard.*

I've shown you how to write an event procedure by hand and how to use Script Wizard to automatically generate one. The final decision is up to you. I think it is easiest to use Script Wizard to discover all the possible events but to type my event procedures by hand.

  IP   As you will soon see, many event procedures are like the DblClick event procedure in that they can work with extra information, or *parameters*. (You'll see a lot more about parameters in the next few chapters.) To find out what parameters can be used by an event procedure, select the event in the left pane and then switch to the Code View option. Script Wizard shows you any parameters in parentheses on the first line of the event procedure.

If you think of Script Wizard as an aid to writing code, you'll be fine. If you think of it as a substitute for reading the rest of this book, well, good luck!

Fundamentals of VBScript Programming

The last chapter dealt mostly with the mechanics of integrating VBScript code with HTML code. You also saw how easy it is to insert ActiveX controls into your Web pages by using Microsoft ActiveX Control Pad. I hope I've convinced you that not only is it easy to customize a Web page by adding controls and setting their properties, it is also amazing how much can be done with a few lines of VBScript code in the head section for your page (either inside or outside an event procedure). However, the code and event procedures you've seen are still limited in what they can do. To do more, you must become comfortable with the VBScript programming language. This chapter covers the basics of the language. You'll learn more about its more sophisticated parts in later chapters.

Anatomy of a VBScript Program

Successful VBScript programming depends on realizing that your code must be broken up into two parts: code that is executed before the user's browser loads your Web page and code that is activated in response to various events.

Code that is executed before the page is loaded is where you put the Document.Write commands that let you build a Web page on the fly. However, this kind of code is far less flexible than code that is activated in response to various events.

These events can be as simple as the browser loading the page or as sophisticated as the user moving the mouse to a specific location. The point to keep in mind is this—if you think of a VBScript program as a set of independent pieces that "wake up" only in response to events they have been told to recognize, you usually won't go wrong. On the other hand, if you think of the script as having a starting line and an ending line and moving from top to bottom, you often will.

Statements in VBScript

Think of a statement in VBScript as a complete sentence; it contains all the necessary parts to express a complete thought.

It is helpful to think that just as sentences are composed of words and proper nouns, VBScript statements are composed of the words of the VBScript language and the names of the items you need to use, such as ActiveX controls, numbers, sections of text, and so on. The numbers and text themselves are often called *literals* because they are interpreted literally by VBScript (that is, they are not the names of anything else). There are also verbs, which are called *methods* in VBScript. These are the commands that tell VBScript what to do. For example, the following statement tells VBScript to apply the Write method (verb) to the Document object (noun):

```
Document.Write "<H1>Hello World!</H1>"
```

VBScript also has connecting words that fill other parts of its statement structure. These are *keywords* such as If and For. Keywords are also called *reserved words* because each one is reserved for a specific purpose by VBScript and can't be used for anything else. (See Appendix B for a list of reserved words in VBScript.)

 OTE Remember that VBScript statements live in HTML source code. However, you can use any of several different ways to write the HTML code along with its VBScript statements. For example, you can use ActiveX Control Pad, a text editor such as Notepad, or even Microsoft Word 97 (if you save the file as an HTML document). Appendix A explains how to use Microsoft Visual Basic version 5 to write your VBScript code.

Over the next few pages, I'll give you the basic rules and show you lots of examples of what constitutes acceptable "grammar" for your VBScript statements. I won't be totally thorough in the way that a computer scientist might like, but as anyone who has tried to learn the rules of English grammar knows, too formal an approach is self-defeating for most of us! I like to think of programming as being a lot like writing; from my point of view, examples plus a few rules are better than any attempt to give a complete rule book. Luckily, complete formality isn't needed because, as you saw in Chapter 2, VBScript will tell you if it doesn't understand something you wrote. You can then make the appropriate changes.

Let's begin with some generalities. First, white space within a line doesn't matter to VBScript. (Extra blank lines don't matter either.) This means you can use an indentation pattern that makes your code clearer. I like to use two spaces for the code inside my event procedures, for example:

```
Sub cmdButton1_Click
  MsgBox "Hello World!"
End Sub
```

Second, a statement in VBScript isn't restricted to only one physical line on your screen, although it usually ends up that way. If a statement must span more than one physical line, place an underscore at the end of the line. The underscore acts as a *line continuation character*. Be aware, however, that the underscore can't be inside quotation marks. Here are two examples of what you can and can't do using the underscore to join two pieces of text together:

```
txtBox1.Text = "This is an example of using the underscore " _
  & "that is OK."
```

```
txtBox1.Text = "This is an example of using the underscore _
  that is not OK."
```

The problem with the second example is that the underscore is inside the quotes. As I mentioned earlier, text inside quotes is interpreted literally, so the underscore in this case is interpreted as part of the text and not as a line continuation character.

OTE   If you don't use an underscore, VBScript regards the end of the line as occurring where you press the Enter key. If you type a very long line that is wider than your screen, you will have to use horizontal scrolling to see the whole line. Most people use the underscore rather than horizontal scrolling.

The third and final generalization is that you can combine statements on a single line by inserting a colon between them. I wouldn't recommend doing this unless the lines are obviously related. Most of the time, your programs are clearer if each line corresponds to one VBScript statement.

Commenting Your Code

The first kind of VBScript statement I want to discuss might seem a bit strange because it doesn't do anything. VBScript doesn't interpret these *comment statements* at all; instead, you put them there for the people who will be reading your code (including yourself). The purpose of comment statements is to explain how your code works. Why do you want to do this? Well, programmers have learned from bitter experience that the code they write today is often difficult (and sometimes impossible) to understand even a few months later—often by the programmers themselves but especially by others. Commenting your code makes it more maintainable (that is, easier to modify).

In VBScript, comment statements are also called *remark statements*. There are two ways to indicate a remark statement. The most common is to use a single quotation mark ('). This is not the apostrophe found below the tilde (~) but the one usually found below the double quotation mark ("). Here is an example:

```
Sub cmdButton1_Click
   'Comments describing the event procedure should go here
   'and probably here too
End Sub
```

You can also use the Rem keyword, as shown in the following example:

```
Sub cmdButton1_Click
   Rem Comments describing the event procedure should go here
   Rem and probably here too
End Sub
```

Notice that I indent the programming lines in both cases to improve readability.

If you want to add comments to the ends of lines, it is easier to use the single quotation mark because the Rem keyword requires a preceding colon. For example:

```
txtName = ""    'blank out the text box
txtName = ""    :Rem blank out the text box
```

Everything on a line following the single quote or the Rem keyword is ignored. This is true regardless of whether it is an executable VBScript statement. As you will see in Chapter 7, commenting out executable statements is a common technique for debugging your programs.

Since comments are downloaded with the rest of your Web page, there might be times when you want to maintain two versions of the same script, one with comments and one without. The advantage to the version without comments is that it will be faster to download.

Assigning Properties

One reason for using a scripting language rather than plain old HTML is that a scripting language is dynamic—you can make changes to your Web page in response to events. This requires changing the property settings of existing VBScript objects. You have already seen examples of how to do this using the Script Wizard in ActiveX Control Pad. For example, you have seen how the Script Wizard can generate code that looks like this in order to change the text that appears in the text box named txtBox1:

```
txtBox1.Text = "This is the new text."
```

Generally, if you want to change a property setting for a VBScript object, place the object's name (that is, the value of its ID property), a period, and the name of the property on the left side of the equal sign, and then put the new value on the right-hand side, as shown in the following model:

```
objectID.property = value
```

For example, suppose you have a text box named txtBlank and you want to blank it out (that is, delete all its text). You need only to have a line like this in an event procedure:

```
txtBlank.Text = ""
```

You can use code to change an object's property setting as often as necessary. For example, if you wanted to change the caption on a command button named cmdYesNo to No and then to Yes, you would use lines such as these:

```
cmdYesNo = "No"
cmdYesNo = "Yes"
```

A simple example

The following example shows you the steps needed to develop a simple VBScript project by first using ActiveX Control Pad to add the controls and then entering the VBScript code directly into the ActiveX Control Pad editing window.

Using ActiveX Control Pad this way is actually one of the most popular ways of developing a Web page that includes VBScript code.

This example has a command button and a text box. Every time you click the button, VBScript adds an exclamation point to whatever is currently in the text box. Figure 3-1 shows a picture of what the Web page will look like.

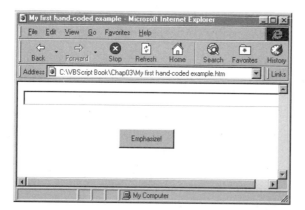

Figure 3-1.   *A simple Web page.*

Here are the steps you need to follow:

1. Open ActiveX Control Pad.

2. Select Insert ActiveX Control from the Edit menu, and add a Microsoft Forms 2.0 TextBox control.

3. Close the Properties window, enlarge the Edit ActiveX Control window so that a hefty portion of the screen is covered, and then widen the text box so that you'll be able to enter a large amount of text.

4. Close the Edit ActiveX Control window.

5. In the Page1 window, type two
 HTML tags to add two blank lines. Then type the <CENTER> tag so that the command button, which you are about to insert, will be centered.

6. Select Insert ActiveX Control from the Edit menu, and add a Microsoft Forms 2.0 CommandButton control.

7. Using the Properties window, change the Caption to *Emphasize!* and the ID property to *cmdEmphasize*.

8. Close the Properties window and the Edit ActiveX Control window.

9. Type the </CENTER> tag after the </OBJECT> tag to finish centering the command button.

10. Change the title from *New Page* to *My first hand-coded example.*

Your script should look like this so far (although, depending on how wide you made the text box, the values for its width and size might be different):

```
<HTML>
<HEAD>
<TITLE>My first hand-coded example</TITLE>
</HEAD>
<BODY>

<OBJECT ID="TextBox1" WIDTH=720 HEIGHT=24
CLASSID="CLSID:8BD21D10-EC42-11CE-9E0D-00AA006002F3">
  <PARAM NAME="VariousPropertyBits" VALUE="746604571">
  <PARAM NAME="Size" VALUE="19050;635">
  <PARAM NAME="FontCharSet" VALUE="0">
  <PARAM NAME="FontPitchAndFamily" VALUE="2">
  <PARAM NAME="FontWeight" VALUE="0">
</OBJECT>

<BR><BR>

<CENTER>
<OBJECT ID="cmdEmphasize" WIDTH=96 HEIGHT=32
```

(continued)

67

```
CLASSID="CLSID:D7053240-CE69-11CD-A777-00DD01143C57">
  <PARAM NAME="Caption" VALUE="Emphasize!">
  <PARAM NAME="Size" VALUE="2540;846">
  <PARAM NAME="FontCharSet" VALUE="0">
  <PARAM NAME="FontPitchAndFamily" VALUE="2">
  <PARAM NAME="ParagraphAlign" VALUE="3">
  <PARAM NAME="FontWeight" VALUE="0">
</OBJECT>
</CENTER>

</BODY>
</HTML>
```

Now it's time to add the VBScript code for the event procedure that adds the exclamation point to whatever text is in the text box.

1. Move the cursor to the beginning of the line containing the </HEAD> tag, and press the Enter key three times to create three blank lines.

2. In the blank area you just created, type the following code (leaving one blank line above the new code and one blank line below):

```
<SCRIPT LANGUAGE="VBSCRIPT">
<!--

   Sub cmdEmphasize_Click
      TextBox1.Text = TextBox1.Text & "!"
   End Sub

-->
</SCRIPT>
```

Look at the key line:

```
TextBox1.Text = TextBox1.Text & "!"
```

You need to remember that the ampersand joins text together. But even having said that, it is worth going over this simple statement in more detail. Notice that the left-hand side of the assignment statement contains the name of the property that gets the value, but it seems that the name of the property occurs on the right-hand side as well. How can this be?

What happens is that VBScript analyzes the right-hand side of any assignment statement first and extracts a value from it. Think of what it is doing as fetching and then storing the current contents of the text box in a sort of scratchpad area in its memory. Only after it has done this does it look to the left-hand side of the assignment statement. VBScript then changes the old text (which it is keeping in its scratchpad area) by adding an extra exclamation point to whatever text was there. It then reassigns the new text as the value of the Text property of the box. The result is that the text in the box now has an extra exclamation point.

All this can be a little confusing. Some people find it helpful to remember that the right-hand side of an assignment statement is there for the value it yields—only the left-hand side gets changed.

By the way, if you haven't already done so, you'll want to try your script. Save the script by selecting Save As from the File menu, and then close ActiveX Control Pad. Open the file in Microsoft Internet Explorer, click the text box to place the cursor there, enter some text, and then click the button. You'll see an exclamation point added to the text.

Boolean properties

Properties that take only the values True and False are called Boolean properties, as described in Chapter 2. You have seen many Boolean properties in the Properties window of ActiveX Control Pad. For example, Boolean properties specify whether a command button is visible and enabled. The following statement disables the command button named cmdButton1:

```
cmdButton1.Enabled = False
```

The control stays disabled until VBScript processes the following statement:

```
cmdButton1.Enabled = True
```

The usual way to *toggle* a Boolean property is with the Not operator. Suppose you have a statement such as this in an event procedure:

```
cmdButton1.Enabled = Not(cmdButton1.Enabled)
```

The statement works as follows: VBScript finds the current value of the cmdButton1.Enabled property, and then the Not operator reverses this value; that is, if the value was True, it changes to False, and vice versa.

Variables

Variables in VBScript hold information (values). Whenever you use a variable, VBScript sets up an area in the computer's memory to store the information. Variable names in VBScript must follow these rules:

- Begin with a letter

- Be up to 255 characters long

- Include any combination of letters, numbers, and underscores

VBScript is not case-sensitive. To VBScript, MyName and myname are the same variable name.

The following list contains some possible variable names and indicates whether they are acceptable.

OnFirst	Acceptable
1stOn	Not acceptable (first character is not a letter)
First.1	Not acceptable (uses a period)
First 1	Not acceptable (includes a space inside the name)
ThisIsKindOfLongButIsTheoreticallyOK	Acceptable (less than 255 characters but probably too cumbersome for a realistic program)

All characters in a variable name are significant. Base is a different variable from Base1, and both are different from Base_1.

Choosing meaningful variable names helps document your program and makes the inevitable debugging process easier. Meaningful variable names are an excellent way to clarify the point of many program statements and often provide the best form of documentation.

For a list of reserved words, see Appendix B.

You can't use names reserved by VBScript for variable names; for example, Sub is not acceptable as a variable name. However, you can embed reserved words within a variable's name. For example, Substitute is a perfectly acceptable variable name. VBScript shows you an error message when you try to use a reserved word as a variable name. The one you will most often see looks like the one shown in Figure 3-2.

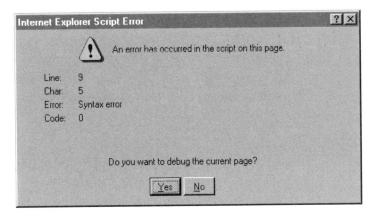

Figure 3-2. *Error message due to assigning a reserved word as a variable name.*

Variable Types

Your programs need to be able to handle different kinds of information. There can be integers such as 1, 2, and 3; strings of text such as "Help"; numbers with decimal places; and the Boolean values True and False. The different kinds of information are called *data types*.

VBScript's Basic Data Types

VBScript handles 16 standard types of variables. This section describes the ones you will use for most of your work.

String

Strings hold characters of text. As you have seen, the easiest way to define a string variable is to surround the string with quotes. Theoretically, string variables can hold up to 2 billion or so characters! In any case, a specific machine might hold less due to memory constraints, system overhead requirements, or the number of strings used on the Web page.

Integer

Integer variables hold relatively small integer values (between −32,768 and +32,767).

Long

The long integer variable is a type that holds integers between −2,147,483,648 and +2,147,483,647.

Double

This is the type of variable VBScript uses if you use a decimal point in your number. Double-precision variables hold numbers with up to 15 places of accuracy and allow more than 300 digits. Calculations are approximate for these variables; you can rely on the first 15 digits only. Calculations are also relatively slow with double-precision numbers compared with integers or long integers.

Single

These are also numbers with decimal points, but VBScript doesn't normally use this format. (In fact, VBScript uses this format only if you explicitly tell it to, by using the CSng conversion function described later in this chapter.) Single-precision variables limit numbers to 7 places of accuracy and can contain up to 40 digits.

Date

The Date data type gives you a convenient way to store both date and time information for any time between midnight on January 1, 100, and midnight on December 31, 9999. Dates and times must be placed between pound signs (#). For example, if you are using the United States style of dates, you would enter this:

```
Millennium = #January 1, 2000#
```

If you do not include a time, VBScript assumes it is midnight. To add a time, use either AM/PM or a 24-hour clock:

```
CloseToMillennium = #December 31, 1999 11:59PM#
CloseToMillennium = #December 31, 1999 23:59#
```

Variable Name Prefixes

Many programmers advocate using a prefix at the beginning of a variable name to indicate what type of information the variable holds. The following table has some suggested conventions:

Type	Prefix	Example
Boolean	bin	binDoIt
Date/Time	dtm	dtmBirthday
Double	dbl	dblTolerance
Integer	int	intAge
Long	lng	lngDistanceToS
Single	sng	sngAverage
String	str	strName

The trouble with doing this is that unless you force the issue by using one of the conversion functions described later, you can't be sure that VBScript will store the information in the form you want. I won't be using these conventions in this book.

Fine Points of Variables

One of the most common bugs in a program is the misspelled variable name. Unless you take appropriate steps, you'll find your VBScript programs are prone to this. The problem is that VBScript allows you to create variables on the fly by merely using a variable name on a line in a program. Misspell the name for a variable that already exists in your program, and VBScript will just create a new variable that has nothing to do with the one you wanted to work with—giving it a default value that will inevitably cause bugs. This implicit variable creation makes it very difficult to track down bugs because you have to find the misspelled variable name.

The way around this is to require your VBScript program to *declare* its variables before you can use them. Then you will be notified if a variable name is spelled incorrectly. The designers of VBScript give you this option but do not force you to use it.

The statement for declaring a variable is called, naturally enough, a *declaration statement*. Declaration statements use the VBScript keyword *Dim*, as in the following example:

```
Dim SalesTax
```

You can declare more than one variable at a time by separating variables with commas, as shown in the following example:

```
Dim Counter, EndValue
```

You can declare a variable name only once within a procedure.

The statement for requiring declarations is *Option Explicit.* It is the first example of a statement that you do not ever find within event procedures. It should be used right after the HTML comment tag that starts your VBScript code:

```
<SCRIPT LANGUAGE="VBSCRIPT">
<!--
Option Explicit
```

After VBScript processes an Option Explicit statement, it will no longer allow you to use a variable unless you declare it first. If you try to use a variable without declaring it, an error message will appear, as shown in Figure 3-3.

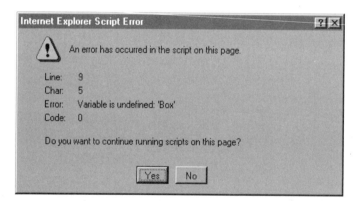

Figure 3-3.   *Error message caused by using an undeclared variable.*

Finally, the first time you use a variable, VBScript temporarily assigns it the default value "empty." This basically means that the variable doesn't contain a value. The "empty" value disappears the moment you assign a value to the variable. You shouldn't hesitate to assign initial values to your variables. Otherwise, you risk creating a breeding ground for hard-to-find bugs. It is therefore quite common to use the first few statements in an event procedure to initialize the variables.

Swapping

A common task within an event procedure is *swapping,* or interchanging, the values of two variables. Suppose you have two variables, Old and New, and you try to swap their values like this:

```
Old = New
New = Old
```

This doesn't work, and it is important that you understand why. What goes wrong is that the first assignment gives the current value of New to the variable Old, but this wipes out the previous value of Old. The result is that the second statement merely copies the original value of New. The solution is to use a temporary variable:

```
Temp = Old    'copy value of Old to Temp
Old = New     'Old now gets the value of New
New = Temp    'retrieve the original value of Old, and assign it to New
```

Scope of Variables

When programmers discuss the availability of a variable used in one part of the program to the other parts of the program, they refer to the *scope* of variables. In older programming languages, where *all* variables were available to *all* parts, keeping variable names straight was always a problem. If, in a complicated program, you had two variables named Total, the values could (and would) contaminate each other.

 OTE   You might want to give two variables the same name if they have the same purpose. For example, you might be totaling two different sets of numbers in two different event procedures in your program. It would be a good idea to name both variables Total.

The solution in modern programming languages such as VBScript is to isolate variables within event procedures. Unless you specifically arrange it, changing the value of a variable named Total in one event procedure will not affect another variable with the same name in another procedure. The technical explanation for this is that variables are *local* to procedures unless specified otherwise. In particular, an event procedure will not normally have access to the value of a variable changed in another event procedure.

As always, it is not a good programming practice to rely on defaults. If you want to be sure that a variable is local within an event procedure, use the Dim statement inside the event procedure to declare all its variables.

Sharing values across procedures

Occasionally you will want the value of a variable to be available to all the VBScript code for your Web page. For example, if an application is designed to perform a calculation involving a single interest rate at a time, that rate should be available to all the procedures for the page. Variables that are shared in this way are called *script-level* variables.

Just as with the Option Explicit statement, you put the declaration statements for script-level variables outside any event procedures. Most programmers place the declarations for script-level variables right after the Option Explicit statement, as shown in the following example:

```
<SCRIPT LANGUAGE="VBSCRIPT">
<!--

   Option Explicit
   Dim SalesTax    'this is a script-level variable
   'event procedures go here

-->
</SCRIPT>
```

In the above example:

- The value of the variable named SalesTax will be visible to all the event procedures for the Web page.

- Any changes made to this variable in one event procedure will persist and show up in the other event procedures.

The last point means you have to be careful when assigning values to script-level variables. Any information passed between event procedures can easily introduce programming bugs. Moreover, these errors are often hard to pinpoint.

OTE Because of the added possibility of bugs when using script-level (or *global*, as they are sometimes called) variables, many programmers like to use a prefix such as "g" (for global) to identify their script-level variables. I think this is a very good programming practice and will adopt it from this point on. Thus, I would prefer to use this:

```
Dim gSalesTax    'script-level variable for sales tax
```

Although most programmers don't think it is a good idea, you can use the same variable name as both a local and a script-level variable. A Dim statement contained in an event procedure takes precedence over a script-level declaration. Duplicating a name in this way makes the script-level variable invisible to the procedure. This means you lose the ability to use the information contained in the script-level variable. VBScript doesn't tell you whether a script-level variable has been declared with the same name as a local variable. This is one more reason to make sure that variables you want to be local really are local, by declaring them inside the procedure. It should also give you more incentive to use the "g" prefix to identify your script-level variables.

Input Boxes

A text box is the normal way for a VBScript application to accept data. However, there is one other technique that is occasionally useful. An input box is a dialog box that the user must close before continuing. This is the principal advantage of using an input box over a text box; it is sometimes necessary to insist that the user supply some necessary data before letting him or her continue to work with the rest of the Web page. The disadvantage is that the dimensions of an input box are fixed by VBScript. Figure 3-4 shows an example of an input box:

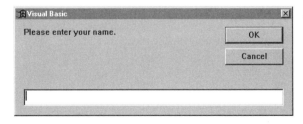

Figure 3-4. *An input box.*

As you can see, input boxes in VBScript have a title bar and four components. The first is the prompt, in this case, "Please enter your name." There are always two command buttons designated OK and Cancel. Finally, there is a text box at the bottom. VBScript always places the cursor here. To display the input box shown in Figure 3-4, use this line of code:

```
YourName = InputBox("Please enter your name.")
```

Here is the general model for displaying an input box:

```
StringVariable = InputBox(prompt)
```

The user types whatever he or she wants in the text box. Pressing the Enter key or clicking the OK button causes whatever is in the text box to become the value of the string variable. Pressing the Esc key or clicking the Cancel button causes VBScript to assign the null string to the variable. You can think of the null string as a placeholder; it is simply a string with no characters and is represented by two double quotation marks with no spaces between them ("").

You can jazz up your input boxes. For example, the following line of code displays the titled input box shown in Figure 3-5:

```
YourName = InputBox("Please enter your name.", "Welcome to VBScript")
```

The second string is what the user sees in the title bar.

Figure 3-5.   *A titled input box.*

You can specify quite a few criteria for an input box. The full range of possibilities is shown in the VBScript documentation, which you can find on the companion CD. (Open the file Vbstoc.htm in the VBSdocs folder. For the most up-to-date version of the VBScript documentation, see Microsoft's VBScript Web page.) Figure 3-6 shows what the InputBox page looks like.

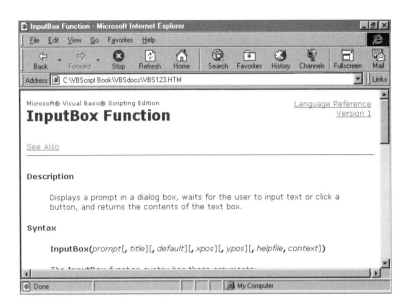

Figure 3-6. *The InputBox page in the VBScript documentation.*

The syntax for the InputBox function is as follows (you'll see a lot more about functions in Chapter 5):

```
StringVariable = InputBox(prompt[, title][, default][, xpos][, ypos]
  [, helpfile, context])
```

I want to go over the above syntax. First, the terms in italics are descriptive placeholders; you substitute your own data for each of these terms. For example, you can substitute "Please enter your name" for *prompt*. Second, the square brackets indicate that what is inside them is optional; you don't include the square brackets themselves in your code. This means that the following syntax is the minimum required for the InputBox function:

```
StringVariable = InputBox(prompt)
```

You could also use any of the following lines:

```
StringVariable = InputBox(prompt, title)
StringVariable = InputBox(prompt, title, default)
StringVariable = InputBox(prompt, title, default, xpos)
StringVariable = InputBox(prompt, title, default, xpos, ypos)
StringVariable = InputBox(prompt, title, default, xpos, ypos, _
  helpfile, context)
```

Notice that because *helpfile* and *context* are contained in one set of square brackets, they must be both included or both excluded.

Since I find that the VBScript documentation is sometimes a little too formal and condensed, here are my paraphrases of what it gives you. To begin with, the terms inside the parentheses are called *parameters* or *arguments*.

The *prompt* parameter is a string (text inside quotes) or a string variable (the name of a variable containing text) whose value VBScript displays in the dialog box. It is limited to roughly 1024 characters. The prompt string will wrap to the next line when it no longer fits, but you can put in your own line breaks if you want by using the Chr(13) and Chr(10) characters that I discuss in the next section.

You saw the *title* parameter in the previous example. The title parameter contains the string used in the title bar. If you omit this parameter, VBScript just puts "Visual Basic" in the title bar.

The *default* parameter lets you display default text in the text box where the user will be entering information. If you omit this parameter, the text box starts out blank.

The *xpos* and *ypos* parameters are either integers or expressions that VBScript can evaluate to integers. The *xpos* parameter specifies the distance in twips between the left edge of the input box and the left edge of the screen. The *ypos* parameter specifies the distance in twips between the top of the input box and the top of the screen. A twip is one-twentieth of a printer's point. (Points are used to measure fonts; this book is set in 10.5-point type. There are 1440 twips to an inch.) If you omit the *xpos* parameter, the input box will be horizontally centered; if you omit the *ypos* parameter, it will be displayed about one-third of the way down the screen.

The parameters *helpfile* and *context* are used together if you want a Help button to appear in the input box—an advanced topic that I won't cover in this book.

The notation presented in the InputBox syntax statement might seem cryptic at first, but it is a good idea to get used to it. It is, after all, the notation used in the VBScript documentation. With this notation, as I mentioned earlier, anything in square brackets is optional. For example, notice that the parentheses, which are required, are *outside* the square brackets. Next, notice the commas that separate the parameters. Although they are inside the square brackets and are therefore optional, there is a little "gotcha." If you want to skip one of the parameters, you still have to use a comma as a separator. How else would VBScript know which parameter belongs where? For example, the following line seems to contain an extra comma:

```
Color = InputBox("Favorite color?", "Welcome to VBScript", , 100, 100)
```

This line sets the prompt of the input box to "Favorite color?" and the title bar to "Welcome to VBScript." It also starts the input box with no default string and moves the input box away from the center of the screen and closer to the top. Notice the comma that marks the place where the default string would go.

Characters (ANSI Codes)

A computer doesn't have one kind of memory for text and another kind for numbers. Anything stored in a computer's memory is changed into a number. The program keeps track of whether or not the memory patterns are codes for text. The code for translating text to numbers within VBScript is called the ANSI (American National Standards Institute) code. The ANSI code associates a displayable or a control character with each number from 0 through 255. (A control character is not an actual character but causes some action to take place. For example, the bell character causes your computer to beep.) The control characters, and such special keys as the Tab key, have numbers less than 32.

Every font has a unique set of ANSI codes. Although ANSI codes are always numbers from 0 through 255, the characters that these numbers represent vary among the different fonts. The value of the function Chr(n) is the character with the ANSI code n in the font currently in use. For example, the following statement displays the character ã if you are using the Times New Roman font but displays ↖ if you are using Wingdings:

```
txtBox1.Text = Chr(227)
```

As I mentioned in the discussion of the InputBox function, a common use of the Chr function is to add line breaks in your text strings. The value of Chr(13) is a Carriage Return (move the cursor down one line), and the value of Chr(10) is a Line Feed (move the cursor to the beginning of the line). Combining the two gives you what you usually get by pressing the Enter key, as shown in the following example:

```
Msg = "This will be on line 1"
Msg = Msg & Chr(13) & Chr(10) & "This will be on line 2"
InputBox(Msg)
```

 OTE VBScript has a *built-in constant* for the Chr(13) & Chr(10) combination. (See below for more about built-in constants.) You can use vbCrLf in its place. So a shorter version of the second line above is:

```
Msg = Msg & vbCrLf & "This will be on line 2"
```

Constants

A program is easiest to debug when it's readable. Try to prevent the "my eyes glaze over" syndrome that is all too common when a program has lots of mysterious numbers sprinkled about. It's a lot easier to read a line of code such as

```
Tax = txtCurrentPrice.Text * SalesTax
```

which identifies the text box and uses a descriptive term for the sales tax, than if you use

```
Tax = txtBox1.Text * .825    '.825 what's that?
                             'and what's txtBox1?
```

even though both will have the same effect.

Programming languages have the notion of *constants* to help prevent the "my eyes glaze over" syndrome. The idea is that once you define a constant, you can't—even by mistake—change it later in your program. The keyword for telling VBScript that something is a constant is simply Const, as shown in the following example:

```
Const PI = 3.14159
```

You might also set up string constants using the same keyword:

```
Const USER_NAME = "B. Smith"
Const SCRIPT_LANGUAGE = "VBScript"
```

(I use the convention that the names of the constants I create are always uppercase.) If you place a constant inside an event procedure, only that event procedure can see it. If you place a constant right after the HTML comment tag (where your VBScript code begins), all your VBScript code can see it and use it.

VBScript comes with lots of useful built-in constants. These are constants such as vbRed and vbYellow for colors, and vbSunday and vbMonday for date functions. (Obviously, VBScript does not follow the convention that built-in constants are uppercase.) There is also the vbCrLf built-in constant, discussed earlier, which you can use for the Chr(13) & Chr(10) combination. You should check the VBScript documentation for a complete list of built-in constants.

Numbers

A number in VBScript cannot use commas to mark off thousands. It can have a decimal point unless you want it to be an integer. (And once it has a decimal point, it ceases to be an integer.) If you need to give a numeric value to a variable, place the number on the right-hand side of the assignment statement, as shown in this example:

```
SalesTax = .0825
```

Operations on Numbers

The following table gives you the symbols for the five fundamental arithmetic operations and for two special operations you will occasionally need:

Operator	Operation
+	Addition
-	Subtraction (and to denote negative numbers)
*	Multiplication
/	Division
^	Exponentiation
\	Integer division
Mod	The remainder after integer division

The ordinary division symbol (/) gives you a value that has a decimal point. The integer division symbol (\) throws away the remainder in order to give you an integer. For example, $7\backslash3 = 2$. Since ordinary division always produces a number with a decimal point, use integer division or the Mod operator if you really want to work with integers.

 OTE VBScript has ways to format numbers containing a decimal point. (See the next chapter.) Unless you use one of these formatting techniques, the result of a calculation will inevitably have too many digits after the decimal point.

The Mod operator gives you the remainder after integer division. For example, 7 Mod 3 = 1. When one integer perfectly divides another, there is no remainder, so the Mod operator gives 0: 8 Mod 4 = 0.

The term for a combination of numbers, variables, and operators from which VBScript can extract a value is *numeric expression*.

Arithmetic on date variables

VBScript makes it easy to do calculations with date variables. If you add or subtract an integer, you add or subtract that many days. Adding a fraction changes the time within a day. You can use the function Now to retrieve the current date and time.

The following example displays today's date and time and then displays the date and time 10,000 days ago:

```
Dim Today, LongTimeAgo

Today = Now
MsgBox(Today)
LongTimeAgo = Today - 10000
MsgBox(LongTimeAgo)
```

(See Chapter 5 for more on the functions that VBScript has for dealing with dates.)

Parentheses and precedence

When you do calculations, you have two ways to indicate the order in which you want operations to occur. The first way is by using parentheses, and you may well prefer this method. Parentheses let you easily specify the order in which operations will occur. The expression 3 + (4 * 5) gives 23 because VBScript does the operation within the parentheses (4 * 5) first and only then adds the 3. On the other hand, (3 + 4) * 5 gives 35 because VBScript adds the 3 and the 4 first to get 7 and only then multiplies by 5.

VBScript allows you to avoid parentheses, provided you carefully follow rules that determine the precedence of the mathematical operations. For example, multiplication takes precedence over addition. This means that 3 + 4 ∗ 5 is 23 rather than 35 because the multiplication (4 ∗ 5) is done before the addition.

The following list shows the hierarchy of arithmetic operations:

1. Negation (making a number negative)

2. Exponentiation

3. Multiplication and division

4. Integer division and the remainder (Mod) operation

5. Addition and subtraction

For example, −4 ^ 2 gives 16 because VBScript first does the negation (−4) and only then does the exponentiation.

Think of the above hierarchy as denoting levels. Operations on the same level are done from left to right, so 96 / 4 ∗ 2 is 48. Because division and multiplication are on the same level, first the division is done, giving 24, and then the multiplication is done. On the other hand, 96 / 4 ^ 2 is 6. This is because the exponentiation is done first, yielding 16, and only then is the division done.

To show you how obscure using the hierarchy of operations can make your programs, try to figure out what VBScript would do with this:

```
4 * 2 + 16 / 8 + 2 ^ 3
```

Here's what happens: first the exponent is computed (2 ^ 3 = 8), then the multiplication and division are done from left to right (4 ∗ 2 = 8; 16 / 8 = 2), and then the addition is done (8 + 2 + 8 = 18).

Examples such as this one should convince you that using parentheses will make your programs clearer!

More on Numbers in VBScript

If you've tried any calculations involving large numbers in VBScript, you've probably discovered that the program often doesn't bother displaying large numbers but often does display answers using a ridiculous number of digits after the decimal point. Even disregarding the abundance of digits, you might have seen something strange if you asked VBScript to display large numbers. It doesn't print a lot of zeros. Instead, it uses a variation of *scientific notation*. For example, let's say you use the following statement to display a 1 followed by 25 zeros:

```
txtBox1.Text = 10 ^ 25
```

What you see instead is 1E+25. If you are not familiar with this notation, think of the E+ as meaning "move the decimal point to the right, adding zeros if necessary." The number of places is exactly the number following the E. If a negative number follows the E, move the decimal point to the left. For example, 2.1E–5 gives you .000021. You can enter a number using the E notation if it's convenient; VBScript doesn't care whether you enter 1000, 1E3, or 1E+3.

Type conversions

Once in a while, you need to tell VBScript that a data type is something different from what it appears to be, say a string of digits rather than a number. For example, VBScript would interpret an ordinary zip code as a number. (The string "12345" is different from the number 12345.) You can (assuming it makes sense) override how VBScript thinks the information stored in one of its variables should be regarded. (By "makes sense," I mean that you can't expect to convert a string of letters to a number, for example, although you can always convert a number to a string.)

You do this with a conversion function. The following table summarizes these functions. (There are two types listed that you haven't seen yet: Currency and Byte. I'll explain them shortly.)

Conversion Function	What It Does
CInt	Converts an expression to an integer, rounding if necessary
CLng	Converts an expression to a long integer, rounding if necessary
CSng	Converts an expression to a single-precision number
CDbl	Converts an expression to a double-precision number
CCur	Converts an expression to a variable of type Currency
CStr	Converts an expression to a string
CBool	Converts an expression to a Boolean value (True or False)
CByte	Converts an expression to a variable of type Byte
CDate	Converts a string to a variable of type Date

For example, the following line ensures that VBScript regards the zip code as a text string and not as a number:

```
ZipCode = CStr(22203)
```

The Byte type is rarely used in VBScript; it simply lets you pack small numbers (0 through 255) in the minimum amount of memory possible. The Currency type, on the other hand, is both interesting and useful. The Currency type allows you to use numbers with greater accuracy than is possible even with the Double or Long type. You often need this degree of accuracy to handle financial transactions. For example, when you use the Double type, it is theoretically possible to have an account be off by, say, .01—which makes some people very unhappy! With the Currency type, this kind of error is essentially impossible. The trade-off, though, is that calculations with the Currency type are the slowest of all. Because of this, VBScript uses the Currency type only if you explicitly tell it to, as shown in this example:

```
MyCheckbookBalance = CCur(1000.01)
```

Sample Program: A Mortgage Calculator

You now have seen enough of VBScript to write some really useful programs. This sample, which is in the file Mortgage.htm on the companion CD, is a mortgage calculator. It won't be the most elegant way to write a program to compute mortgages, but it does show you how much progress you have made so far.

The program provides three text boxes so that the user can enter the amount of the mortgage, the interest rate, and the term in years. Then the program calculates the monthly mortgage payment by using a standard formula.

To create this sample from scratch, the first thing to do is design the Web page. Figure 3-7 shows the page with four labels, four text boxes, and one command button. It uses the default sizes for all the controls.

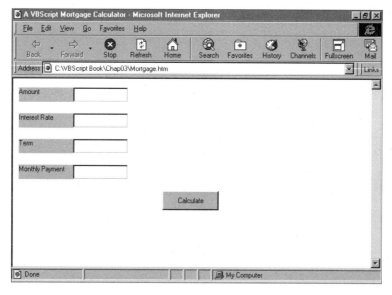

Figure 3-7.   *A mortgage calculator.*

The following table lists the ActiveX controls in the order you should add them to the Web page and describes the property values you need to change.

ActiveX Control	Property	Value
Microsoft Forms 2.0 Label	Caption ID	Amount Label1
Microsoft Forms 2.0 TextBox	ID	txtMortgageAmount
Microsoft Forms 2.0 Label	Caption ID	Interest Rate Label2
Microsoft Forms 2.0 TextBox	ID	txtInterestRate
Microsoft Forms 2.0 Label	Caption ID	Term Label3
Microsoft Forms 2.0 TextBox	ID	txtMortgageTerm
Microsoft Forms 2.0 Label	Caption ID	Monthly Payment Label4
Microsoft Forms 2.0 TextBox	ID	txtMortgagePayment
Microsoft Forms 2.0 CommandButton	Caption ID	Calculate cmdCalculate

The code to calculate the monthly mortgage payment is a bit more complicated than you might expect. Here is the formula:

```
Payment = Principal * MonthInt / (1-(1/(1+MonthInt)) ^ (Years * 12))
```

The variable MonthInt is the annual interest rate divided by 12. Because entering this formula is prone to error, I'll break it up into a numerator and a denominator in the sample. Here's the whole HTML file:

```
<HTML>
<HEAD>

  <TITLE>A VBScript Mortgage Calculator</TITLE>
  <SCRIPT LANGUAGE="VBSCRIPT">
  <!--

    Option Explicit

    Sub cmdCalculate_Click
      'Calculates the monthly mortgage payment by using this formula:
      'Principal * MonthInt / (1-(1/(1+MonthInt)) ^ (Years * 12))
```

(continued)

```
        Dim Years, Principal
        Dim Percent, MonthInt
        Dim Numerator, Denominator
        Dim Payment

        'Get info
        Years = txtMortgageTerm.Text
        Principal = txtMortgageAmount.Text
        Percent = txtInterestRate.Text / 100
        MonthInt = Percent / 12

        Numerator = Principal * MonthInt
        Denominator = 1-(1/(1+MonthInt)) ^ (Years * 12)
        Payment = Numerator / Denominator
        txtMortgagePayment.Text = Payment
      End Sub

    -->
    </SCRIPT>

</HEAD>
<BODY>

<OBJECT ID="Label1" WIDTH=96 HEIGHT=24
CLASSID="CLSID:978C9E23-D4B0-11CE-BF2D-00AA003F40D0">
  <PARAM NAME="Caption" VALUE="Amount">
  <PARAM NAME="Size" VALUE="2540;635">
  <PARAM NAME="FontCharSet" VALUE="0">
  <PARAM NAME="FontPitchAndFamily" VALUE="2">
  <PARAM NAME="FontWeight" VALUE="0">
</OBJECT>

<OBJECT ID="txtMortgageAmount" WIDTH=96 HEIGHT=24
CLASSID="CLSID:8BD21D10-EC42-11CE-9E0D-00AA006002F3">
  <PARAM NAME="VariousPropertyBits" VALUE="746604571">
  <PARAM NAME="Size" VALUE="2540;635">
  <PARAM NAME="FontCharSet" VALUE="0">
  <PARAM NAME="FontPitchAndFamily" VALUE="2">
  <PARAM NAME="FontWeight" VALUE="0">
</OBJECT>

<BR><BR>

<OBJECT ID="Label2" WIDTH=96 HEIGHT=24
CLASSID="CLSID:978C9E23-D4B0-11CE-BF2D-00AA003F40D0">
  <PARAM NAME="Caption" VALUE="Interest Rate">
  <PARAM NAME="Size" VALUE="2540;635">
  <PARAM NAME="FontCharSet" VALUE="0">
```

```
    <PARAM NAME="FontPitchAndFamily" VALUE="2">
    <PARAM NAME="FontWeight" VALUE="0">
</OBJECT>

<OBJECT ID="txtInterestRate" WIDTH=96 HEIGHT=24
CLASSID="CLSID:8BD21D10-EC42-11CE-9E0D-00AA006002F3">
    <PARAM NAME="VariousPropertyBits" VALUE="746604571">
    <PARAM NAME="Size" VALUE="2540;635">
    <PARAM NAME="FontCharSet" VALUE="0">
    <PARAM NAME="FontPitchAndFamily" VALUE="2">
    <PARAM NAME="FontWeight" VALUE="0">
</OBJECT>

<BR><BR>

<OBJECT ID="Label3" WIDTH=96 HEIGHT=24
CLASSID="CLSID:978C9E23-D4B0-11CE-BF2D-00AA003F40D0">
    <PARAM NAME="Caption" VALUE="Term">
    <PARAM NAME="Size" VALUE="2540;635">
    <PARAM NAME="FontCharSet" VALUE="0">
    <PARAM NAME="FontPitchAndFamily" VALUE="2">
    <PARAM NAME="FontWeight" VALUE="0">
</OBJECT>

<OBJECT ID="txtMortgageTerm" WIDTH=96 HEIGHT=24
CLASSID="CLSID:8BD21D10-EC42-11CE-9E0D-00AA006002F3">
    <PARAM NAME="VariousPropertyBits" VALUE="746604571">
    <PARAM NAME="Size" VALUE="2540;635">
    <PARAM NAME="FontCharSet" VALUE="0">
    <PARAM NAME="FontPitchAndFamily" VALUE="2">
    <PARAM NAME="FontWeight" VALUE="0">
</OBJECT>

<BR><BR>

<OBJECT ID="Label4" WIDTH=96 HEIGHT=24
CLASSID="CLSID:978C9E23-D4B0-11CE-BF2D-00AA003F40D0">
    <PARAM NAME="Caption" VALUE="Monthly Payment">
    <PARAM NAME="Size" VALUE="2540;635">
    <PARAM NAME="FontCharSet" VALUE="0">
    <PARAM NAME="FontPitchAndFamily" VALUE="2">
    <PARAM NAME="FontWeight" VALUE="0">
</OBJECT>

<OBJECT ID="txtMortgagePayment" WIDTH=96 HEIGHT=24
CLASSID="CLSID:8BD21D10-EC42-11CE-9E0D-00AA006002F3">
    <PARAM NAME="VariousPropertyBits" VALUE="746604571">
```

(continued)

```
      <PARAM NAME="Size" VALUE="2540;635">
      <PARAM NAME="FontCharSet" VALUE="0">
      <PARAM NAME="FontPitchAndFamily" VALUE="2">
      <PARAM NAME="FontWeight" VALUE="0">
</OBJECT>

<BR><BR>

<CENTER>
<OBJECT ID="cmdCalculate" WIDTH=96 HEIGHT=32
CLASSID="CLSID:D7053240-CE69-11CD-A777-00DD01143C57">
   <PARAM NAME="Caption" VALUE="Calculate">
   <PARAM NAME="Size" VALUE="2540;846">
   <PARAM NAME="FontCharSet" VALUE="0">
   <PARAM NAME="FontPitchAndFamily" VALUE="2">
   <PARAM NAME="ParagraphAlign" VALUE="3">
   <PARAM NAME="FontWeight" VALUE="0">
</OBJECT>
</CENTER>

</BODY>
</HTML>
```

It's pretty long, isn't it? For this reason, from now on, I won't always give you the complete HTML source code. I'll just assume that you can get it from the companion CD. Instead, I'll show you only the important parts of the code.

Improvements to the Mortgage Calculator

There are lots of ways to improve the mortgage calculator. One way is to get rid of all those silly numbers that show up after the decimal point in the monthly payment. You'll see these if you open the program file in Internet Explorer; enter an amount, an interest rate, and a term; and then click the Calculate button. Another important improvement would be making the program more "bulletproof." Inexperienced users often enter information in the wrong form. You might want to prevent them from entering anything but digits, for example. You could also make the program more friendly by allowing users to enter commas or dollar signs in the mortgage amount. In the next chapter, you'll see how to write the code to do this.

For now, though, suppose you want to add a command button that increases the interest rate by $\frac{1}{8}$ percent and then redoes the calculations. (You could also add a command button that decreases the interest rate.)

Go back to the Web page and add another command button. Change the button's ID property to cmdIncrease and the Caption property to Increase. Add the following simple event procedure, which will be executed when you click the new button:

```
Sub cmdIncrease_Click
   txtInterestRate.Text = txtInterestRate.Text + .125
   cmdCalculate_Click
End Sub
```

Take a look at the following key statement:

```
cmdCalculate_Click
```

This is the first example you've seen of one event procedure using (the technical term is *calling*) another event procedure. As your programs get more sophisticated, event procedures become more and more interrelated. Chapter 6 discusses this in depth. What happens here is that when VBScript calls the cmdCalculate_Click event procedure you wrote earlier, it uses the current contents of the text boxes. Because the following line changes the contents of the text box directly, the cmdCalculate_Click event procedure has new data to work with:

```
txtInterestRate.Text = txtInterestRate.Text + .125
```

As this example indicates, you call an event procedure by using its name. More complicated event procedures (those that have parameters) are still called by using their names—you just need to supply the required parameters.

2

Beyond the Basics

Controlling Program Flow

Two of the most useful things that computers can do are to repeat thousands of operations quickly and to change what they are doing based on user input.

This chapter shows you two features of VBScript (and of most programming languages): loops and conditional statements. A loop allows a computer program to repeat operations; a conditional statement allows a program to take different actions depending on whether a condition, such as whether the user entered required information into a text box, is True or False.

Repeating Operations (Loops)

In programming, as in real life, you might want to repeat an operation until one of the following situations occur:

- The operation has been repeated a fixed number of times
- A predetermined goal has been reached
- Certain initial conditions have changed

You use a *determinate loop* for the first situation and two different kinds of *indeterminate loops* for the latter two.

Determinate Loops

There are times when you need different heading levels on your Web page. You could write code like this:

```
<H1>This is heading level 1</H1>
<H2>This is heading level 2</H2>
```

However, combining the Document.Write method with a little bit of code, you can do it automatically. Before I show you how, I'll start with a simpler example. When the Web page starts, let's display a list of the numbers 10 down to 1 (counting backward) followed by a message box that says, "Blastoff!" The simplest way to do this is to place the following lines of code in the head section:

```
For I = 1 To 10
  Document.Write 11 - I
  Document.Write "<BR>"
Next
Document.Write "Blastoff!"
```

In the preceding example, the line with the For and To keywords means "for every value from 1 through 10 of the variable I." Think of a For-Next loop as winding up a wheel inside the computer so the wheel will spin a fixed number of times. You can tell the computer what you want it to do during each spin of the wheel. In this case, the Document.Write method displays information directly on the screen.

 OTE The example uses subtraction inside the loop. You'll see a simpler way to count down in the section "More on For-Next Loops" later in this chapter.

For and Next are keywords that must be used together. The statements between the For and the Next are called the body of the loop, and the whole control structure is called, naturally enough, a For-Next loop.

The keyword For sets up a counter variable. In the preceding example, the counter is the integer variable I. In this example, the counter's starting value is set to 1 and the ending value is set to 10. First VBScript sets the counter variable to the starting value. Then it checks whether the value for the counter is less than or equal to the ending value. If the value is greater than the ending value, nothing is done. If the starting value is less than or equal to the ending value, VBScript processes subsequent statements until it comes to the keyword Next. At that point, it adds 1 to the counter variable and starts the process again. The process continues until the counter variable is greater than the ending value. At that point, the loop is finished, and VBScript moves past it. Figure 4-1 shows a flow diagram of the For-Next loop.

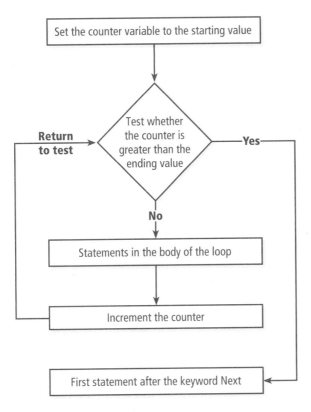

Figure 4-1. *Flow diagram of the For-Next loop.*

Finally, you might have noticed that the body of the For-Next loop is indented. As always, the purpose of the spacing in a program is to make the program more readable and therefore easier to debug. I always find it easier to have the body of a loop indented from the controlling code.

Here's the example that displays the heading levels. The only tricky part is assembling the correct tags using the ampersand (&) symbol—you saw simpler versions of this in Chapter 3:

```
<HTML>
<HEAD>

  <TITLE>Display heading levels</TITLE>
  <SCRIPT LANGUAGE="VBSCRIPT">
  <!--

    Option Explicit

    Dim I, BeginHeading, EndHeading

    For I = 1 To 6
      BeginHeading = "<H" & I & ">"
      EndHeading = "</H" & I & ">"
      Document.Write BeginHeading & "This is heading level " _
        & I & EndHeading
    Next

  -->
  </SCRIPT>

</HEAD>
<BODY>

</BODY>
</HTML>
```

Example: A retirement calculator

With For-Next loops, you can compute many interesting values that would otherwise require sophisticated mathematics. For example, suppose you wanted to write a program that would allow users to enter the following information:

■ A fixed amount of money they think they can put away each year for retirement

■ The interest rate they expect to get each year

■ The number of years until their retirement

The program would then tell them how much money they will have when they retire. There are sophisticated formulas involving geometric progressions for this sort of calculation, but common sense (and a simple For-Next loop) suffices. What happens is that each year you get interest on the previous amount, and you add the new amount to it. Let's assume that the interest is compounded annually. Then this program will need four text boxes, four labels, and a command button. Figure 4-2 shows the Web page. As I mentioned in the last chapter, I won't give you all the source code here—but it's on the companion CD in the file Retire.htm.

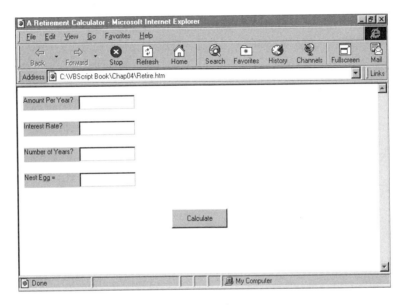

Figure 4-2.   *Web page for calculating retirement income.*

The following table lists the ActiveX controls in the order you should add them to the Web page and describes the property values you need to change. The only property I haven't discussed before is the Locked property. Setting the Locked property of the txtNestEgg text box to True prevents the user from entering anything in this text box, which is where the program puts the retirement income.

ActiveX Control	Property	Value
Microsoft Forms 2.0 Label	Caption	Amount Per Year?
Microsoft Forms 2.0 TextBox	ID	txtAmountPerYear
Microsoft Forms 2.0 Label	Caption	Interest Rate?
Microsoft Forms 2.0 TextBox	ID	txtInterestRate
Microsoft Forms 2.0 Label	Caption	Number of Years?
Microsoft Forms 2.0 TextBox	ID	txtNumberOfYears
Microsoft Forms 2.0 Label	Caption	Nest Egg =
Microsoft Forms 2.0 TextBox	ID Locked	txtNestEgg True
Microsoft Forms 2.0 CommandButton	ID Caption	cmdCalculate Calculate

Here is the cmdCalculate_Click event procedure that does the actual calculation:

```
Sub cmdCalculate_Click
  'Calculate retirement income assuming
  'fixed deposit and fixed interest rate

  Dim Total, Amount
  Dim Interest, Years
  Dim I

  Total = 0
  Amount = txtAmountPerYear.Text
  Interest = txtInterestRate.Text / 100
  Years = txtNumberOfYears.Text

  For I = 1 To Years
    Total = Amount + Total + (Total * Interest)
  Next

  txtNestEgg.Text = Total
End Sub
```

The key line inside the For-Next loop is this:

```
Total = Amount + Total + (Total * Interest)
```

The key line gets a new total by adding this year's amount and the interest earned to the previous total amount.

Errors with Loops

Changing the counter variable inside a loop is one sure source of errors. VBScript will cheerfully use the new value, and you will no longer know how many times your loop will run. For example, you can't be sure how many times the following code will run:

```
For Count = 1 To 10
  Count = InputBox("How many items did you count?")
Next
```

 WARNING Changing the counter can also give you an *infinite loop*. Infinite loops theoretically run forever because the counter never reaches the ending value. In practice, the browser will notify you or you will get tired of waiting and end the browser task by using, for example, the Ctrl-Alt-Del key combination.

Probably the most common type of error in using loops is called an *off-by-one error,* or *fence post error.* This affects even the most experienced programmer occasionally. When this error occurs, instead of performing an operation, say, 500 times as you had planned, the program performs it 499 or 501 times. If your program suffers from this problem, keep in mind that the loop terminates only when the counter exceeds (not equals) the ending value.

 NOTE Why is it called a fence post error? Well, the common answer to questions such as how many shelves does it take to make a bookcase or how many fence posts does it take to make a fence is often "off by one." For example, a bookcase with three shelves needs four pieces of wood because of the extra shelf needed for the top, and a fence with 10 holes between the posts needs 11 pieces of wood.

More on For-Next Loops

You don't always count by ones. Sometimes it's necessary to count by twos, by fractions, or backward. You do this by adding the Step keyword to a For-Next loop. The Step keyword tells VBScript to change the counter by the specified amount rather than by one, as was done previously. For example, instead of doing subtraction inside a loop, it is faster to do this:

```
For I = 10 To 1 Step -1
  Document.Write "It's t minus " & I & " and counting."
  Document.Write "<BR>"
Next
Document.Write "<H1>" & "Blastoff!" & "</H1>"
```

 IP   When you use a negative step value, the body of the For-Next loop continues until the counter is less than (instead of greater than) the ending value.

Example: a mortgage table calculator

As a more serious example, let's take the mortgage calculator from the previous chapter and add a For-Next loop so that it can calculate several mortgage payments instead of just one. When the user clicks the button, the program will calculate mortgages for a range of interest rates. The range will be within +/−1 percent of the rate entered by the user, in increments of $1/8$ percent. We will use a list box to display the table of results. The only new programming feature in this example is a method named *AddItem* that lets us add items to a list box. The simplest syntax for this method (and the one we use in this example) is this:

`ListBoxID.AddItem(Text)`

You substitute the value of the ID property of the list box for *ListBoxID*; you substitute the text string you want to add for *Text*. The following table lists the ActiveX controls in the order you should add them to the Web page and describes the property values you need to change.

ActiveX Control	Property	Value
Microsoft Forms 2.0 Label	Caption	Amount
Microsoft Forms 2.0 TextBox	ID	txtMortgageAmount
Microsoft Forms 2.0 Label	Caption	Interest Rate
Microsoft Forms 2.0 TextBox	ID	txtInterestRate
Microsoft Forms 2.0 Label	Caption	Term
Microsoft Forms 2.0 TextBox	ID	txtMortgageTerm
Microsoft Forms 2.0 ListBox	ID	lstMortgage
	Width	333
Microsoft Forms 2.0 CommandButton	ID	cmdCalculate
	Caption	Calculate

Figure 4-3 shows the Web page.

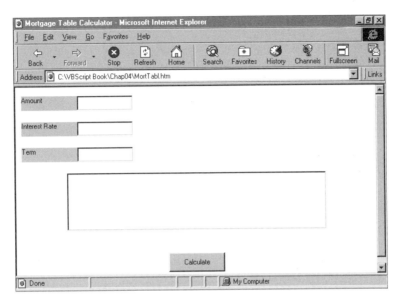

Figure 4-3. *The mortgage table calculator.*

Here's the code for the cmdCalculate_Click event procedure, which you can find in the file MortTabl.htm on the companion CD:

```
Sub cmdCalculate_Click
  'Calculates a table of mortgage amounts for a range
  'of interest rates (+/-1 percent of the interest rate
  'entered by the user, in increments of 0.125 percent);
  'puts the information in a list box

  Dim Years, Principal
  Dim Percent, MonthInt
  Dim Payment, Interest
  Dim StartInterest, EndInterest

  'Get info
  Years = txtMortgageTerm.Text
  Principal = txtMortgageAmount.Text
  Percent = txtInterestRate.Text / 100
  StartInterest = Percent - .01    '1 percent change
  EndInterest = Percent + .01
```

(continued)

```
For Interest = StartInterest To EndInterest Step .00125
  MonthInt = Interest / 12
  Payment = Principal * MonthInt / (1-(1/(1+MonthInt)) _
    ^ (Years * 12))
  1stMortgage.AddItem("At the rate of " & Interest & _
    ", payment is " & Payment)
Next
```

```
End Sub
```

The For-Next loop simply recalculates the mortgage payment for each interest rate in a repetitive fashion. (As before, the answers are displayed with too many decimal places. I'll show you how to clean this up in the next chapter.)

 OTE   The answers in the list box stop at +0.875 percent instead of +1 percent because, as I mentioned in Chapter 3, VBScript uses approximations for decimal numbers. The approximation it uses for 0.00875 is actually a little larger than 0.00875, so adding another 0.00125 sends it past 0.01!

Nested For-Next Loops

A lot of information is presented in tabular form, from a simple multiplication table to a sophisticated mortgage table that allows a range of interest rates across the top and a range of amounts down the side.

To see the kind of VBScript code you need to create these types of tables, let's start with the simpler example of a multiplication table. A fragment such as this one gives you the "twos" table:

```
For I = 1 To 9
  Document.Write 2 * I
Next I
```

To get an entire multiplication table, you need to enclose this loop with another one that changes the 2 to a 3, the 3 to a 4, and so on. In other words, the final table requires one loop *nested* inside the other. For example, if you place the following code in the head section, you'll see a multiplication table. (The numbers will be a bit out of alignment because of the different numbers of digits involved.

```
<SCRIPT LANGUAGE="VBSCRIPT">
<!--

  Option Explicit

  Dim I, J

  For J = 1 To 9
    For I = 1 to 9
      Document.Write I * J & "      "    'add spaces
    Next
    Document.Write "<BR>"                'to new line after each row
  Next

-->
</SCRIPT>
```

Here's what is happening: The value of J starts out at 1, and then VBScript enters the inner loop. The value of I starts out at 1 as well. VBScript makes 9 passes through the inner loop before it finishes. On each pass, it displays the number along with a few spaces after the number. Once it finishes a whole pass through the inner loop, it processes the extra Document.Write statement that moves down to a new line. After that, it processes the second Next statement. At this point, VBScript changes the value of J to 2 and starts the process all over again.

Sometimes it's helpful to think of the inner loop in a nested For-Next loop as really doing one thing—that is, as a statement in VBScript a bit more complicated than the usual ones. If you think of the inner loop as accomplishing one task, you won't have many problems. Nested loops have a reputation for being hard to program and hard to understand, and for being a breeding ground for bugs. This need not be true. All you have to do is outline the loops on a piece of paper, and then they won't be hard to program. And if you are careful about your indentation pattern, they won't be hard to understand or, therefore, to debug.

The rule for nesting For-Next loops is simple: the inner loop must be completed before the Next statement for the outer loop is encountered. You can have loops nested to three levels (that is, a loop that contains a second loop, which then contains a third loop) or loops nested to four or even more levels. You are limited only by how well you understand the logic of the program, not by VBScript.

Indeterminate Loops

Let's go back to the retirement calculator discussed earlier in this chapter. Instead of asking how much money a person will have at the end of a specified number of years, let's ask how long it will be until the person has $1,000,000—again assuming that the same amount of money is put away each year and that the interest rate doesn't change. You could use trial and error with the previous program, but there is a more direct approach. You'll soon see how to resolve this and many similar problems.

This modified retirement calculator offers a good example of a task that comes up repeatedly in programming. Loops must either keep on repeating an operation or not, depending on the results obtained within the loop. Such loops are indeterminate—that is, not executed a fixed number of times—by their very nature. You use the following pattern when you write this type of loop in VBScript:

```
Do
    VBScript statements
Until condition is met
```

Figure 4-4 shows what VBScript does in a Do-Until loop.

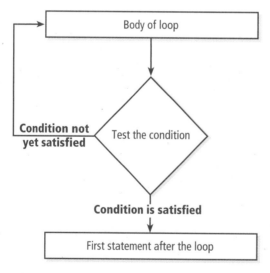

Figure 4-4.   *Flow diagram for a Do-Until loop (test the condition at the end).*

If necessary, use the Ctrl-Alt-Del key combination to end the Internet Explorer task.

When you write an indeterminate loop, something must change; otherwise, the test will always fail and you'll be stuck with an infinite loop. Microsoft Internet Explorer tells you when it thinks it is trapped in an infinite loop by displaying a dialog box that says the script has been running for a long time. The dialog box asks you whether you want to stop the script, as shown in Figure 4-5.

Figure 4-5.   *Message for an infinite loop.*

If this dialog box appears, try clicking the Yes button.

Relational operators

The keys to making indeterminate loops work are called *relational operators*. The simplest one, of course, tests for equality. This uses the same equal (=) sign you probably remember from school and have already seen used for assigning values to variables and properties. In more sophisticated scripts, you need ways to check for something besides equality. You do this by means of the other relational operators. The relational operators are listed here:

Symbol	Meaning
=	Equals
< >	Is not equal to
<	Is less than
<=	Is less than or equal to
>	Is greater than
>=	Is greater than or equal to

For strings, these operators test for ANSI order. This means that "A" comes before "B" and "B" comes before "C." The uppercase letters come before the lowercase letters, so "Z" comes before "a." Within the lowercase letters, as you might expect, "a" comes before "b" and "b" comes before "c." The string "aBCD" comes after the string "CDE" because uppercase letters come before lowercase letters. A space comes before any letter, number, or other displayable character.

As an example, suppose you want to prevent a "divide-by-zero" error when a user enters data in a text box. Use a fragment like this:

```
Do
    Number = InputBox("Please enter a nonzero number.")
Loop Until Number <> 0
```

The section "What Is It?" on page 122 in this chapter has more on checking input.

Writing this kind of loop is the first step in stopping a user from entering the wrong kind of data. Testing input data is one way to begin to bullet-proof a program. In fact, a large part of bulletproofing a program (the jargon is "making it robust") involves making it tolerant of input errors. Instead of behaving strangely because of a user's typo, the program checks that the data entered is usable. If not, it warns the user. The more robust a program is, the less likely it is to behave strangely for an inexperienced user.

 NOTE   One of the big advantages of VBScript is that the user's computer does the work of *input validation* (checking what the user typed). As I discussed in Chapter 1, you no longer need to send the data over the net, thus wasting the server's time on this task.

You can even monitor keystrokes as they are typed into any control that accepts input. To see how to do this, see the section "Using the KeyPress Event Procedure" in Chapter 9.

We are now ready to look at the revised retirement calculator mentioned at the beginning of this section. You enter the amount saved per year and the interest rate, and then you click the Calculate button. A message box informing you how long it will take to accumulate $1,000,000 is then displayed, as shown in Figure 4-6.

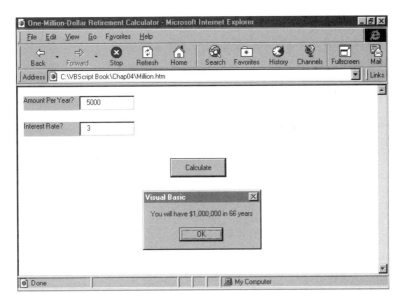

Figure 4-6. *The revised retirement calculator.*

Here is the cmdCalculate_Click event procedure, which you can find in the file Million.htm on the companion CD, that determines how long it will take to accumulate $1,000,000:

```
Sub cmdCalculate_Click
  'Calculate how many years it will
  'take to save $1,000,000, assuming
  'fixed deposit and fixed interest rate

  Dim Amount, Interest
  Dim Years, Total

  Amount = txtAmountPerYear.Text
  Interest = txtInterestRate.Text / 100
  Years = 0
  Total = 0

  Do
    Total = Amount + Total + (Total * Interest)
    Years = Years + 1
  Loop Until Total >= 1000000

  MsgBox ("You will have $1,000,000 in " & Years & " years")
End Sub
```

The body of the loop is much like the one in the retirement calculator from the beginning of this chapter—it figures the yearly change and adds it to the previous total to get a new total. This time, however, the variable Years keeps track of the number of years. Finally, the loop continues as long as the value of the variable Total is less than 1,000,000. The moment the total equals or exceeds this target, the loop ends and VBScript reports the results in a message box.

Possible missteps

You should be aware of a problem that frequently occurs with these new kinds of loops. Consider (but don't run) this fragment:

```
Total = 0
PassNumber = 0

Do
  Total = Total + .1
  PassNumber = PassNumber + 1
  Document.Write "At " PassNumber & " the total is: " & Total & "<BR>"
Loop Until Total = 1
```

You might think this program would end after ten passes through the loop, but it doesn't, and it's important to understand why. In fact, this fragment results in an *infinite* loop, and either you will be warned by Internet Explorer (via the dialog box that you saw earlier) or you will need to use the Ctrl-Alt-Del key combination to end the Internet Explorer task.

This infinite loop occurs for a subtle but important reason. As you saw with the mortgage table calculator that stopped too early, *once you use a decimal point in your VBScript numbers, these numbers are only approximations.* VBScript's internal characterization of 0.1 is off by a little in, say, the seventh place. As VBScript adds 0.1 to the total, tiny errors accumulate, and the resulting total, although it comes very close to 1, never exactly equals 1.

The moral is that when you use numbers with decimal points, you should not use equality (or inequality) as the condition for the loop to end. Instead, allow for tiny errors by using one of the other relational operators, for example:

```
Loop Until Total > .99999999
```

Or, to be sure that the total is at least 1, do the following:

```
Loop Until Total >= 1
```

This ensures that the program really will stop after ten passes through the loop.

Sophisticated indeterminate loops

A common task is reading names that a user enters, keeping count all the while. You need a way to know when the user is finished entering names. Suppose you stop when the user enters ZZZZ. (You'll see how to store the names in Chapter 6; for now, just follow along with this example, even though we are throwing away a lot of information that the user is so laboriously entering.)

This seems pretty easy—you use an indeterminate loop that keeps track of the number of entries and that ends when the user enters ZZZZ:

```
NameCount = 0

Do
   Name = InputBox("Please enter the next name:")
   NameCount = NameCount + 1
Loop Until Name = "ZZZZ"

Document.Write "The number of names you entered is " & NameCount
```

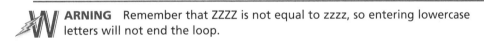

WARNING Remember that ZZZZ is not equal to zzzz, so entering lowercase letters will not end the loop.

Although this fragment might seem like a prototype for code that reads in a list of items until the last one is encountered, it has a problem. In fact, it suffers from an off-by-one error! Why? Imagine that the list consists of only one name besides the ZZZZ. What happens? Let's work through this program step by step. The user types the first name, and NameCount increases to 1. Next the user types ZZZZ. Because the test is done at the end of the loop, NameCount increases to 2 before the test is done. Therefore, when the loop ends, the count is 2 when we want it to be 1. One possible cure is to subtract 1 from NameCount after the loop ends. However, this is a bit silly when VBScript makes the cure so easy—move the test to the beginning of the loop. Consider the following:

```
NameCount = 0
Name = InputBox("Please enter the next name:")

Do Until Name = "ZZZZ"
  NameCount = NameCount + 1
  Name = InputBox("Please enter the next name:")
Loop
```

Now the user types the first name before the loop starts. Once this is done, the loop is entered. The program does an initial test, and NameCount increases by 1 only if the test fails. (Notice that this kind of loop also works if the user enters nothing but ZZZZ. In this case, NameCount equals 0, just as it should.) Figure 4-7 shows a picture of what VBScript does in this type of loop.

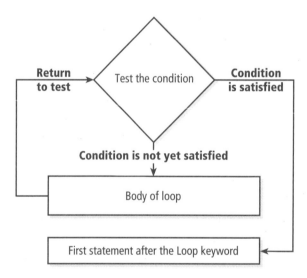

Figure 4-7.   *Flow diagram for a Do-Until loop (test the condition at the beginning).*

 IP   A good rule of thumb is that if you do not want to keep the final entry (such as ZZZZ) as part of your list of entries, put the test at the beginning of the loop. Otherwise, put the test at the end.

With the test at the end, the loop is always executed at least once; with the test at the beginning, the loop might not be executed at all. Also, remember that when the test is at the beginning, you obviously must have something to test. Therefore, make sure that, before the loop starts, you initialize the variable to be tested. Finally, don't forget that you usually need two assignment statements when the test is at the beginning—the first before the loop starts and the second (to keep the process going) inside the loop.

When nesting Do loops, you must follow a rule similar to the rule you follow for nesting For-Next loops—the inner loop must be finished before the outer loop is tested. Choose a reasonable indenting pattern, and you won't have any problems.

Finally, keep in mind that all arithmetic operators have higher precedence than relational operators. VBScript has no trouble interpreting the following code as meaning first do the multiplication and then do the greater-than test:

```
Loop Until TheNumber * 10 > 100
```

But, as always, parentheses make things clearer, so I would write this as:

```
Loop Until (TheNumber * 10) > 100
```

The Do-While loop

VBScript has other kinds of loops. These loops consist of replacing the keyword Until with the keyword While. This new kind of loop might seem superfluous since you can always change a Do-While loop into a Do-Until loop by reversing the relational operator. For example,

```
Do
Loop While txtBox1.Text = ""
```

is the same as

```
Do
Loop Until txtBox1.Text <> ""
```

and

```
Do
Loop While YourGuess <= 100
```

is the same as

```
Do
Loop Until YourGuess > 100
```

Given this, why bother learning this new type of loop? There are two reasons why the Do-While loop isn't superfluous. The first is that, as much as possible, you want to write a program conforming to the way your mind works. Sometimes you will think of an operation as going on until something happens, while other times you think of it as continuing indefinitely. The richness of VBScript's programming language makes the fit better between your thought patterns and the computer program you're trying to write. In fact, psychologists have found that tests with positive conditions are easier to understand.

```
Do While Number = 0
```

is easier for most people to process than its counterpart,

```
Do Until Number <> 0
```

Do loops with And, Or, and Not

The previous section gave you one reason to use both Do-Until and Do-While loops, but this is not the only reason. Probably the best reason to learn both kinds of loops comes when you have to combine conditions. Let's say you want to have $1,000,000 before you are 50 years old, for example.

In VBScript, you can combine conditions using the ordinary English words And, Or, and Not. These three keywords, which are called *logical operators*, work in VBScript pretty much as they do in English. You can continue a process as long as both conditions are True or stop it when one becomes False. For example, you might use the following code to stop an operation when it has been done 10 times or when the total is large enough:

```
Do While (Count <= 10) And (Total < 100)
```

On the other hand, you would use this code to ensure that the operation was done at least 10 times and that the total reached at least 100:

```
Do While (Count <= 10) Or (Total < 100)
```

If this is confusing, think about it this way: If the count is 11 but the total is only 99, ordinary English usage tells us that we still need to continue the operation.

Finally, imagine that ButtonPressed is a variable that has the value True or False. The following code allows you to continue an operation as long as the ButtonPressed variable is not yet True:

```
Do While Not(ButtonPressed)
```

As you can see, the logical operators are used exactly the way they are in English. However, it becomes increasingly confusing to try to force combinations of the And, Or, and Not operators into loops that they don't seem to fit. For example, suppose you want to continue a process while a number is greater than 0 and a text box is empty. It is much easier to say

```
Do While (Number > 0) And (txtBox1.Text = "")
```

than to say

```
Do Until (Number <= 0) Or (txtBox1.Text <> "")
```

although they both mean the same thing.

Making Decisions (Conditional Statements)

At this point, your scripts can only decide whether to repeat a group of statements. They can't as yet change what they do depending on new information. The next few sections take care of this. All the statements in these sections deal with turning a phrase such as this into VBScript code:

If *condition* Then *do something different...*

VBScript uses the If-Then statement in much the same way that you do in normal English. For example, to warn a user that a text box must not be empty, use a line like this:

```
If txtBox1.Text = "" Then MsgBox "You must enter something!"
```

More generally, when VBScript encounters an If-Then statement, it checks whether the first clause (called, naturally enough, the If clause) is True. If that clause is True, the computer does whatever follows (called the Then clause). If the test fails, processing skips to the next statement.

You can use the If-Then statement to compare strings or numbers. For example, a statement such as the following tests for ANSI order:

```
If String1 < String2 Then MsgBox(String1 & " comes before " & String2)
```

If the variables N1 and N2 both hold numbers, this statement tests for numeric order:

```
If N1 < N2 Then MsgBox(N1 & " comes before " & N2)
```

The If-Then Statement with And, Or, and Not

You can also use the keywords And, Or, and Not in an If-Then statement. These keywords let you check two conditions at once. For example, suppose you have to check whether a number is between 0 and 9:

```
If (Digit >= 0) And (Digit <= 9) Then MsgBox "OK"
```

 ARNING In both speaking and writing, we sometimes say something like, "If my average is greater than 80 and less than 90, then…" Translating this sentence construction directly into VBScript code won't work. You must repeat the variable each time you want to test something. To do the translation from English to VBScript, say, "If my average is greater than 80 and my average is less than 90, then…"

A final note on using the And, Or, and Not operators—you do not have to use the same variable in all conditions. A statement such as this one is a perfectly good VBScript statement:

```
If (Grade4 > Grade3) And (Average > 60) Then MsgBox "Improving!"
```

The parentheses are there only to improve readability; they are not necessary. VBScript processes relational operators before worrying about the logical operators such as And.

Using the keyword Or in an If-Then statement is similar. The test is successful if either one of the conditions is True. Suppose you had to test whether at least one of two numbers was nonzero. You would use a statement such as this:

```
If (A <> 0) Or (B <> 0) Then…
```

Choosing to use the Not statement depends a lot on personal taste (like deciding between the Do-While and Do-Until loops). Most people find it easier just to change the relational operator. For example:

```
If Not (Salary > 62700) Then…
```

is exactly the same as

```
If Salary <= 62700 Then…
```

Similarly,

```
If Not (A = "Internet Explorer") Then…
```

is harder to write than

```
If A <> "Internet Explorer" Then…
```

If you prefer to use the Not operator, be sure you use parentheses; without them your program is apt to be unreadable.

Since VBScript is really testing for a Boolean value in the If clause, you can actually place any Boolean property there. For example, in the following statement, VBScript processes the Then clause only if the Enabled property of the txtBox1 text box is set to True:

```
If txtBox1.Enabled Then…
```

Other Logical Operators

There are other, somewhat less common, ways of combining tests. For example, you can use the Eqv (equivalence) operator. This lets you test whether two conditions are both True or both False. For example:

```
If (X=True And Y=True) Or (X=False And Y=False) Then…
```

is the same as

```
If (X Eqv Y) Then…
```

Another useful operator (especially for graphics and file security scripts) is Xor (exclusive Or). This corresponds to the English "if A or B but not both."

The If-Then-Else Statement

Suppose you need to write a social security tax calculator. The way this tax works is that you pay (in 1997) 6.2 percent of the amount you make, up to $65,400. After that, whether you make $66,000 or $5,550,000 per year, you pay no more social security tax than $4,054.80. To write the code for this calculator, you need to use a line such as this:

```
If Wages < 65400 Then SSTax = .062 * Wages Else SSTax = 4054.80
```

When VBScript processes an If-Then-Else statement, if the test succeeds, VBScript processes the statement that follows the keyword Then (the Then clause). If the test fails, VBScript processes the statement that follows the keyword Else (the Else clause). Figure 4-8 shows you, in flow-diagram style, what VBScript does with an If-Then-Else statement.

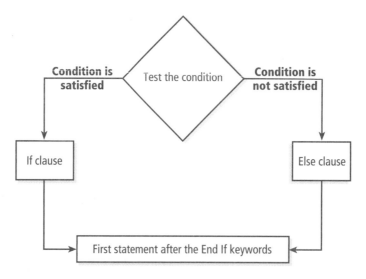

Figure 4-8.   *Flow diagram for an If-Then-Else statement.*

The Block If-Then-Else Statement

More often than not, you will want to process multiple statements if a condition is True or False. To do this, you need the most powerful form of the If-Then-Else statement, the *block If-Then-Else* statement. This lets you process as many statements as you like in response to a True condition, as shown in the following outline:

```
If Savings > one year's income
   buy stock
   buy bonds
   go on vacation
```

Here there are three statements in response to something being True. To write this in VBScript, you use a slightly different format than the usual If-Then-Else statement. The block If-Then-Else statement looks like this:

```
If condition to test Then
   lots of statements
Else
   lots more statements
End If
```

You do not put anything on the line with the keyword Then; press the Enter key immediately after typing it. This bare Then keyword is how VBScript knows it's beginning a block. The Else keyword is optional; putting it there (again, alone on a line) means that another block of statements will follow, to be processed only if the If clause is False. However, whether the Else clause is there or not, the block If-Then-Else statement must end with the keywords End If.

For an example of this, let's expand the original mortgage calculator from Chapter 3 so that the program checks whether the user wants to calculate the monthly payment or the maximum amount he or she can borrow, depending on which text box is empty. The comments in the following program give the formula you need for this. (You have to do a little algebra on the original formula.) We will use exactly the same Web page design that we used in Chapter 3. Here is the new cmdCalculate_Click event procedure, which you can find in the file ExpMort.htm on the companion CD:

```
Sub cmdCalculate_Click
   'Calculates either the monthly mortgage payment,
   'using the formula:
   'Payment = Principal * MonthInt / (1-(1/(1+MonthInt))^(Years*12))
   'or the maximum you can borrow, using the formula:
   'Principal = Payment * (1-(1/(1+MonthInt))^(Years*12)) / MonthInt

   Dim Years, Principal
   Dim Payment, Percent
   Dim MonthInt
   Dim Numerator, Denominator
```

(continued)

```
'Get info
Years = txtMortgageTerm.Text
Principal = txtMortgageAmount.Text
Payment = txtMortgagePayment.Text
Percent = txtInterestRate.Text / 100
MonthInt = Percent / 12

If txtMortgagePayment.Text = "" Then
  Numerator = Principal * MonthInt
  Denominator = (1-(1/(1+MonthInt))^(Years*12))
  Payment = Numerator / Denominator
  txtMortgagePayment.Text = Payment
Else
  Numerator = Payment * (1-(1/(1+MonthInt))^(Years*12))
  Denominator = MonthInt
  Principal = Numerator / Denominator
  txtMortgageAmount.Text = Principal
End If

End Sub
```

What Is It?

It's easy to use the If-Then-Else statement to determine whether the user has entered a string in the form of a date or a number. This is the first step in the process of input validation. The technique depends on two Boolean functions built into VBScript. The built-in function IsDate tells you whether an expression is in the right form to be used as a date. Consider the following code:

```
Input = txtBox1.Text
If IsDate(Input) Then
  'do whatever you want with the date
Else
  MsgBox "Please enter the text in the form of a date."
End If
```

Similarly, you can use the IsNumeric function to determine whether a variable contains a number. This gives you a quick way of checking whether the user accidentally entered a letter, for example:

```
Input = txtBox1.Text
If IsNumeric(Input) Then
  'do whatever you want with the number
Else
  MsgBox "Please enter a number."
End If
```

122

Using the If-Then-Else Statement with a Message Box

The If-Then-Else statement can also be used to determine which button the user clicked in a message box. If you assign the value of the MsgBox function to a variable, you can use an If-Then-Else statement to check the value. You can include buttons in a message box by adding a second parameter to the MsgBox function call. VBScript comes with built-in constants for these values. For example, using the constant vbYesNo displays a message box with two buttons—Yes and No. You can then check which button the user clicked by using a built-in constant such as vbYes, as shown in the following example:

```
X = MsgBox("Yes or No?", vbYesNo)
If X = vbYes Then
  MsgBox "The Yes button was clicked."
Else
  MsgBox "The No button was clicked."
End If
```

Notice that you need to use parentheses when using the MsgBox function in this way. The following table lists the built-in constants for the various buttons you can display in a message box.

Constant	Value	Description
vbOKOnly	0	Display OK button only
vbOKCancel	1	Display OK and Cancel buttons
vbAbortRetryIgnore	2	Display Abort, Retry, and Ignore buttons
vbYesNoCancel	3	Display Yes, No, and Cancel buttons
vbYesNo	4	Display Yes and No buttons
vbRetryCancel	5	Display Retry and Cancel buttons

The following table lists the built-in constants you can use to display icons, rather than buttons, in a message box.

Constant	Value	Description
vbCritical	16	Display Critical Message icon
vbQuestion	32	Display Warning Query icon
vbExclamation	48	Display Warning Message icon
vbInformation	64	Display Information Message icon

You can combine the values in these two tables by adding the constants together. For example, the following code gives you the message box shown in Figure 4-9:

```
X = MsgBox("Yes or No?", vbYesNo + VbInformation)
```

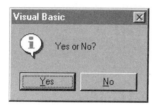

Figure 4-9.   *A message box with buttons and an icon.*

The following table lists the built-in constants you use to identify which button the user clicked. You saw an example of this earlier.

Constant	Value	Description
vbOK	1	OK button was clicked
vbCancel	2	Cancel button was clicked
vbAbort	3	Abort button was clicked
vbRetry	4	Retry button was clicked
vbIgnore	5	Ignore button was clicked
vbYes	6	Yes button was clicked
vbNo	7	No button was clicked

There's a lot more you can do with message boxes. For example, you can change which button is the default button by adding one of the constants shown in the following table to the constants you are already using. The first button is normally the default.

Constant	Value	Description
vbDefaultButton1	0	First button is the default
vbDefaultButton2	256	Second button is the default
vbDefaultButton3	512	Third button is the default
vbDefaultButton4	768	Fourth button is the default

Finally, you can prevent the user from continuing to work with Internet Explorer or even from switching to another application until he or she responds to the message box. (Not to be done casually!) This is done by adding one of the constants in the following table to the constants you are already using.

Constant	Value	Description
vbApplicationModal	0	Application modal. The user must respond to the message box before continuing work in the current application. This is the default.
VbSystemModal	4096	System modal. All applications are suspended until the user responds to the message box.

Combining the If-Then-Else Statement with Loops

Suppose you wanted to modify the program that calculates how long it takes to build up a $1,000,000 nest egg so that the program ends when one of these conditions is met:

■ The $1,000,000 goal is reached

■ The number of years until you retire reaches some maximum

It's easy to write the loop that continues until either condition occurs. Let's say, however, that you want to display a message box that says which condition caused the loop to end. To do this, you need to use an If-Then-Else statement following the loop. Here is the new cmdCalculate_Click event procedure, which you can find in the file MaxYears.htm on the companion CD:

```
Sub cmdCalculate_Click

  Const GOAL = 1000000
  Const NUMBER_OF_YEARS = 30

  Dim Amount, Interest
  Dim Years, Total
```

(continued)

```
Amount = txtAmountPerYear.Text
Interest = txtInterestRate.Text / 100
Years = 0
Total = 0

Do Until (Total >= GOAL) Or (Years = NUMBER_OF_YEARS)
  Total = Amount + Total + (Total * Interest)
  Years = Years + 1
Loop

If Years < NUMBER_OF_YEARS Then
  MsgBox("Congratulations! You will reach your goal in " _
    & Years & " years.")
Else
  MsgBox("You have only $" & Total & " to retire on.")
End If

End Sub
```

The Select-Case Statement

Suppose you were designing a program to decide whether to hire people for programming jobs based on their grades on the final exam in their VBScript programming course. You'll make an offer to those who received an A; you'll bring those who received a B in for an interview; you won't consider anybody else. Although you can use the If-Then-Else statement to program this, having multiple cases to consider is so common that VBScript has another control structure designed exactly for it. It's called the Select-Case statement. To use this statement, you start with something you want to test. For example, you could write this:

```
If Grade = "A" Then MsgBox "We would like to hire you!"
If Grade = "B" Then MsgBox "Please schedule an interview."
If (Grade <> "A") And (Grade <> "B") Then _
  MsgBox "I am sorry, we won't be able to consider your application."
```

Using the Select-Case statement, however, you can write this:

```
Select Case Grade
  Case "A"
    MsgBox "We would like to hire you!"
  Case "B"
    MsgBox "Please schedule an interview."
  Case "C"
    MsgBox "I am sorry, we won't be able to consider your application."
End Select
```

The Select-Case statement makes it clear that a program has reached a point with many branches; multiple If-Then statements do not. (And the clearer a program is, the easier it is to debug.)

 NOTE Only one clause of a Select-Case statement can be activated.

What follows the keywords Select Case is a variable or an expression, and what VBScript is going to do depends on the value of that variable or expression. The keyword Case is shorthand for "In the case that the variable or the expression equals."

The Case-Else clause should always come last in a Select-Case statement.

The elimination of all cases that require special testing is so common that VBScript has a way of lumping all the remaining cases into one. This is represented (naturally enough) by the keywords Case Else, which you should think of as shorthand for, "Do this case if none of the other cases hold." In the previous example, if somebody with a grade of D or F applies, the program fragment won't even dignify the applicant with a response! This is because there are no cases for a D or an F grade. The following example shows a better way to write the hiring program:

```
Select Case Grade
  Case "A"
    MsgBox "We would like to hire you!"
  Case "B"
    MsgBox "Please schedule an interview."
  Case Else
    MsgBox "I am sorry, we won't be able to consider your application."
End Select
```

Now you have taken care of all possibilities.

Finally, the Select-Case statement allows you to combine cases. Instead of creating five separate cases to test for the five different vowels, you could write this:

```
Case "A", "E", "I", "O", "U"
  MsgBox "This letter is a vowel."
```

Finishing Up with the If-Then-Else Statement

The Select-Case statement allows multiple branches of action but can test for equality only—whether the expression on the first line of the statement equals the value in any of the Case clauses. But suppose you want to use other relational operators. For example, let's say you are keeping track of the number of items your salespeople sell. A person who sells more than 10 items receives a bonus; a person who sells fewer than 10 items receives a salary deduction; nothing happens if exactly 10 items are sold. Your outline might look like this:

```
If ItemsSold > 10 Then do something
If ItemsSold = 10 Then do something else
If ItemsSold < 10 Then do a third thing
```

So far so good. Now imagine that you want to reset the ItemsSold variable in all three cases so that in the first case the salesperson will start out with credit for the excess over 10 sales, in the second case the salesperson will start out at 0, and in the third case the salesperson will start out with a debit. Can you see what will go wrong? The answer is that we could inadvertently activate the third If-Then statement, causing a debit for a salesperson who sold 10 or more items! For example, imagine how unhappy your employees would be if you ran the following code:

```
If ItemsSold > 10 Then
  MsgBox "You have earned a $500 bonus!"
  MsgBox "Am setting back your items sold count."
  ItemsSold = ItemsSold - 10    'credit for excess over 10 sales
End If

If ItemsSold = 10 Then
  MsgBox "Good work but not quite enough for a bonus."
  MsgBox "Am setting your items sold count back to 0."
  ItemsSold = 0
End If

If ItemsSold < 10 Then
  MsgBox "Deducting $500 from your salary " & _
    "because you didn't make your quota."
  MsgBox "And you'll need to make up the gap!"
  ItemsSold = ItemsSold - 10    'note that this will be negative
End If
```

You will make your best employees unhappy by telling them you are deducting $500 from their salaries! (Try to think through the above code. For example, imagine that a salesperson sold 15 items. The code sets back the items sold count to 5—but this activates the last If-Then statement.)

This is a very common situation. The action taken in an If-Then statement unintentionally affects the condition to be tested in a subsequent If-Then statement. The solution is to use the keyword ElseIf. Here is the correct translation of the outline:

```
If ItemsSold > 10 Then
  MsgBox "You have earned a $500 bonus!"
  MsgBox "Am setting back your items sold count."
  ItemsSold = ItemsSold - 10   'credit for excess over 10 sales

ElseIf ItemsSold = 10 Then
  MsgBox "Good work but not quite enough for a bonus."
  MsgBox "Am setting your items sold count back to 0."
  ItemsSold = 0

Else   'ItemsSold < 10
  MsgBox "Deducting $500 from your salary " & _
    "because you didn't make your quota."
  MsgBox "And you'll need to make up the gap!"
  ItemsSold = ItemsSold - 10   'note that this will be negative
End If
```

Now everything is tied together. And just as in the If-Then-Else and Select-Case statements, VBScript activates at most one clause. In particular, if ItemsSold is 10 or greater, the Else clause is never activated and you won't have a lot of irate employees on your hands.

A block If-Then-Else statement can have as many ElseIf clauses as you like; the final Else clause is not required, but it must be the last clause if you do include it. The limit on the number of ElseIf clauses is essentially determined by how much your brain can process. That's why it's preferable to use the Select-Case statement if you are checking for equality only. Although any Select-Case statement can be transformed into an If-Then-ElseIf statement, the latter is usually much harder to read and therefore to debug.

The final point worth noting is that the block If-Then-Else statement is extremely flexible. You can put any VBScript statement following the keyword Then—in particular, another If-Then-Else statement. Consider the following, which a teacher might use if he or she did not regard the final exam as being all-important:

```
If FinalExam < 65 Then
  MsgBox "You failed the final exam."
  If Average > 70 Then
    MsgBox "However, you passed the course."
  Else
    MsgBox "I'm sorry, you failed the course."
  End If
End If
```

Is it clear (forgetting the indentation pattern for a moment) that the Else clause belongs to the inner If-Then-Else statement? The way to see this is to "play computer." For the Else clause to belong to the outer If-Then statement, the inner If-Then-Else statement must have already finished. But it hasn't because, up to that point, no End If keywords have been processed. The first set of End If keywords finishes the inner If-Then-Else statement, while the second set finishes the outer If-Then statement. Therefore, the Else clause must belong to the inner If-Then-Else statement. Of course, you should use a consistent indentation pattern to make it obvious at a glance where nested If-Then-Else statements belong.

Functions and Arrays

This chapter covers the most frequently used built-in functions found in VBScript. These functions can help in situations as common as analyzing the text that a user enters or as uncommon as your needing a trigonometry function. There are more than 80 built-in functions, so I won't try to cover them all in detail in this chapter. Instead, I'll place special emphasis on the string functions as well as on the Rnd function and the Randomize statement. The string functions are especially important because much of what you do with VBScript consists of analyzing text that a user enters. The Rnd function and the Randomize statement, on the other hand, allow you to build an element of chance into your programs. Using these random number tools is the way you'll program, for example, games of chance or simulations, and even make certain kinds of eye-catching Web pages.

Along the way, I'll also show you more about the list box control. This will require you to learn about *arrays.* An array is VBScript's equivalent of a list or table. For this reason, an array is a convenient way to organize information. For example, if you allow a user to add items to a list box, you need a way to get at the new items. (It turns out that VBScript stores all the items in a list box in an array.) Besides their use in working with list boxes, arrays are often needed when working with some of VBScript's more powerful string handling functions. I'll show you how to use these string functions as well.

String Functions

You have already seen that you can join two strings together with the & operator. (You can also use a plus sign, but this is not recommended since you might run into problems when combining numbers and strings.) In this section, you'll see some of VBScript's more useful string-handling functions.

Some Useful String Functions

VBScript has many built-in functions for handling strings. I'll begin with some of the simpler (but still useful) ones and show you the more so-phisticated ones later in this chapter.

String

Often you will need to build a string consisting of repeated instances of the same character. The String function creates this type of string:

```
String(Number, Character)
```

You replace the parameter *Number* with the number of characters you want in the string. You replace the parameter *Character* with the character you want to repeat (or with the character's ANSI code, if you happen to remember it). For example, the following script displays a line of 60 aster-isks across your screen:

```
<HTML>
<HEAD>

  <TITLE>Asterisks</TITLE>
  <SCRIPT LANGUAGE="VBSCRIPT">
  <!--

    Option Explicit

    Dim Asterisks

    Asterisks = String(60, "*")
    Document.Write Asterisks

  -->
  </SCRIPT>
```

```
</HEAD>
<BODY>

</BODY>
</HTML>
```

LCase, UCase

As you might expect from its name, the LCase function forces all the characters in a string to be lowercase. Similarly, the UCase function forces all the characters in a string to be uppercase. These functions are used when you want to disregard the case inside a string. For example, suppose you want to check a string that a user entered, but you don't care whether or not the Caps Lock key was used. Instead of checking for equality between two strings, check if there is equality between the uppercase (or the lowercase) versions:

```
If UCase(txtBox1.Text) = UCase(UserName) Then
  MsgBox "Welcome " & UserName
Else
  MsgBox "Sorry, I don't recognize your name."
End If
```

StrComp

This function can be used instead of a relational operator (such as < or >) to compare two strings. It tells you immediately which of three possibilities you have: the first string is less than the second string, the two strings are equal, or the second string is greater than the first. For example, in the following code, A and B are the two strings to be compared:

```
X = StrComp(A, B)
```

The following table shows the possible values for X:

If	Then the value of X is set to
A < B	-1
A = B	0
A > B	1
A or B is an empty string	Null (a built-in constant)

IP By adding a third parameter to the call to StrComp, you can control whether the comparison is case sensitive. If you use StrComp(A, B, 1), then the comparison is not case sensitive; for StrComp(A, B, 0), it is. (The default is a case-sensitive comparison.)

Trim, LTrim, RTrim

It's easy to accidentally insert extra spaces when typing in data. Although you have to work a little bit to pull out extra spaces from inside a string, you don't have to do much to eliminate spaces at the beginning or end of a string. The Trim function removes spaces from both the left and right sides of a string, as shown in the following example:

```
BadInput = "   This is it.     "
GoodInput = Trim(BadInput)
```

The variable GoodInput now contains the string, "This is it." Similarly, LTrim removes all the spaces from the left side only, while RTrim removes all the spaces from the right.

Analyzing Strings

Suppose you want to examine what the user has typed into a text box, character by character. The code needs to look like this:

```
For each character
  do what you want with the character
Next
```

Translating this outline into VBScript code requires a For-Next loop that uses character *positions* for the starting and ending values. The first character in a string is at position 1, the second character is at position 2, and so on. The starting value for the loop obviously must be 1, but what's not so obvious is that you must determine the length of the string to know what the ending value should be.

Using the Len, Mid, Left, and Right Functions to Analyze Strings

In VBScript, you use the Len function to determine the length of a string. The syntax for this function is:

```
Len(String)
```

You substitute the actual string (or string variable) for the parameter named *String*.

Next you need a function that lets you look at an individual character in a string, based on the character's position. The most important of these functions is the Mid function, which also lets you look at a chunk of characters within a string. The syntax for this function is:

```
Mid(String, Start [, Length])
```

The first parameter is the string (or string variable) you want to analyze. Next comes the position of the character (or of the first character in the chunk) that you want to retrieve. The optional last parameter specifies the number of characters to extract. Here are some examples of how to use this function:

```
LanguageName = "Visual Basic Scripting Edition"
X = Mid(LanguageName, 1, 6)   'X = "Visual"
Y = Mid(LanguageName, 1, 7)   'Y = "Visual "   note the space!
Z = Mid(LanguageName, 8, 5)   'Z = Basic"
```

If you leave out the last parameter, you get a copy of the rest of the string—starting, of course, from the position specified by the second parameter:

```
LanguageName = "Visual Basic Scripting Edition"
X = Mid(LanguageName, 8)   'X = "Basic Scripting Edition"
```

Here is an example that counts the number of spaces in a string by using the Len and Mid functions in a For-Next loop:

```
Dim MyString, SpaceCount, Length, Position

MyString = txtBox1.Text
SpaceCount = 0
Length = Len(MyString)

For Position = 1 To Length
  If Mid(Mystring, Position, 1) = Chr(32) Then
    SpaceCount = SpaceCount + 1
  End If
Next
```

Chr(32) equals the space character.

On each pass through the For-Next loop:

- The character position used by the Mid function increases by one because the variable Position is the loop counter

- Exactly one character is extracted because the third parameter remains the same

---

 IP You could use a line like this in the code above:

```
If Mid(MyString, Position, 1) = " " Then
```

However, there is a potential problem when doing so—you have to be careful to have exactly *one* space inside the quotes. It is safer to use Chr(32) as the space character whenever you need to test for a space.

The Mid function has two cousins that are occasionally useful: Left and Right. As the names suggest, Left extracts characters from the beginning of a string and Right extracts characters from the end. Of the two, the Right function is more commonly used. It avoids a subtraction inside the Mid function and can work a bit faster as a result. For example, the following lines all retrieve the last 4 characters from the string A:

```
Mid(A, Len(A) - 3, 4)
Mid(A, Len(A) - 3)
Right(A, 4)
```

The Left function works the same way but only saves you from using a 1 as the second parameter to the Mid function. If you want the first 10 characters in a string, use one of the following:

```
Mid(A, 1, 10)
Left(A, 10)
```

The Replace Function

Suppose you want to change just part of an existing string. You can do it in an instant with VBScript's new Replace function. For example, suppose you want to change the string "Java is the best programming language" to read "VBScript is the best programming language" instead.

Here's the code fragment that will do this:

```
Test = "Java is the best programming language"
Test = Replace(Test, "Java", "VBScript")
```

Remember that you usually use the Replace function by assigning its result to a variable. Usually it will be the same variable as the one you are working with, though it doesn't have to be. For example, the following code keeps intact the variable YourOpinionIs and only changes the variable MyOpinionIs:

```
YourOpinionIs = "Java is the best programming language"
MyOpinionIs = Replace(YourOpinionIs, "Java", "VBScript")
```

The Replace function has a lot more power, so I'll go over its features by using them in various kinds of examples. Before I do that, though, here's the syntax for the Replace function:

```
Replace(Expression, Find, Replacewith[, Start[, Count[, Compare]]])
```

You have just seen examples of the first three parameters. The optional Start parameter lets you tell VBScript the position at which to start looking for the string that needs to be replaced. (The Start parameter is usually combined with the InStr function, which I'll discuss later in this chapter.) If you omit the Start parameter, as I did in the examples above, the Replace function starts looking at the first character in the string.

The optional Count parameter specifies the number of times you want to do the substitution if VBScript encounters multiple copies of the same string. If you omit this parameter, the default behavior of the Replace function is to replace *all* occurrences of the string. For example, the following code uses a Start parameter of 1 and a Count parameter of 1 to replace only the first letter A with the letter B:

```
TestString = "AAAAAA"
TestString = Replace(TestString, "A", "B", 1, 1)
```

The string "BAAAAA" is the resulting value of TestString.

The optional Compare parameter is convenient because it means you can do a replacement that is not case sensitive. All you have to do is use one of the following built-in constants:

Constant	Value	Description
vbBinaryCompare	0	In spite of its name, this constant means that the replacement should be done only if the case matches perfectly.
vbTextCompare	1	This constant means ignore case.

Finally, there are rare instances when you want to use somewhat strange values as the parameters to the Replace function. The most common of these is when you want to remove something from an expression. To do this, set the Replacewith parameter to the empty (or zero-length) string as shown below:

```
LackOfLetterI = Replace("Mississippi", "i", "")
```

The string "Mssssppp" is the resulting value of LackOfLetterI.

The following table summarizes the results from other special situations:

If	The resulting string is
The original string (Expression parameter) is an empty string ("").	An empty string ("")
The string that you want to replace (Find parameter) is an empty string.	The original string
The Start parameter is greater than the length of the original string.	An empty string
The Count parameter is 0.	The original string
The original string is Null.	An error (See Chapter 7 for more on Null and VBScript-error handling powers.)

Using the InStr and InStrRev Functions to Find Substrings

You already saw the various Trim functions that let you remove extra spaces at the ends of a string. Suppose you want to make sure that there are no double or triple spaces *inside* a string. Your first instinct might be to use a line like this:

```
SpacesGone = Replace(StringWithSpaces, "  ", " ")
```

This goes through the string and replaces every occurrence of two spaces by a single space. The problem is that you might have to repeat the process—all this line can do is reduce the number of consecutive spaces by one each time you use it. You need to program something that can be described as follows:

```
Do While there are still areas with more than one space
  Use Replace(StringWithSpaces, "  ", " ")
Loop
```

To change this outline into actual VBScript code, you need a function that tells you whether one string is part of another string. That is, you need to know whether one string is a *substring* of another. The VBScript function that does this is named Instr (short for "in string"). When you use Instr, VBScript searches the original string, starting at the first position, until it finds the substring.

The syntax for the Instr function is this:

```
Instr([Start, ] OriginalString, Substring[, Compare])
```

The optional first parameter specifies from which position to start the search. If you omit this parameter, the search automatically starts from the first position. The OriginalString and SubString parameters specify the original string to search and the substring to find, respectively. The optional Compare parameter lets you specify whether or not the search should be case sensitive. You can use the same built-in constants that the Replace function allows for this parameter: vbBinaryCompare for a case-sensitive search and vbTextCompare to ignore case. Like the Replace function, the Instr function does a case-sensitive search if you omit this parameter.

If VBScript doesn't find the substring, it returns the value 0. This is exactly what you need to use to remove all occurrences of multiple spaces inside a string. Here is the code:

```
SpacesGone = Replace(OriginalString, "  ", " ")
Do While Instr(SpacesGone, "  ") <> 0
  SpacesGone = Replace(SpacesGone, "  ", " ")
Loop
```

In VBScript, the built-in constant False is equal to 0, and the built-in constant True is equal to –1. Conversely, if you include a number in a Boolean expression, 0 evaluates to False while any nonzero number evaluates to True. Since the Instr function returns the value 0 (False) when VBScript doesn't find a character, or a nonzero value (True) when it does, you will often find yourself writing If-Then-Else statements or Do loops using the Instr function to do the test. For example, you can write an If-Then-Else statement like the following:

```
If Instr(NumericExpression, ".") Then
  MsgBox "Decimal point found."
Else
  MsgBox "No decimal point found."
End If
```

You also could have written this:

```
If Instr(NumericExpression, ".") <> 0 Then
  MsgBox "Decimal point found."
Else
  MsgBox "No decimal point found."
End If
```

 IP   The loop pattern I used in the code to eliminate extra spaces is extremely common for working with repeated occurrences of a substring. Taking advantage of the fact that 0 evaluates to False while nonzero numbers evaluate to True, many people prefer to use a "Found" helper variable to make the code clearer. In this case, the outline looks like this:

```
Found = Instr(OriginalString, Substring)
Do Until Not Found
   do whatever you need; next instance of substring was found
   Found = Instr(OriginalString, Substring)
Loop
```

The idea is that the variable Found will switch to False when the substring is no longer to be found. This in turn will let VBScript stop the Do loop.

Finally, there is also an InStrRev function that returns the position of one string within another, but this time it starts from the back end of the string. The syntax for the InStrRev function is this:

```
InstrRev(OriginalString, Substring[, Start[, Compare]])
```

One sample use of InStrRev would be to check the extension at the end of a filename that a user typed. For example, to check that a filename has a .jpg extension (used for the jpeg picture format), you could use a line like this:

```
If InStrRev(Filename, ".jpg") = Len(Filename) - 4 Then
```

Arrays

When you write the code that validates information that the user enters on a Web page, often you will need to take a string apart into logical pieces and examine the components. For example, you might need to break the user's name into the first name, middle initial, and last name. This is called *parsing* a string. To learn how to use VBScript's powerful string-parsing functions, you need to know how to use *arrays*. Arrays are also necessary when working with list boxes. In fact, let's start by using an array in this situation.

Consider the Web page shown in Figure 5-1 on the next page. We want to allow the user to add an item to the list box if it is not already there. You know how to add an item to a list box—simply call the AddItem method. But how can you find out if an item is already in the list box? We need to do something that can be described by the following outline:

```
Look at each item already in the list box
If the new item is found, stop looking
If the new item is not found, add it
```

To change this outline into actual VBScript code, you need to know that all the items in a list box are stored in a special property of the list box called, naturally enough, the List property. The List property is the first example you have seen of an array. The idea is that a *list* (or, as it is more technically called, a one-dimensional array) has slots for data. Unfortunately, the slots are numbered starting at 0 rather than 1. You get at the slots by using parentheses containing the slot number. For example, lstBox1.List(0) is the item in the first slot, which is the first item in the List array and the first item displayed in the list box; lstBox1.List(1) is the second item in the list box, and so on.

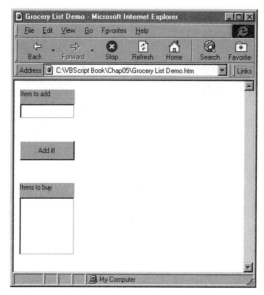

Figure 5-1. *A Web page with a list box.*

The ListCount property of a list box tells you how many items there are in the list box. This, of course, is the same as the number of items in the List array.

 ARNING Since the items in a List array are numbered starting at 0, the last item in a List array is this:

```
lstBox1.List(ListCount-1)
```

It is not, as you might expect, this:

```
lstBox1.List(ListCount)
```

Here's the Click event procedure for the command button on the Web page shown in Figure 5-1:

```
Sub cmdButton1_Click
  Dim I    'counter
  Dim Found

  If Trim(txtBox1.Text) = "" Then Exit Sub

  Found = False
  I = 0
  Do Until Found Or I = lstBox1.ListCount
    If lstBox1.List(I) = txtBox1.Text Then
```

```
      Found = True
    Else
      I = I + 1
    End If
  Loop

  If Not Found Then lstBox1.AddItem txtBox1.Text
  txtBox1.Text = ""

End Sub
```

 OTE   In the preceding code, I used a new language feature of VBScript—the Exit Sub statement. This statement causes the event procedure to exit prematurely; it is the equivalent of skipping directly to the End Sub statement. In this case, the Exit Sub statement is executed if the user has not entered anything (or has entered only spaces) in the text box.

In general, a list (or one-dimensional array) is a way to group items so that you can refer to each item individually by means of its *index*. The index is simply the number you place inside the parentheses; it is the position of the item in the array.

The name of the list has to follow VBScript's rules for variable names. You tell VBScript that you will be working with a list by using a variation of the Dim statement that you have already seen. The only difference is that you need to add the parentheses with the maximum index. For example, the following statement could be used to identify the sales for a year:

```
Dim SalesInMonth(11)
```

This Dim statement would tell VBScript to set aside 12 slots in memory. Those slots would be identified as:

```
SalesInMonth(0) = some number    'for sales in January
SalesInMonth(1) = some number    'for sales in February
  ⋮
SalesInMonth(11) = some number   'for sales in December
```

Notice the advantage of using a list. The following code is cumbersome:

```
Dim SalesInJan, SalesInFeb, SalesInMar, SalesInApr,
Dim SalesInMay, SalesInJun, SalesInJul, SalesInAug,
Dim SalesInSep, SalesInOct, SalesInNov, SalesInDec
```

(continued)

```
SalesInJan = InputBox("Enter the sales for the next month:")
SalesInFeb = InputBox("Enter the sales for the next month:")
SalesInMar = InputBox("Enter the sales for the next month:")
SalesInApr = InputBox("Enter the sales for the next month:")
SalesInMay = InputBox("Enter the sales for the next month:")
SalesInJun = InputBox("Enter the sales for the next month:")
SalesInJul = InputBox("Enter the sales for the next month:")
SalesInAug = InputBox("Enter the sales for the next month:")
SalesInSep = InputBox("Enter the sales for the next month:")
SalesInOct = InputBox("Enter the sales for the next month:")
SalesInNov = InputBox("Enter the sales for the next month:")
SalesInDec = InputBox("Enter the sales for the next month:")
```

But with a list, you can use this code:

```
Dim I
Dim SalesInMonth(11)    'set up 12 slots

For I = 0 To 11
  SalesInMonth(I) = InputBox("Enter the sales for the next month:")
Next
```

Dynamic Versus Fixed Arrays

The SalesInMonth array is an example of a *fixed array*. That's because we fixed its size in the Dim statement. However, you might need an array whose size can change while the program is running. This is called a *dynamic array*. To create a dynamic array whose size you can change inside any event procedure, simply use parentheses without the maximum index and make sure that the array is a script-level variable:

```
Dim gThingsToDo()
```

Now suppose, for example, we want to activate the Web page shown in Figure 5-2 on the next page and we want to store the contents of the To Do list in an array. We need to change the size of the array each time the user adds or removes an item. This can be done with the ReDim statement:

```
ReDim gThingsToDo(lstBox1.ListCount - 1 )
```

 OTE   Using ReDim erases the contents of the array. You can also use a special version of the ReDim statement that keeps the data intact. It's named ReDim Preserve.

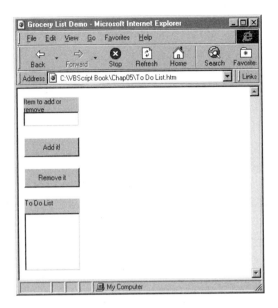

Figure 5-2. *A To Do Web page.*

When you start enlarging or shrinking the size of an array, it becomes vital (in For-Next loops, for example) to have a way of knowing the current upper bound. This is done with the UBound function. A For-Next loop whose code starts like this will go through all the elements in the array:

```
For I = 0 To UBound(AnArray)
```

Finally, by using the ReDim statement inside an event procedure, you can change the size of an array that is *local* to that procedure. For example:

```
Sub cmdSetNumberOfItems_Click

   Dim NumberOfItems

   NumberOfItems = InputBox("How many items today?")
   ReDim Items(NumberOfItems)
   ⋮
```

Each time the user clicks the button, VBScript creates a new array (because we didn't use ReDim Preserve) of a size specified by the value entered in the input box.

Always keep in mind the difference between the following two actions: first, using the Dim statement *outside* all procedures and then using a ReDim statement *inside* a procedure to set its size; second, using only the ReDim statement inside a procedure to create a local array.

In the first case, the array can be seen by all the event procedures in your script, and so any changes you make to the array in one procedure will affect the array in all other procedures. In the second case, the array can't be seen outside the particular event procedure. (The more widely data is available to the different parts of your script, the easier it is to introduce hard-to-track-down bugs.)

Multidimensional Arrays

Just as lists lead to one-dimensional arrays, tables lead to *multidimensional arrays*. For example, to make a two-dimensional array for the multiplication tables, you would write this:

```
Dim MultiplicationTable(9,9)
```

This sets aside 10 rows and 10 columns for a total of 100 slots. (Remember that arrays start with a slot at position 0.) To actually fill the table, use a nested For-Next loop:

```
For I = 0 To 9
  For J = 0 To 9
    MultiplicationTable(I,J) = (I+1) * (J+1)
  Next
Next
```

Converting Variables to Arrays

One of VBScript's most amazing abilities regarding arrays is that you can assign an array to a variable that doesn't use parentheses in its definition, and then treat the variable just like an ordinary array. VBScript provides two ways to do this. The first is with the Array function, which simply turns a bunch of data into an array:

```
Dim A
A = Array(1, 2, 3, 4)
```

Now A(0) gives you 1, A(1) gives you 2, and so on. You can also declare an array and then simply assign it to another variable:

```
Dim ATable, MultiplicationTable(9,9)
ATable = MultiplicationTable
```

You can even use a variable to temporarily hold an array in order to "swap" two arrays. (Check out the next chapter for an example of this.)

Although I said earlier that the List property of a list box is an array, this is true only in a restricted sense. It works exactly like an array as far as element access (via the index), but you cannot assign the List property of a list box to a variable. This is a shame, since you end up needing to write a For-Next loop in order to transfer the contents of a list box to an array for future processing:

```
Dim I

ReDim ArrayForListContents(lstBox1.ListCount-1)
For I = 0 To lstBox1.ListCount-1
  ArrayForListContents(I) = lstBox.List(I)
Next
```

If you could assign the List property as I mentioned earlier, you could do this instead:

```
ArrayForListContents = lstBox1.List
```

Oh well, maybe they will add this feature in the next version of VBScript.

Parsing and Building Strings

You have already seen the Mid function that you can use to break down a string on a character-by-character basis. If you are willing to write the code, every possible string manipulation can be done with Mid. The code can get complex, so VBScript has many powerful labor-saving functions for building up and breaking down strings. These functions all work with arrays. For example, the Join function takes an array of strings and in one fell swoop makes a new string out of it. This saves you the work of coding a For-Next loop to join together the individual strings—and it even works faster.

Here's an example of the Join function. Let's suppose I have previously stored a list of names in an array, as shown in the following code:

```
Dim MyNieces(5)

MyNieces (0) = "Shara "
MyNieces(1) = "Rebecca "
  ⋮
```

Now I can simply write one line of code to display all their names in a message box, as shown here:

```
Msgbox "Hello " & Join(MyNieces)
```

The real stars of the group of functions that build up and break down strings, however, are the Split and Filter functions. I'll discuss the Split Function first. For example, suppose you have somebody's name:

Bertrand Arthur William Russell

The Split function can take this string and return an array of four strings:

- First array entry (at index 0) = "Bertrand"

- Second array entry = "Arthur"

- Third array entry = "William"

- Last array entry = "Russell"

Here's the code to do this and also to display the results in successive message boxes (note the use of the UBound function):

```
Dim Test, A, I

Test = "Bertrand Arthur William Russell"
A = Split(Test)

For I = 0 To UBound(A)
  MsgBox A(I)
Next
```

Notice how this code uses an ordinary variable (a variable not declared as an array) to hold the array returned by the Split function. You will have to use a variable in this way whenever you use the Split function.

The simplest form of the Split function breaks down a string into the parts that are separated by individual spaces. However, it doesn't work very well if the user has inadvertently added multiple spaces. For example, if you change the code to read as follows, it will display a bunch of "empty" message boxes because of the extra spaces:

```
Dim, Test, A, I

Test = "Bertrand     Arthur    William Russell"
A = Split(Test)

For I = 0 To UBound(A)
  MsgBox A(I)
Next
```

The easiest solution is to simply use the Replace function to remove extra spaces, as you saw earlier, *before* using the Split function.

The full power of the split function

Although the Split function defaults to splitting a string at its spaces, you can do more when you use some of its optional parameters. For example, you can tell the Split function that backslashes mark the breaks. (Whatever character you specify is called the *delimiter*.) This lets you easily analyze the full path of a filename. The following code splits a filename into its separate path components:

```
A = Split(Filename, "\")
For I = 0 To UBound(A)
  MsgBox A(I)
Next
```

The full syntax for the Split function looks like this:

```
Split(Expression[, Delimiter[, Count[, Compare]]])
```

The Delimiter parameter is the string that marks the breaks. (It doesn't have to be a single character, by the way.) If you omit it, VBScript assumes you want the string split at the space characters. The optional Count parameter tells VBScript how many substrings you want in the array. Omitting it (or using −1) tells VBScript to return all the substrings. The Compare parameter works as before; it determines case sensitivity if the delimiter is alphabetic.

 OTE You might see the individual substrings that result from using the Split function referred to as *tokens*.

The Filter Function

The Filter function takes an array of strings and returns a new array by including only those entries that satisfy the filter or only those that do not. (You often apply the Filter function to an array that resulted from using the Split function.)

 N|**OTE** Just as the List property of a list box cannot be used directly in an assignment statement (even though this property is an array), it also cannot be used directly by the Filter function. For that matter, it cannot be used by any function that needs an array.

For example, suppose that an array named NewsgroupNames contains the names of Internet newsgroups. Internet newsgroup names include dots— for example, rec.art.dance or comp.lang.basic. The first part of the name (up to the first dot) defines the *hierarchy*. You want to filter out all the newsgroups in the alt hierarchy because this is the hierarchy containing newsgroups with messages you don't want your children to see. Here's all the code that you need:

```
FilteredNewsgroups = Filter(NewsgroupNames, "alt.", False)
```

Now the FilteredNewsgroups array contains exactly what you want.

In this example, I created the new array by eliminating entries that contained the search string. This was controlled by the third parameter. If you change it to True, you include the entries that contain the search string:

```
AltNewsgroups = Filter(NewsgroupNames, "alt.", True)
```

The syntax for the Filter function looks like this:

```
Filter(InputStrings, Value[, Include[, Compare]])
```

The default for the Include parameter is True, and the Compare parameter works as before.

Formatting Output

VBScript provides the following functions to format numbers for display:

- FormatNumber
- FormatPercent
- FormatCurrency
- FormatDateTime

Let's work first with the FormatNumber function, as it is the most common of the four. For example, suppose you want to always show two places after the decimal point for a variable named TheNumber. All you have to do is use this:

```
MsgBoxFormatNumber(TheNumber, 2)
```

 OTE The FormatNumber function returns a string rather than a number, but you can convert the results back to a number either by explicitly using a conversion function or by letting VBScript do its automatic conversion. (VBScript automatically converts a string to a number when necessary—for example, in a numeric calculation. I don't recommend this—letting VBScript automatically convert a string of digits to a number is a sure breeding ground for bugs.)

As another example, to modify the mortgage table calculator from Chapter 4 to format the results instead of leaving them in a form with far too many decimal places, all you have to do is change the statement:

```
1stMortgage.AddItem("At a rate of " & Interest & __
  ", payment is " & Payment)
```

to

```
1stMortgage.AddItem("At a rate of " & Interest & _
  ", payment is " & FormatNumber(Payment, 2))
```

Of course, this is still not perfect because the result looks like Figure 5-3 on the next page.

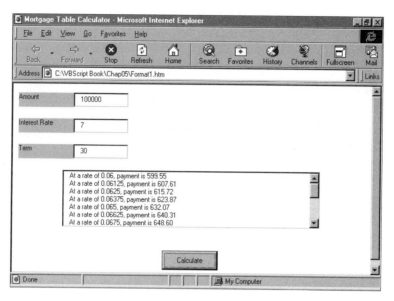

Figure 5-3. *Formatted payments in the mortgage table.*

It would be nice to change the interest rates to display as percentages. This can be done with the FormatPercent function, which converts a decimal number to a percentage. The most common form of the FormatPercent function is this:

```
FormatPercent(Expression, NumDigitsAfterDecimal)
```

You use the second parameter to indicate the number of decimal places you want. For example, the result of using the following statement in the mortgage table calculator is shown in Figure 5-4:

```
lstMortgage.AddItem("At a rate of " & _
    FormatPercent(Interest, 2) & _
    ", payment is " & _
    FormatNumber(Payment, 2))
```

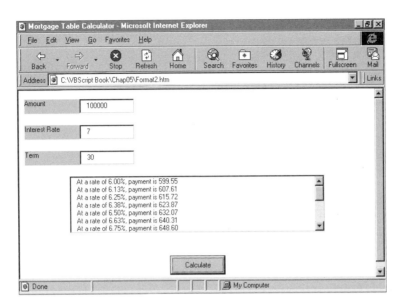

Figure 5-4. *Formatted interest rates in the mortgage table.*

Of course, some people would like to see the payments formatted as currency. This can be done by replacing the FormatNumber function with the FormatCurrency function, which returns a string with whatever currency symbol is defined by the user's system. As an example, the result of using the following statement is shown in Figure 5-5 on the next page:

```
1stMortgage.addItem("At a rate of " & _
  FormatPercent(Interest, 2) & _
  ", payment is " & _
  FormatCurrency(Payment, 2))
```

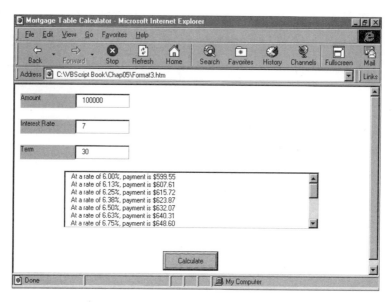

Figure 5-5.   *A properly formatted mortgage table.*

Finally, the FormatDateTime function is a little different. The idea is that you give it a date expression (something that VBScript can interpret as a date, such as #1/1/98# or Now + 100) and a named format, as shown in the following code:

```
MsgBox FormatDateTime(Now, vbGeneralDate)
```

The result is shown in Figure 5-6.

Figure 5-6.   *The general date format in a message box.*

The following table describes the constants you can use for the second parameter and the results of using them:

Constant	Example of result
vbLongDate	Wednesday, July 08, 1997 (the long date format from your computer's regional settings)
vbShortDate	7/8/97 (the short date format from your computer's regional settings)
vbLongTime	8:01:01 PM (the time format specified in your computer's regional settings)
vbShortTime	20:01 (a 24-hour clock)
vbGeneralDate	7/8/97 3:31:03PM (a combination of the short date and the long time)

The Rnd Function and the Randomize Statement

In card games and most other games, the play is unpredictable. This is exactly what is meant by a game of chance. On the other hand, computers are machines, and the behavior of machines is (well, at least should be) predictable. To write a program in VBScript that allows you, for example, to draw lottery numbers or simulate the throwing of a die, you need a function that makes the behavior of the computer seem random. You do this by means of the function Rnd. For example, run the following little script:

```
<HTML>
<HEAD>

  <TITLE>Random Number Example</TITLE>
  <SCRIPT LANGUAGE="VBSCRIPT">
  <!--

    Option Explicit

    Dim I

    For I = 1 To 10
      Document.Write Rnd
      Document.Write "<BR>"
    Next
```

(continued)

```
    -->
    </SCRIPT>

</HEAD>
<BODY>

</BODY>
</HTML>
```

You'll see the screen shown in Figure 5-7.

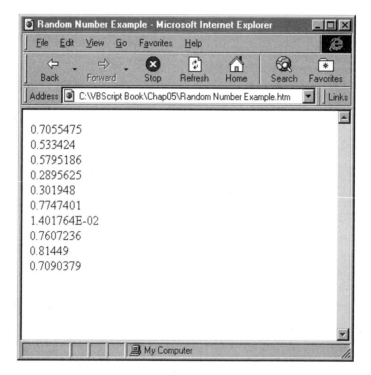

```
0.7055475
0.533424
0.5795186
0.2895625
0.301948
0.7747401
1.401764E-02
0.7607236
0.81449
0.7090379
```

Figure 5-7.   *A random number example.*

As you can see, 10 strange numbers between 0 and 1 fill the screen. These numbers seem to follow no pattern—they're random. They also have many, but not all, of the sophisticated statistical properties that scientists expect of random numbers.

Each time VBScript processes the line containing the statement "Document.Write Rnd," a different number between 0 and 1 is produced. The number can be 0, but it can never be 1. Often you simply want to store the value of the random number into a variable, as follows:

```
RandomNumber = Rnd
```

It's natural to wonder what a strange-looking number with up to seven
decimal places is good for. Suppose, for example, you wanted to write a
program that simulates a coin toss. There are three possibilities: it could
be heads, it could be tails—or it could stand on edge. (Don't wait up for
this last possibility to happen.) The code to simulate a coin toss might
look like this:

```
<HTML>
<HEAD>
<TITLE>A coin toss simulator</TITLE>

  <SCRIPT LANGUAGE="VBSCRIPT">
  <!--

    Option Explicit

    Dim CoinToss

    CoinToss = Rnd

    If CoinToss < .5 Then
      MsgBox "Heads"
    ElseIf CoinToss = .5 Then
      MsgBox "Stood on edge!!!!"
    Else
      MsgBox "Tails"
    End If

  -->
  </SCRIPT>

</HEAD>
<BODY>

</BODY>
</HTML>
```

This seems to work, but if you reload this page a few times (by clicking the
Refresh button or pressing the F5 key), notice how you always get the same
result! This would certainly be unusual behavior for an honest coin. What
is happening?

In fact, the numbers you get from using the Rnd function are only pseudo-random. *Pseudo* means "apparently true," and you've just seen one of the problems of pseudorandom numbers. Every time you start a script that uses pseudorandom numbers, you get the same sequence of pseudorandom numbers. The script operates as if the computer's memory contains a book of these numbers, and after each script is over, the book gets turned back to page 1. The book always starts at the same place, and the numbers are always in the same order; therefore, the results are fixed. You need a way to shuffle the pages each time the program starts. You can do this in many ways, but the easiest way is to use the Randomize statement before you use the Rnd function, as shown in the following code:

```
Dim CoinToss

Randomize    'shuffle the deck
CoinToss = Rnd

If CoinToss < .5 Then
   MsgBox "Heads"
ElseIf CoinToss = .5 Then
   MsgBox "Stood on edge!!!!"
Else
   MsgBox "Tails"
End If
```

Scaling

Numbers between 0 and 1 might (with a little work) be good for imitating a coin toss, but the method used earlier would be cumbersome for, say, a lottery-drawing program with 48 numbers. The outline would need to be something like this:

```
If the random number is less than 1/48, make it a 1
If the random number is at least 1/48 but is less than 2/48, make it a 2
If the random number is at least 2/48 but is less than 3/48, make it a 3
⋮
```

Thinking about this outline leads to a simple trick called *scaling* that more or less automates this process. Suppose you take a number between 0 and 1 and multiply it by 48. If it was less than $1/48$ to start with, it will now be less than 1; if it was at least $1/48$ but less than $2/48$, it will now be between 1 and 2 (but never quite 2), and so on. To get a lottery number, all you need to do is multiply the number by 48 and move up to the next integer.

Unfortunately, there's no VBScript function that moves up to the next integer. The easiest way to do this is with the Fix function, which just throws away the decimal part of a number. For example:

- Fix(4.456) = 4

- Fix(−9.9998) = −9

- Fix(8) = 8

By adding one to the result of "fixing" a positive number, you move to the next highest positive integer. For example, look at the following fragment:

```
'A die simulation using the Fix function

Randomize

Die = Fix(6 * Rnd) + 1
MsgBox "You rolled a " & Die
```

The key to the fragment is that the number inside the parentheses—6*Rnd—is always between 0 and 6, but it can't be exactly 6 because the value of Rnd is never 1. Applying the Fix function gives you an integer between 0 and 5 (that is, 0, 1, 2, 3, 4, or 5), and then you only have to add 1 to make it a proper-looking die.

Up to this point, all the random integers you've used have started from 0 or 1. Sometimes it's convenient to have random integers that span a range. For example, how do you get a random integer between 65 and 90 (the range of ANSI codes for the uppercase alphabet)? To get a random integer in this range, perform the following steps:

1. Generate a random integer between 0 and 25.

2. Add 65 to the random integer to get the ANSI value of an uppercase letter.

Here is a translation of this into code:

```
CharNum = Fix(26 * Rnd) + 65
```

The Lottery Picker as a Script

Actually, writing a script that lets someone generate lottery numbers turns out to be a little tricky. The problem is that you need a way to keep track of the numbers you have already generated. The easiest way to do this is to set up an array and "mark" the numbers you have used. Here's the code that displays a message box with six different numbers between 1 and 48 every time you click the button. Although the code listing is short, it's a little tricky, so I will go over it line by line after you've had a chance to look it over:

```
Sub cmdButton1_Click

  Dim NumbersUsed(47), NumbersToPlay(5), ANumber, NumberFound, I

  Randomize

  For I = 0 To 47
    NumbersUsed(I) = I + 1
  Next

  For I = 0 To 5
    NumberFound = False
    Do Until NumberFound
      ANumber = Fix(48 * Rnd)
      If NumbersUsed(ANumber) <> 0 Then
        NumbersToPlay(I) = NumbersUsed(ANumber)
        NumbersUsed(ANumber) = 0
        NumberFound = True
      End If
    Loop
  Next

  MsgBox "Pick these numbers: " & Join(NumbersToPlay)

End Sub
```

The call to the Randomize function tells VBScript to make sure that each time you click the button you get different choices. Next we fill an array with the numbers in the lottery (1 to 48 in this case). Every time someone clicks the button, we refill the numbers again so we can start all over. We now need to choose six numbers to fill the array for the numbers chosen.

The real work is done in the Do loop. What it does is generate a new random number between 0 and 47. The code then checks the NumbersUsed array; if the entry there is not 0, we copy it to the NumbersToPlay array *and then make it 0*. That way, a subsequent try to get this number won't work—the If clause won't be True anymore. We also set the NumberFound variable to True in order to tell the Do loop to stop. After the Do loop, VBScript encounters the "Next" keyword. This starts the process all over until we get our six numbers. Finally, I use the Join function to display all the numbers we found, as shown in Figure 5-8.

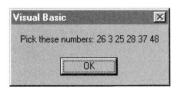

Figure 5-8.   *Results of the lottery picker.*

More on Rnd and Randomize

In addition to using Rnd to generate a random number, VBScript gives you the ability to get back the last random number it generated. You do this by using Rnd(0). This is useful when trying to debug a program. Imagine trying to debug a program if an important number changes each time you run the program.

Next, suppose there is a negative number inside the parentheses for the Rnd function. (The number inside the parentheses is usually called the *seed*.) You can think of the seed as the number from which the random numbers grow. Each time you use the same negative seed, you get the same pseudorandom number.

This is another important debugging tool. It lets you rerun a program, keeping the pseudorandom numbers temporarily stable. A good way to think about what a negative seed does is to imagine that there is a list of pseudorandom numbers, each one corresponding to a different negative seed.

Finally, the Randomize statement can also be a useful debugging tool. This is because you can use any numeric expression in the Randomize statement. If you first use the Rnd function with a negative number to "reseed" the random number generator and then issue a Randomize statement with a number, your program will always get the same set of random numbers. Therefore, use code like this to generate a repeatable sequence of random numbers:

```
x = Rnd(-1)     'or any negative number to reseed the generator
Randomize 37    'or any number after the Randomize keyword

For I = 1 To 10
  MsgBox Rnd
Next
```

The Int Function

There's another function that works much the same way as Fix—the Int function. Int gives the *floor* of a number—the first integer that's smaller than or equal to the number. Thinking of it as the floor function makes it easy to remember what happens for negative numbers. With negative numbers, you move down. For example, Int(–3.5) is –4, Int(–4.1) is –5, and so on. You can see that Fix and Int work the same way for positive numbers but are different for negative ones. Using Int and adding 1 always changes the number to the next largest integer.

Example: Calculating the Postage Due

The Fix and Int functions turn out to have a lot of other uses. Consider the Web page shown in Figure 5-9. As part of a United States Postal Web site, this page could be used to calculate the postage for an item.

Activating this Web page provides a good example of using the Int function. For example, the cost for first-class mail is 32 cents for the first ounce and 23 cents for each additional ounce or fraction thereof. Suppose an item weighs 4.4 ounces. The cost would be 32 cents for the first ounce and 92 (4 * 23) cents for the additional ounces, counting the fraction. The cost is:

```
.32 + .23 * Int(4.4)
```

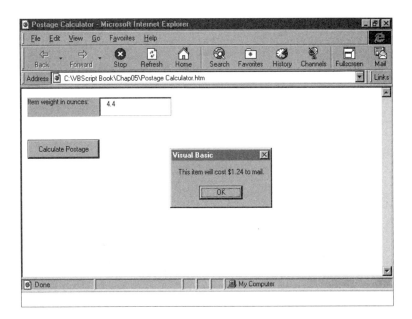

Figure 5-9. *A postage calculator.*

The following code activates the page shown in Figure 5-9. The only tricky part is that we need to convert the number back to a string in order to test whether it is equal to the string we started with. The CStr function lets us do this:

```
Sub cmdCalculate_Click
  Dim Weight, Cost

  Weight = txtBox1.Text

  If CStr(Int(Weight)) = Weight Then
    Cost = .32 + .23 * (Weight - 1)
  Else
    Cost = .32 + .23 * (Int(Weight))
  End If

  MsgBox "This item will cost " & FormatCurrency(Cost) & " to mail."
End Sub
```

Date and Time Functions

You have already seen the FormatDateTime function, which lets you format date and time values. VBScript has many other built-in functions you can use to work with date and time variables. For example, you already saw the Now function that returns the current date and time. The Date function, on the other hand, returns the current date only; the usual form is mm/dd/yy.

The month and day use one or two digits; the year uses two digits for years between 1900 and 1999, and it uses four digits for all other years (for example, 1/1/96 for January 1, 1996, and 10/10/2001 for October 10, 2001). The Time function gives you the current time but not the date. Thus, you can think of:

```
Now = Date & Time
```

Next, to do financial calculations accurately, your programs must be able to calculate the number of days that have passed between two dates—taking leap years into account, if possible. VBScript makes this easy (and does take leap years into account, by the way).

You simply store the information in two date variables, subtract them, and you're done. (Remember, you surround the information in a date variable with pound signs.) For example, suppose you want to create a Web page that lets someone calculate how long it is until January 1, 2000. This Web page is shown in Figure 5-10.

The millenium countdown calculator has a label, a text box named txtDaysToGo, and a button named cmdCalculate. The code needed is almost trivial:

```
Sub cmdCalculate_Click
  txtDaysToGo = #1/1/2000# - Date
End Sub
```

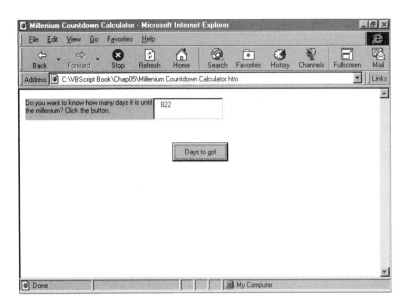

Figure 5-10. *A millennium countdown calculator.*

Miscellaneous Date and Time Functions

Occasionally, you will need the DateSerial function. Its syntax is this:

```
DateSerial(Year, Month, Day)
```

Year is a number between 100 and 9999, inclusive. *Month* is a number between 1 and 12, and *Day* is a number between 1 and 31, depending on the month. If you go beyond these limits for the month or day, VBScript wraps the date. For example, the following line of code displays a date in February:

```
MsgBox DateSerial(1998, 1, 35)
```

If you ask VBScript to do a calculation for a date, it will do this in a special way. For example, the following line of code gives you the day before the first day of two months before August (or May 31, 1998):

```
DateSerial(1998, 8-2, 1-1)
```

A handful of other functions let you process dates and times. These are useful when you need to write applications that work on a day-to-day or even a minute-to-minute basis. The following table lists all the date and time functions (for more details, see the online Help):

Function	Description
Date	Returns the current date
DateAdd	Lets you add a specified time interval to a date
DateDiff	Lets you find the difference between two dates
DatePart	Returns either the year, quarter, month, day of year, day, weekday, week of year, hour, minute, or second of a given date
DateSerial	Returns a date variable corresponding to the specified day, month, and year
DateValue	Takes a string representing a date and returns a date variable
Day	Returns a number corresponding to the day portion of a date
Hour	Returns a number corresponding to the hour portion of a time
Minute	Returns a number corresponding to the minutes portion of a time
Month	Returns a number corresponding to the month portion of a date
MonthName	Returns a string corresponding to the specified month
Now	Returns the current date and time
Second	Returns a number corresponding to the seconds portion of a time
Time	Returns the current time
TimeSerial	Returns a date variable corresponding to the specified hour, minute, and second
Weekday	Returns a number corresponding to the week portion of a date
WeekdayName	Returns a string corresponding to the specified week
Year	Returns a number corresponding to the year portion of a date

> **NOTE** All the functions that return strings get their information from the user's machine (not from the machine on which you wrote the code). For example, the MonthName function returns "January" on a machine using English but "Janvier" on a machine using French. Thus, it is better to use these functions than to create your own strings in your programs.

Numeric Functions

If you don't do a lot of scientific work, it's unlikely that you will use the information in this section very much. All I do here is summarize the numeric functions available to you in VBScript.

Round

The Round function does what its name suggests—it simply rounds the number inside the parentheses:

Round(4.1) = 4

Round(4.7) = 5

For even numbers, it rounds down at .5:

Round(4.5) = 4

For odd numbers, it rounds up at .5

Round(5.5) = 6

You can also give the Round function a second parameter that tells it how many decimal places are included in the rounding:

Round(4.567, 2) = 4.57

Sgn

The Sgn function returns 1 if the number inside the parentheses is positive, −1 if the number is negative, and 0 if the number is 0. One nonobvious use of this function is in a For-Next loop that starts in this way:

```
For I = A To B Step Sgn(B - A)
```

As long as A does not equal B, VBScript executes the body of the For-Next loop the correct number of times, regardless of whether A is greater or less than B.

Abs

The Abs function gives the absolute value of whatever is inside the parentheses. All this function does is remove a minus sign:

Abs(−5) = 5

Abs(5) = 5

One common use of the absolute value function is Abs(B−A). This gives the distance between the numbers A and B. For example, suppose A = 13 and B = 41. Then Abs(B−A) = Abs(A−B) = 28 because 13 and 41 are 28 numbers apart.

IP   You often use the Abs function to set up a tolerance test in a Do loop. A tolerance test is used to test whether an empirical value is within a certain range of the true answer. For example, the following line of code sets up a loop that stops when the empirical value is within .001 of the true answer:

```
Do Until Abs(TrueAnswer - EmpiricalValue) < .001
```

Sqr

The Sqr function returns the square root of the numeric expression inside the parentheses, which must be nonnegative.

Exp

The Exp function gives *e* (*e* is roughly 2.7182) to the power *x*, where *e* is the base for natural logarithms. The answer is a double-precision number.

Log

The Log function gives the natural logarithm of a number. To find the common logarithm (log to base 10), use Log(x)/Log(10).

IP   One quick way to find the number of digits in a number greater than 1 is to use Int(Log(x)/Log(10))+1.

Trigonometric Functions

For those who need them, VBScript has most of the standard trigonometric functions. You have Sin (sine), Cos (cosine), Tan (tangent), and Atn (arctangent). The only problem is that VBScript expects the angle inside the parentheses to be in radian measure. To convert from degrees to radians, you need the value of p. The formula is radians = degrees$* \pi/_{180}$.

 IP The easiest way to find the value of π is to create a script-level variable using the Atn (arctangent) function as follows:

```
Dim PI
PI = 4 * Atn(1)
```

This works because the arctangent of 1 is $\pi/_4$.

Writing Your Own Functions and Subprocedures

The last chapter showed you how to use VBScript's built-in functions; this chapter shows you how to write your own *reusable* functions and subprocedures. (See below for more about subprocedures.) The reason to do so is simple—nobody likes to reinvent the wheel. When you write programs, certain tasks occur time and time again. For example, you might need to do one of the following tasks:

- Verify that a user has entered something in a textbox instead of leaving it blank.

- Search through a list or sort it alphabetically.

- Verify the format of a phone number or social security number.

Once you write the code to do one of these tasks, you don't want to have to write it again! In fact, the more you program, the more you begin to see that the same problems recur under different guises. To solve a new problem, you often can simply "glue" together pieces of code that you have already written.

There's another reason to write your own functions and subprocedures. Event procedures are the heart of VBScript, but they shouldn't be made too complicated. If an event procedure is much longer than one screen length, it might be too long to debug easily. (See the next chapter for debugging techniques.) Consider farming out the work to one or more general functions or subprocedures in order to *modularize* your scripts. (To modularize is to break a program down into smaller, more manageable pieces. See the last section in this chapter for more on modularizing.)

Functions and Subprocedures

A *procedure* is a named chunk of code that does a specific task. A procedure can be called (executed) from other procedures or from the main part of your program. There are two kinds of procedures in VBScript: *functions* and *subprocedures.* You've already seen VBScript's built-in functions, but VBScript also allows you to write your own functions. As with built-in functions, the functions you write perform a task *and then return a value.*

A subprocedure (sometimes called a subroutine or routine) is a generalization of the event procedures you have already seen. Like an event procedure, a subprocedure doesn't return a value—it simply does something. An event procedure is a special type of subprocedure because an event procedure is executed automatically in response to an event, such as a button being clicked or a key being pressed.

You can send data to both functions and subprocedures by passing them parameters. Usually, functions don't change the data they are sent; they are written primarily to return a value. If you do write a function that changes the information sent to it, the value the function returns is normally used to indicate success or failure. Subprocedures that accept data, on the other hand, are usually written to *process* that data. Therefore, if you direct it to do so, a subprocedure changes the data it is sent.

Often there is a function and a subprocedure that are related. For example, consider again the problem of eliminating multiple spaces inside a string of text. Do you want to create a second version of the string, with all the spaces removed, while keeping a copy of the original string? In this case, you would write a function that returns a new string. Do you want to permanently modify the original string so that its spaces are gone for good? In this case, you would write a subprocedure that accepts the string and then changes it.

Functions

You might want to create your own function when you use a sequence of statements more than once in your program. For example, suppose you need to eliminate the extra spaces inside some text more than once. You saw the code for this in the last chapter:

```
ExtraSpacesGone = Replace(Test, "  ", " ")
Do While Instr(ExtraSpacesGone, "  ") <> 0
  ExtraSpacesGone = Replace(ExtraSpacesGone, "  ", " ")
Loop
```

Here's how you make a reusable function out of the above lines of code:

```
Function RemoveExtraSpaces(TheText)
  Dim ExtraSpacesGone, DoubleSpace
  DoubleSpace = Chr(32) & Chr(32)

  ExtraSpacesGone = Replace(TheText, DoubleSpace, Chr(32))
  Do While Instr(ExtraSpacesGone, DoubleSpace) <> 0
    ExtraSpacesGone = Replace(ExtraSpacesGone, DoubleSpace, Chr(32))
  Loop

  RemoveExtraSpaces = ExtraSpacesGone
End Function
```

 OTE I replaced occurrences of a single space (" ") by Chr(32) and a double space (" ") by a variable named DoubleSpace, which contains Chr(32) & Chr(32). This makes the function a bit easier to read as well as to modify into a function that eliminates occurrences of any doubled text, as you'll see later in this chapter.

As you will soon see, after you enter this code in the script for your Web page, you can use RemoveExtraSpaces just like a built-in function. (I like to put all my functions at the beginning of my script in the head section. However, provided a function is enclosed within the pair of <SCRIPT> </SCRIPT> tags, VBScript is smart enough to find it no matter where you put it.) The point is that at the cost of a few extra lines of bookkeeping you will be able to reuse the code easily.

Let's go over this example since the framework is the same for all the functions you write. The first line contains the keyword Function, the name of the function, and any parameters inside parentheses. The first line of this function is:

```
Function RemoveExtraSpaces(TheText)
```

In this case, the name of the function is RemoveExtraSpaces. The parameter named TheText inside the parentheses is the key to the function working smoothly. It is called a *formal parameter,* but it is easiest to think of it as a placeholder. As you have seen with VBScript's built-in functions, you call the function with different values for the placeholder. For example:

```
NewText = RemoveExtraSpaces(txtBox1.Text)
```

The code between the first and last lines is called the *body* of the function. Inside the body, you need to include at least one assignment that looks like this:

```
NameOfFunction = SomeValue
```

In the above example, I used this line:

```
RemoveExtraSpaces = ExtraSpacesGone
```

VBScript uses this type of assignment statement to define the return value of the function.

Here's another example. If we were writing our own version of the built-in absolute value function (that always gives you the positive value of a number), it would look like this:

```
Function MyAbsoluteValue(X)

  If X > 0 Then
    MyAbsoluteValue = X
  Else
    MyAbsoluteValue = -X
  End If

End Function
```

The point is that VBScript uses whichever assignment statement it actually processed to set the return value of the function. In the above code, the return value is either the number or the opposite of the number, depending on the number's sign.

Function parameters

You have already seen parameters in various built-in functions. In general, to call a function, you replace the formal parameter (the placeholder) with an expression. VBScript then replaces all occurrences of the placeholder in the body of the function with the value of the expression. For example, assume you've written this:

```
A = "This is a test. "
B = " Will it work?"
```

(Note the extra space at the beginning of B.)

The following lines of code will have the same result:

```
FullText = RemoveExtraSpaces(A & B)
FullText = RemoveExtraSpaces("This is a test.  Will it work?")
```

Next it is important to keep in mind the difference between these two statements:

```
NewText = RemoveExtraSpaces(txtBox1.Text)
txtBox1.Text = RemoveExtraSpaces(txtBox1.Text)
```

In the first case, we are simply storing the new value for future use in a variable named NewText. In the second case, we will actually change the contents of the text box.

Finally, always remember that the formal parameters of a function have no independent existence as variables. If you write a function with a formal parameter named TheText and you declare a variable named TheText somewhere else in your program—even as a script-level variable—the variable will never have an effect on the function's behavior.

 ARNING Be careful about placing a formal parameter on the left side of an assignment statement in the body of the function. Any changes you make to the parameters will affect the original variables. (See "Passing by Reference versus Passing by Value" later in this chapter for more on this.)

Example: a function-based approach for calculating U.S. postage

Let's redo the postage calculator from the last chapter. If we just modified the code to create a function, it would look like this:

```
Function Postage(Weight)
  'Calculate the cost, in cents, of mailing a
  'first-class letter of a given weight in ounces

  If CStr(Int(Weight)) = Weight Then
    Postage = .32 + .23*(Weight -1)
  Else
    Postage = .32 + .23*(Int(Weight))
  End If

End Function
```

Other terms describing this use of numbers are hardwired numbers and magic numbers.

However, this is not a good way to write a reusable function: after all, postage rates might go up, and if you want to reuse this function after a rate change you would need to go back and change the numbers in more than one place. This function, in fact, uses two examples of what programmers call *hard-coded numbers* (.32 and .23). It is better to write functions that use constants instead. That way, when a change is necessary you have to change the constants in only one place (usually right at the beginning of your program); you won't have to search for all occurrences of the hard-coded numbers. (Trust me—it is easy to miss an occurrence of a hard-coded number in a complicated function.)

In addition, constants with descriptive names make the code more readable.

Here's a better way to write the previous function:

```
Function Postage(Weight)
  'Calculate the cost, in cents, of mailing a
  'first-class letter of a given weight in ounces

  Const FIRST_OUNCE_COST = .32
  Const ADDITIONAL_OUNCE_COST = .23

  If CStr(Int(Weight)) = Weight Then
    Postage = FIRST_OUNCE_COST + ADDITIONAL_OUNCE_COST*(Weight - 1)
  Else
    Postage = FIRST_OUNCE_COST + ADDITIONAL_OUNCE_COST*(Int(Weight))
  End If

End Function
```

How can you use this function? As an example of the kind of "client-side validation" that you will be doing so often with VBScript, you will certainly want to check that what the user enters is a number greater than 0.

Here's one version of code that does this:

```
Sub cmdCalculate_Click
  Dim WeightOfLetter

  If Not IsNumeric(txtBox1.Text) Then
    MsgBox "Please enter a number."
    txt Box1.Text = ""
  ElseIf txtBox1.Text < 0 Then
    MsgBox "Please enter a positive number."
    txtBox1.Text = ""
  Else
    MsgBox "This will cost you " & Postage(txtBox1.Text) _
      & " to mail."
  End If

End Sub
```

Exiting a function prematurely

Occasionally, you will want to exit a function prematurely without assigning a return value. In that case, the default return value is 0 for numbers and "" for strings. The statement that lets you do this is the Exit Function statement.

A good example of where I would use the Exit Function statement is in a function that determines whether the user neglected to enter information in a text box—something you constantly need to be on the alert for. Your first instinct might be to simply use this:

```
Function TextNotOk(TheText)

  If TheText = "" Then
    TextNotOk = True
  Else
    TextNotOk = False
  End If

End Function
```

The trouble with this function is that the user might inadvertently have hit the Spacebar. In this case, the function says that the text is okay when it clearly is not. After all, a text box containing only space characters has not been filled in. Here's a function that not only checks whether a text string contains any characters at all but also whether it contains only white space characters:

```
Function IsWhiteSpace(TheText)
  Dim I

  For I = 1 To Len(TheText)

    Select Case Mid(TheText, I, 1)
      Case Chr(32), vbCr, vbLf, vbTab
        'these are white space characters (space, carriage return,
        'line feed, tab) so just continue the loop
      Case Else
        'found a character that isn't white space
        IsWhiteSpace = False
        Exit Function
    End Select

  Next

  'only get here if we did not execute the Exit Function statement
  '(if there were no characters or if all characters were white space)
  IsWhiteSpace = True

End Function
```

Some programmers don't like using the Exit Function statement; they argue that a function should have only one entry point and one exit point. I understand their reasoning; a function with multiple exit points is often harder to understand than a function with only one exit point. In this particular case, I am not convinced that an approach that avoids the Exit Function statement is any clearer. Here's a version of the code that avoids the Exit Function statement. Why don't you decide which one you find easier to understand?

```
Function IsWhiteSpace(TheText)
  Dim I, NonWhiteSpaceFound

  NonWhiteSpaceFound = False
  I = 0

  Do Until NonWhiteSpaceFound Or I = Len(TheText)
    I = I + 1    'start with the first character

    Select Case Mid(TheText, I, 1)
      Case Chr(32), vbCr, vbLf, vbTab
        'these are white space characters (space, carriage return,
        'line feed, tab) so just continue the loop
      Case Else
```

```
        'found a character that isn't white space
        NonWhiteSpaceFound = True
    End Select

  Loop

  If NonWhiteSpaceFound Then
    IsWhiteSpace = False
  Else
    IsWhiteSpace = True
  End If

End Function
```

The programming involved in this loop is actually an example of a common situation that occurs when you avoid using the Exit Function statement— you have a Do loop that ends if either one of two possible situations occurs. You test *after* the loop to see what situation actually occurred.

Functions with more than one parameter

The functions we have built so far work with only one parameter; often you will need functions that work with more than one parameter. For example, suppose you wanted to modify the RemoveExtraSpaces function so that it can remove occurrences of any doubled text. You need to pass it two parameters:

- The entire text string

- The substring to be removed

Here's the code:

```
Function RemoveDoubledText(TheText, TextToGo)
  Dim ExtraTextGone, DoubledText
  DoubledText = TextToGo & TextToGo

  ExtraTextGone = Replace(TheText, DoubledText, TextToGo)
  Do While Instr(ExtraTextGone, DoubledText) <> 0
    ExtraTextGone = Replace(ExtraTextGone, DoubledText, TextToGo)
  Loop

  RemoveDoubledText = ExtraTextGone
End Function
```

Next suppose you are creating a Web page that does a computation (such as calculating retirement savings) and you need random integers (such as monthly deposit amounts) in different ranges. At one time, you need the integers to be between 1 and 6, at another time between 100 and 999, and at yet another time between 1000 and 10,000. To get integers between 1 and 6, you need this expression:

```
Int(6*Rnd) + 1
```

To get numbers between 100 and 999, you need this expression:

```
Int(900*Rnd) + 100
```

Remember that the Rnd function returns a decimal number between 0 and 1; the number might be 0, but it will never be exactly 1. The expression 900*Rnd, therefore, produces a number from 0 up to, but not including, 900. Applying the Int function to the expression then produces an integer from 0 through 899. (Remember that the Int function removes the decimal part of a number.) Finally, adding 100 gives you an integer between 100 and 999, inclusive.

How did I come up with the number 900? Not by trial and error! In general, you subtract the smaller number from the larger number of the range you want to end up with and then add 1. In this case, I subtracted 100 from 999 and then added 1 to get 900. Here's a function that does this for any range of positive numbers:

```
Function RandomRangeXToY(X, Y)
   RandomRangeXToY = Int((Y - X + 1) * Rnd) + X
End Function
```

Although this is only a one-line function, it is a little tricky. The best way I know to understand code is to "play computer." Try some specific numbers, and see what happens. For example, what happens with X = 100 and Y = 999?

1. Y - X + 1 = 900.

2. (900 * Rnd) produces a number from 0 up to, but not including, 900.

3. Int(900 * Rnd) produces an integer from 0 through 899, inclusive. (Notice that 899 is Y - X.)

4. Adding X gets you to the desired range of 100 through 999.

Here's another example. You might need a function that counts the number of times a particular character is inside a string. The idea is simple; you use the Mid function and walk through the characters in the string one by one, keeping track of the number of times the character occurs, as shown in this function:

```
Function CountCharOccurrences(TheCharacter, TheString)
  'This function counts the number of
  'times a character is inside a string

  Dim Count, I

  Count = 0
  For I = 1 To Len(TheString)
    If Mid(TheString, I, 1) = TheCharacter Then Count = Count + 1
  Next

  CountCharOccurrences = Count
End Function
```

The For-Next loop walks through the string character by character, adding one to the value of the Count variable if it finds a match. The function then returns the value of the Count variable.

Subprocedures

You write a function to automate a task and then receive a value. Let's suppose, however, that you want to automate a task but you don't need to receive a value. In this case, you would write a subprocedure.

For example, you might want to automate the display of text at a certain heading level. You've gotten tired of writing this:

```
Document.Write "<H" & I & ">" & TheText & "</H>"
```

Here's a subprocedure that has two parameters, one for the heading level and one for the text to display:

```
Sub WriteInHeadingLevel(HeadingLevel, TheText)
  Document.Write "<H" & (HeadingLevel & ">" & TheText & "</H>"
End Sub
```

In general, as this example shows, the first line of a subprocedure has the keyword Sub followed by the subprocedure's name. Like a function name, a subprocedure name must follow the rules for a variable name. Next comes the parameter list, enclosed in parentheses. (If your subprocedure uses no parameters, the parentheses are optional.) After the parameter list come the statements that make up the body of the subprocedure. Finally there are the keywords End Sub, which end the subprocedure.

OTE   Just as there is an Exit Function statement, there is an Exit Sub statement that exits a subprocedure prematurely.

Using a subprocedure

To call a subprocedure, you use its name followed by parameters. If there is more than one parameter, you separate them by commas:

```
WriteInHeadingLevel 2, "This is a level-2 heading"
```

You can also use the keyword Call, which looks like this:

```
Call WriteInHeadingLevel(2, "This is a level-2 heading")
```

If you use the Call keyword, you must use parentheses around the parameter list; if you don't use the Call keyword, omit the parentheses.

IP   You can also call an event procedure directly in this way. For example, the following line calls the Click event procedure for the button named cmdCalculate:

```
cmdCalculate_Click
```

I like the explicitness of using the keyword "Call" here (although this is a matter of taste), so I would use this:

```
Call cmdCalculate_Click()
```

Example: writing a table-making subprocedure

The subprocedure to write some text at a specific heading level was so simple that you could argue it was easy just to do it "inline"—that is, not using a call to a function or subprocedure. Suppose, however, that you wanted to automate the building of HTML tables. The Document.Write statements that you need are a lot of work to create. The following example creates a simple table. The number of rows and columns are set by variables named Rows and Columns, and the table is created with a fairly narrow border and some space between the columns (3 pixels). To make things clearer, I added some code to print the row and column numbers in each cell in the table:

```
Document.Write "<TABLE BORDER=3 CELLPADDING=3>"

For I = 1 to Rows
  Document.Write "<TR>"
  For J = 1 to Cols
    Document.Write "<TD>"
    Document.Write "Row " & I & ", Col " & J
    Document.Write "<TD>"
  Next
  Document.Write "</TD>"
Next

Document.Write "</TABLE>"
```

This cries out to be made into a subprocedure. Ideally, we would like to be able to have the subprocedure take as a parameter a two-dimensional array for the contents of the table, but we will have to leave that improvement until later. Here's the first version of a subprocedure that will grow in both usefulness (and alas, complexity) as this chapter progresses. I included it in the code for a simple Web page so that you can see the effects. I followed the code for the subprocedure with a call to it so that you can see a 4x4 table (you can also find this example in the file Table.htm on the companion CD):

```
<HTML>
<HEAD>
<TITLE>A VBScript table generator</TITLE>

  <SCRIPT LANGUAGE="VBSCRIPT">
  <!--

    Option Explicit

    Sub MakeTable(Rows, Columns, Border, CellPadding)
      Dim Temp, I, J

      Temp = "<TABLE BORDER=" & Border _
        & " CELLPADDING=" & CellPadding & ">"
      Document.Write Temp

      For I = 1 to Rows
        Document.Write "<TR>"
        For J = 1 to Columns
          Document.Write "<TD>"
          Document.Write "Row " & I & ", Col " & J
```

(continued)

```
        Document.Write "<TD>"
     Next
        Document.Write "</TD>"
     Next

     Document.Write "</TABLE>"
   End Sub

   'Call the table generator
   MakeTable 4, 4, 3, 3

  -->
  </SCRIPT>

</HEAD>
<BODY>

</BODY>
</HTML>
```

Passing by Reference Versus Passing by Value

You might have noticed that within the body of a function or subprocedure, I have not placed a parameter on the left side of an assignment statement. This was deliberate—there has never been any code like this:

```
SomeParameter = NewValue
```

The reason is that there are actually two ways to pass a parameter to a function or subprocedure: *passing by reference* and *passing by value.* The distinction can be confusing, but if you keep these two points in mind you won't go wrong:

- When you pass a parameter by reference, any changes to the corresponding parameter inside the function or subprocedure (that is, putting it on the left side of an assignment statement) will change the value of the original variable when the function or subprocedure finishes.

- When you pass a parameter by value, the original variable retains its value after the function or subprocedure terminates—regardless of whether the corresponding parameter was changed inside the function or subprocedure. VBScript simply throws away any changes it might have made.

(Actually, VBScript makes a copy of the value of an original variable. The function or subprocedure then works with the copy rather than with the original variable.)

Here's about the simplest example of the distinction between passing by reference and passing by value:

```
Sub AddTwo(X)
   X = X + 2
   MsgBox "The value of X inside the subprocedure is " & X
End Sub
```

Now suppose you use code like this:

```
Dim X

X = 7
AddTwo X
MsgBox "The value of X is now " & X
```

The value of X is now 9, and that is what you will see. This is because the default in VBScript is to pass by reference! If you write the following code, you will see a 7. Using AddTwo(X) with the parentheses tells VBScript to pass by value:

```
Dim X

X = 7
AddTwo(X)
MsgBox "The value of X is now " & X
```

Here's a more subtle example. We all know that "a bird in the hand…." When it comes to finance, this means that money today is worth more than money 10 years from now. For example, if interest rates are 7 percent, money doubles in about 10 years, so a promise to pay $1,000 today is equivalent in value to a promise to pay $2,000 in 10 years. This is why lotteries are able to offer prizes that seem so big—money paid out over 20 years is worth a whole lot less than a lump sum payment.

One way to figure out how much an amount of money will be worth in the future is with a simple For-Next loop that keeps on adding the interest accumulated to the previous total, as shown in the next example:

```
For I = 1 To Yrs
   CurrentBalance = CurrentBalance + IntRate * CurrentBalance
Next
```

Consider the following function:

```
Function FutureValue(Balance, IntRate, Yrs)
  Dim I

  For I = 1 To Yrs
    Balance = Balance + IntRate * Balance
  Next

  FutureValue = Balance
End Function
```

Suppose we use an input box to get a person's current savings:

```
MySavings = InputBox("How much have you saved?")
```

Now try one of these statements:

```
MyRetirement = FutureValue(MySavings, .07, 30)
MyRetirement = FutureValue((MySavings), .07, 30)
```

The first statement is wrong and will lead to subtle bugs in your program! The reason is that the parameter Balance appears on the left side of an assignment statement inside the function FutureValue, causing the original value of the MySavings variable to change. Its original value will be lost. The second statement works fine; the extra set of parentheses forces VBScript to pass the MySavings variable by value so that changes to it are thrown away.

Figure 6-1 shows the distinction between passing by reference and passing by value.

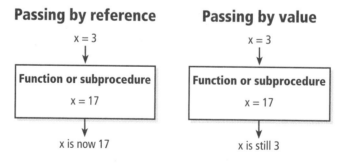

Figure 6-1.   *Passing by reference versus passing by value.*

Forgetting that the default in VBScript is to pass by reference can lead to subtle bugs, so it is worth repeating that variables are always passed by reference unless surrounded by a set of parentheses.

Therefore, when writing functions and subprocedures, make assignments to parameters only when you want to change their original values. Otherwise, you will end up with inadvertent *side effects*.

If you know that a particular parameter should never be passed by reference, you can specify that it is to be passed only by value. To do this, add the ByVal keyword before the parameter in the argument list. Here's an example of the syntax:

```
Function FutureValue(ByVal Balance, ByVal IntRate, ByVal Yrs)
```

Now you will never have to be concerned about the type of side effect I discussed above.

If you pass a parameter by reference to a function or subprocedure and the original variable is changed intentionally, the effect is similar to that created by using a script-level variable. (Remember that one of the main reasons to use a procedure-level variable is that it can't be affected outside the procedure that declares it.) How do you decide whether to use a procedure-level variable that is passed by reference or a script-level variable?

Most programmers follow the convention that script-level variables are for information that should be available to the entire script (for example, the value of π), and therefore you rarely should change the value of these variables inside a procedure. Procedures ideally should change only the values of the variables passed as parameters. The reason for this convention stems from the methods used to debug programs. For more on debugging, see the next chapter.

Using Arrays in Procedures

VBScript makes it easy to use arrays in functions and subprocedures. One way to do this is to make the array a script-level variable. However, passing arrays as parameters is much more common because it avoids the dangers of script-level variables. (Remember that script-level variables are easy to inadvertently contaminate.)

To pass an array as a parameter to a function or subprocedure, simply place the name of the array in the parameter list. For example, a better version of the MakeTable subprocedure from the table generator example you saw earlier includes an array parameter for the contents of the table. Here is the first line of the modified subprocedure:

```
Sub MakeTable(TheEntries, Border, CellPadding)
```

The parameter TheEntries is the array. Note that just as with other types of parameters, array parameters are placeholders; they have no independent existence.

Here's the entire modified subprocedure, which lets you build an HTML table from any two-dimensional array that you pass to it. The key point in the new subprocedure is the use of the UBound function to determine the number of rows and columns. The second parameter to the UBound function indicates which dimension's upper bound is returned. For example, the following lines retrieve the upper bounds for the first and second dimensions, respectively, of the two-dimensional array TheEntries:

```
Rows = UBound(TheEntries, 1)
Columns = UBound(TheEntries, 2)
```

As before, I included the MakeTable subprocedure in the code for a Web page so that you can see the effects. I followed the code for the subprocedure with code that creates a 5x7 array and then passes that array to the subprocedure (you can also find this example in the file Table2.htm on the companion CD):

```
<HTML>
<HEAD>
<TITLE>A better VBScript table generator</TITLE>

  <SCRIPT LANGUAGE="VBSCRIPT">
  <!--

    Option Explicit

    Dim A(5, 7)
    Dim R, C

    Sub MakeTable(TheEntries, Border, CellPadding)
      Dim Temp, I, J, Rows, Columns
```

```
      Temp = "<TABLE BORDER=" & Border _
        & " CELLPADDING=" & CellPadding & ">"
      Document.Write Temp

      Rows = UBound(TheEntries, 1)
      Columns = UBound(TheEntries, 2)

      For I = 1 to Rows
        Document.Write "<TR>"
        For J = 1 to Columns
          Document.Write "<TD>"
          Document.Write TheEntries(I, J)
          Document.Write "<TD>"
        Next
        Document.Write "</TD>"
      Next

      Document.Write "</TABLE>"
    End Sub

    'Create an array, and call the table generator
    For R = 0 To 5
      For C = 0 To 7
        A(R,C) = CStr(R) & ", " & CStr(C)
      Next
    Next

    MakeTable A, 3, 3

  -->
  </SCRIPT>

</HEAD>
<BODY>

</BODY>
</HTML>
```

 IP To make sure that someone doesn't try to use this subprocedure by passing it a parameter that isn't an array, you can add the following line at the beginning of the subprocedure:

```
      If Not IsArray(TheEntries) Then Exit Sub
```

Next suppose you want to write a function that returns the smallest number from a list of numbers. You need a function that has an array as a parameter, as shown in the following outline:

```
Function FindSmallest(TheList)
  set the minimum value to the first entry in the list
  for each entry in the list, if the entry is smaller than the current
    minimum value, then set the current minimum value to the entry
  set the value of the function to the final minimum value
```

Again, the key is the UBound function. If you are thinking that this function will occur in most of your procedures that handle arrays, you are right on target. Here is the above outline turned into VBScript code:

```
Function FindSmallest(TheList)
  Dim NumOfEntries, Smallest, I

  If Not IsArray(TheList) Then
    MsgBox "Please pass me a list."
    Exit Function
  End If

  NumOfEntries = UBound(TheList)
  Smallest = TheList(0)

  For I = 0 To NumOfEntries
    If TheList(I) < Smallest Then Smallest = TheList(I)
  Next

  FindSmallest = Smallest
End Function
```

This function returns the smallest entry in the list (or the first in alphabetical order).

Searching and Sorting

Searching and sorting lists are two of the most common tasks people use computers for. Most scripts don't have to deal with enormous lists containing millions of entries, so I will concentrate on techniques that work well for small lists but don't work so well for very large lists.

Searching

If the list is small, the way to proceed is to write a function that searches the list. Here's a search function that returns True if the target entry is found or False if it is not found:

```
Function FindIt(TheList, TheTarget)
  Dim NumOfEntries I,

  NumOfEntries = UBound(TheList)

  For I = 0 To NumOfEntries
    If TheList(I) = TheTarget Then
      FindIt = True
      Exit Function
    End If
  Next

  FindIt = False
End Function
```

However, if the list is already ordered (alphabetically or numerically, for example), this is not the best way to proceed. After all, if you are looking in a telephone book for a name beginning with K, you don't start at page 1; you open the book roughly in the middle and proceed from there. When the information in the list you're searching is already ordered, you can speed things up by programming something similar to what you would do with a telephone book. This speeds up a search significantly. Here's an outline for a program that searches a list of names that is already in alphabetical order:

```
Function BinarySearch(TheList, WhatToFind)
  as long as there are names left to look at, do this loop:
    divide the list in half
    if the entry at the halfway mark is the name you're looking for,
      you're done
    otherwise, determine whether you have gone too far (does
      the entry at the halfway mark come before or after the
      name you're looking for?)
    if you have gone too far, look at the first half of
      the list; otherwise, look at the second half
```

The point is that each pass through the loop looks at a list that is only half the size of the previous list.

Suppose your list has 500,000 names. After the first pass through the loop, you will start over with a list of 250,000 names. After the second pass through the loop, you have only 125,000 names, and then only 62,500, and so on. After a few more passes, you are down to only 2 names left to search. This type of search is called a *binary search*. The extraordinary feature of the binary search is that it works almost as quickly for large lists as for small. For example, suppose you are searching through the New York City telephone directory, with roughly 10,000,000 entries, to find a name. Just by following this outline (and not doing any estimation of where the letters are), you would find the name, if it is in the directory, in no more than 25 passes through the loop *and* only 5 or so more passes than are needed with a list of 500,000 names.

A function that does a binary search is a bit tricky—the code below is a first attempt that follows the outline exactly. (It has a subtle bug, which you might want to try to find before I explain what it is.)

```
Function BinarySearch(TheList, WhatToFind)
  Dim High, Low, Middle, TargetPosition

  Low = LBound(TheList)
  High = UBound(TheList)
  TargetPosition = -1

  Do
    Middle = (Low + High) \ 2
    If TheList(Middle) = WhatToFind Then
      TargetPosition = Middle
    ElseIf TheList(Middle) > WhatToFind Then
      High = Middle - 1
    Else
      Low = Middle + 1
    End If
  Loop Until TargetPosition <> -1

  BinarySearch = TargetPosition
End Function
```

The function returns the position of the target. Or does it? It seems like the Do loop does what you need. First it finds the middle of the list by using the integer division operator. (List indexes are always integers.) There are three possibilities from the search, so use an If-Then-ElseIf statement to do the checking. For example, if the entry in the middle position is too large, look at the first half of the list. In this case, the target can't be the middle entry (that possibility was eliminated by the first clause of the If statement), so you can move the "High" index down by one. A similar situation holds for the final Else clause.

Here's the problem—the loop stops only if TargetPosition has a value other than –1. In other words, the loop stops if the function finds the target. But suppose the target isn't in the list? The loop never stops; the program is stuck in an infinite loop!

How can you fix this function so that it stops when there are no more entries left to check? Consider the following example: Suppose you are down to a list that consists of two names, say in the 12th and 13th positions, and the 12th entry is too small and the 13th entry too large. What happens? The first time you're in this situation, the value of Middle is set to (12 + 13) \ 2 = 12. Since the value in the 12th position is too small, the value of Low is set to one more than Middle—that is, to 13. The value of Low and High are now the same. What happens next? Both Low and High are the same, and the value of Middle is also the same. Now the entry in the Middle position is too large, so the value of High shrinks by one, to 12— less than the value of Low. This gives you the way to end the loop. Change the line that ends the loop to this:

```
Loop Until (TargetPosition <> -1) Or (High < Low)
```

Remember that it's the strange, unusual cases that often cause the most subtle bugs in a program!

Here's a version of the binary search function that takes care of all the possibilities by returning –1 as the value of the function if the target was not found:

```
Function BinarySearch(TheList, WhatToFind)
  Dim High, Low, Middle, TargetPosition

  Low = LBound(TheList)
  High = UBound(TheList)
  TargetPosition = -1
```

(continued)

```
Do
  Middle = (Low + High) \ 2
  If TheList(Middle) = WhatToFind Then
    TargetPosition = Middle
  ElseIf TheList(Middle) > WhatToFind Then
    High = Middle - 1
  Else
    Low = Middle + 1
  End If
Loop Until (TargetPosition <> -1) Or (High < Low)

  BinarySearch = TargetPosition
End Function
```

Sorting

Ordered lists, such as online dictionaries and telephone books, are sorted because techniques like binary searching work so quickly. This is why sorting data is one of the most common jobs a computer is asked to do. Unfortunately, sorting is also potentially time-consuming. If you work for the Social Security Administration and have a list with a hundred million entries, choosing the wrong sorting method (one optimized only for smaller lists), can cause the sorting process to take weeks! No, I am not kidding.

Because of this, computer scientists have developed literally hundreds of different ways to sort lists. Luckily, VBScript programmers don't need to worry about sorting massive amounts of data, so this section shows you two methods. One works well for small lists (up to about 500 entries), and the other works well for lists of about 100 through 5000 entries.

Sorting Procedures

When you sit down to write a procedure that isn't going to be obvious, it's always a good idea to see if anything you do in real life is analogous to what you want the computer to do. For sorting lists, what comes to my mind is putting the cards in order in my hand when I play hearts or bridge. As far as I can tell, there are two types of people:

- Those who pick up all the cards at once and sort them by first finding the smallest card, then the next smallest, and so on

- Those who pick up one card at a time, scan what they have already sorted, and then immediately place the new card in the correct place

For what it's worth, computer scientists have proved that these two methods of sorting take roughly the same amount of time, with the second method usually being a tiny bit faster. The first one is called a ripple sort; the second one is called an insertion sort. I will show you only the code for the insertion sort.

Insertion sort

The idea is that when you pick up a card (a new entry to add to the list), you look through the cards you already have (the list, starting at what is currently the last entry and moving down to the first) until you find something smaller than the new card. At every stage, you'll have an already sorted hand of cards, but until you are done there will still be cards "left on the table." Unfortunately, unlike the case of a real hand of cards, a list requires you to move some of its entries by one position to make room for the new card. Now, each time you find that the list entry you're looking at is larger than the "card you picked up," you move the list entry to the next highest position in the list. If you do this, you'll be moving a "hole" as you scan the list. When the comparison finally fails, you drop the new card into the hole. Here's the insertion sort subprocedure:

```
Sub InsertionSort(TheList)
  Dim Lowest, Highest, I, J, Temp

  Lowest = LBound(TheList)
  Highest = UBound(TheList)

  For I = Lowest+1 To Highest
    Temp = TheList(I)

    'find a hole
    For J = I-1 To 0 Step -1
      If TheList(J) > Temp Then
        TheList(J + 1) = TheList(J)
      Else
        'nothing to do, so leave the loop
        Exit For
      End If
    Next

    TheList(J + 1) = Temp
  Next

End Sub
```

The inner For-Next loop moves list entries up until conditions are ripe for the Exit For statement. (An Exit For statement gives you a way to leave a For-Next loop prematurely.) This occurs when you have located the position of the hole—in preparation for the following statement, which fills the hole:

```
TheList(J + 1) = Temp
```

Since the insertion sort follows the playing card analogy closely, it isn't that hard to program. Moreover, for small lists, it is reasonably fast. Sorting 250 list entries by using the insertion sort on a Pentium 166 takes about half a second. Unfortunately, sorting 500 entries takes about 2 seconds. The insertion sort has the unfortunate property that doubling the list *quadruples* the time. Sorting a list of 1000 names would take about 8 seconds. This is unacceptable, and Internet Explorer will warn you via a message box that the script is taking too long. (Now you can see why the binary search is so nice—doubling the list adds only one step.)

The next section shows you one of the fastest sorting methods that works well for any list you are likely to see as a VBScript programmer.

Shell sort

The sorting method I'll show you here is called the *Shell sort* because it was discovered by a man named Donald Shell, about 40 years ago. The Shell sort is unusual because while the code is short, it is not easy to understand. This is partially because there is nothing you do in real life that's analogous to the Shell sort and partially because it's a really clever idea. Another problem is that even after you understand how it works, it's unclear why it's so much faster than the ripple or insertion sort.

I find that the best way to understand the Shell sort is to ask myself: what are the advantages and disadvantages of the insertion sort and the ripple sort? Well, the main disadvantage of the insertion sort is that most of the time it moves entries inefficiently. Even when the list is mostly sorted, you still have to move the entries one by one to create the hole. The main advantage of the ripple sort is that it moves objects efficiently. Once the smallest object is placed in the first position, it stays there.

In a sense, then, the insertion and ripple sorts are opposites. Donald Shell decided to create a sort that combined the best features of both. So he tried to improve the insertion sort by moving the entries long distances, as is done in the ripple sort. Consider the following list of numbers to sort:

157, 13, 2, 9, 11, 7, 8, 4, 5, 1, 97, 6

Suppose instead of comparing 157 with 13, you compare it with 8 (that is, you compare the first item with the seventh). Instead of comparing the second item with the third, you compare it with the eighth. The idea is to compare elements that are far away from one another, rather than adjacent. In short, cut up the list into six different lists. Then sort each of these two-item lists. At this point, you'll have six lists, each of which is sorted. In the above example, they look like this:

8, 157

4, 13

2, 5

1, 9

11, 97

6, 7

Of course, the whole list isn't sorted, but now comes Shell's really clever idea. He merges the six smaller lists by placing the first item from each two-item list into a new list and then adding all the second items. The new list then looks like this:

8, 4, 2, 1, 11, 6, 157, 13, 5, 9, 97, 7

Next Shell breaks up the list into three lists of four items each. The first list contains the first, fourth, seventh, and tenth items; the second list contains the second, fifth, eighth, and eleventh items; and so on:

8, 1, 157, 9

4, 11, 13, 97

2, 6, 5, 7

Then he sorts each of these three lists, so he gets this:

1, 8, 9, 157

4, 11, 13, 97

2, 5, 6, 7

Now he merges these three lists using the same technique as before (all the first entries, then all the second entries, and so on). The resulting list looks like this (and is very close to being sorted):

1, 4, 2, 8, 11, 5, 9, 13, 6, 157, 97, 7

Finally he uses an insertion sort (which means comparing adjacent items until all the items have moved to where they belong). The idea is that insertion sort is efficient when you don't have to move items very far, and at this point the items already have been moved to positions close to where they should be.

Here's a version of the Shell sort:

```
Sub ShellSort(TheList)
  Dim NumOfEntries, Increm, I, J, Temp
  NumOfEntries = UBound(TheList)
  Increm = NumOfEntries \ 2
  Do Until Increm < 1
    For I = Increm To NumOfEntries
      Temp = TheList(I)
      For J = I - Increm To 0 Step - Increm
        If Temp >= TheList(J) Then Exit For
        TheList(J + Increm) = TheList(J)
      Next
      TheList(J + Increm) = Temp
    Next
    Increm = Increm \ 2
  Loop
End Sub
```

The Do loop divides the lists into smaller lists. Inside the Do loop, the inner For-Next loop does an insertion sort on the smaller lists. Since each entry in the smaller list differs from the next by the value of the variable Increm, the Step option gives you a way of working with the smaller lists. The Shell sort works well for lists with many thousands of entries, although after about 5000 items it won't be as fast and Internet Explorer will warn you that the script that uses it is taking a long time

---

OTE   The speed of the Shell sort depends somewhat on the numbers you use to split the list into smaller lists. These are usually called the *increments* (the 6, 3, and 1 used in the preceding example), and they should be chosen with care. The numbers used in the example (half the current size of the list) are Shell's original choice. Today we know you can obtain slightly better results with other increments. For the kinds of lists that VBScript programmers will encounter, Shell's original choice works well enough.

Reusability

If you create a stock of functions and subprocedures, Internet Explorer makes it easy to reuse them. You don't have to cut and paste a procedure into every script that needs it. All you have to do is store your procedures in a file with a .vbs extension and add a few lines to your script that look like this (make sure you add these lines as a second set of <SCRIPT></SCRIPT> tags, *outside* the standard <SCRIPT></SCRIPT> tags):

```
<SCRIPT
  LANGUAGE="VBSCRIPT"
  SRC="C:\MyScripts\UsefulStuff.vbs">
</SCRIPT>
```

From this point on, you can use all the VBScript code in the file UsefulStuff.vbs as if you had typed it into the script yourself!

Script Design

I want to end this chapter with a few general words on how I write scripts. The best way to become an efficient programmer is to adapt a modular design to your scripts. Write *lots* of small functions and subprocedures, and keep script-level code to a minimum.

After all, when you have something hard to do, you usually divide it into several smaller jobs. Often these smaller jobs follow a natural order; you pour the foundation of a house before you build the frame. I try to write my scripts starting from the general and moving toward the particular. I begin by looking at the big picture. What controls do I need? What are the event procedures supposed to do? Then I break that down in stages. This lets me keep track of the forest even when there are lots of trees.

Pen and paper outlines help too; my first outline for a sophisticated script lists the controls and the event procedures with the jobs they have to do. I keep refining my outline by adding helper functions and subprocedures until I can easily visualize the code for each function and subprocedure.

Testing, Debugging, and Error Trapping

Until now we have lived in the never-never land of assuming all the code that we write will be "bug free." In reality, programmers must always follow these steps:

1. Test the code (which will almost always reveal bugs).

2. Squash any bugs found (you think).

3. Retest the code.

4. Repeat steps 2–3 as many times as necessary.

The Bug Universe

Actually, there are two species of programming bugs: *syntax errors* and *logic errors*.

Syntax Errors

A syntax error results from a statement that violates the grammatical rules of the VBScript language. Consequently, a syntax error prevents the program from running. Misspelling a keyword is an example of a syntax error, as shown here:

```
Document.Writ "Hello"
```

The corrected line of code looks like this:

```
Document.Write "Hello"
```

In Chapter 2, you saw how Microsoft Internet Explorer version 4 handles syntax errors. You'll see a dialog box, like the one shown in Figure 7-1, which asks whether you want to debug the current page.

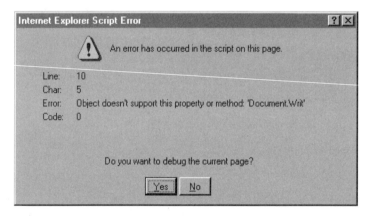

Figure 7-1.   *A dialog box resulting from a syntax error.*

Syntax errors are easy to fix. Here's what I usually do:

1. Click the No button in the dialog box.

2. Open the source code in Notepad by selecting Source from the View menu.

3. Correct the typo.

4. Save the file.

5. In Internet Explorer, click the Refresh button (or press the F5 key) to verify that I squashed the bug.

Logic Errors

A logic error causes a program to produce incorrect results but does not prevent the program from running. Consequently, logic errors are harder to fix than syntax errors. The first problem is finding them; logic errors usually hide, revealing themselves only occasionally and then under special circumstances. For example, your program might seem to work perfectly until the first time a user leaves a text box blank. Then your program goes haywire. *Testing* your program is the only way to make the logic errors come out of hiding. Here are some tips for testing. (It's helpful to have a hard copy of the source code, by the way. You can print the code from Microsoft ActiveX Control Pad or from Notepad.)

Check that random data produces reasonable results

Using our mortgage calculator from Chapter 3 as an example, try several different amounts to see if the results make sense. Assuming you use the same interest rate and term, the monthly payment for a $100,000 mortgage should be twice that for a $50,000 mortgage.

The choice of *test data* is paramount. You must test all possible execution paths inside your code in order to have any hope that it will be bug free. You need lots of possible scenarios to test.

Check the boundary cases

This means that you check what happens if the user forgets to enter something or if he or she enters a value that is at the limits of the possibilities for the program. For example, what happens if a user of a catalog order form mistakenly enters 0 for the number of items to order? (You certainly don't want to be in the position of sending out bills for $0.00!)

Proactive Program Design

Testing is no fun, and debugging is even worse. You can make your life a whole lot easier by breaking your program up into lots of functions and subprocedures, each of which, ideally, does only one task. You can test many individual procedures much more easily than you can test a large piece of code that resembles a plate of spaghetti. In short, it's better to test each function or subprocedure in isolation knowing it is supposed to do one thing—and do it correctly. For example, suppose you need to total several numbers that are stored in an array. If you make a function out of this task, as shown in the following example, it will be easy to check that the function is working correctly:

```
Function SumIt(TheArray)
  Dim I, Total

  For I = 0 To UBound(TheArray)
    Total = Total + TheArray(I)
  Next

  SumIt = Total
End Function
```

You'll know pretty quickly whether you typed a minus sign instead of a plus sign, for example, because the wrong total will be displayed if you use a message box to test the results of calling the function, as shown in the following example:

```
Dim I, A(5)

For I = 1 To 5
  A(I) = I
Next

MsgBox SumIt(A)
```

The same message box technique will display the wrong total if you mistakenly wrote this:

```
For I = 0 To UBound(TheArray)
  Total = TheArray(I)
Next
```

In this case, the total displayed is equal to the last entry in the array!

Or, forgetting that array indexes start at 0 instead of 1, you might have written this:

```
For I = 1 To UBound(TheArray)
  Total = Total + TheArray(I)
Next
```

If this little piece of code was part of a 100-line section of code, how easy do you think this mistake would be to track down? It's better to design your program as a bunch of happily cooperating debugged functions and subprocedures.

The ultimate point of using *modularization,* as this kind of design is called, is to make the testing process easier. The idea is to check that each function and subprocedure can handle correctly all possible parameters that might be passed to it.

You also want to test your procedures to make sure they cause no undesirable side effects. For example, they shouldn't incorrectly change parameters (see the discussion of passing by reference in Chapter 6) or the values of script-level variables. A good practice is to continuously require that your program run correctly, regardless of whether all its features are yet implemented.

By now, you might be wondering how you can ensure that your program runs correctly at each stage of its development. In order to run, the program might need results from a function or subprocedure that you have not yet written. In this case, the best technique to use is to write a *stub.* A stub is a placeholder for a procedure that will eventually be part of the program.

The notion of a stub might seem abstract, so here's an example of how you would use one. Suppose you are writing a program to translate user entry into pig latin. Here are the basic rules:

- A word beginning with a vowel gets the suffix "ay".

- A word beginning with one or more consonants gets the consonants shifted to the end of the word, and then the word gets the suffix "ay".

Oday ouyay understanday ethay ulesray?

This is a fairly complicated program to implement, but for now let's concentrate on the idea of building it from individual functions. First you make a list of the functions you need:

- Function to separate the entire string into words. (This is built into VBScript—see Chapter 5 for a description of the Split function.)

- Function to handle words that begin with consonants. (Shift the initial consonants and add the "ay" suffix.)

- Function to handle words that begin with vowels. (Add the "ay" suffix.)

- Function to put everything back together. (This is built into VBScript—see Chapter 5 for a description of the Join function.)

Your goal is to write a program that works at every stage of its development. How can you do this? First test single words that begin with consonants, making sure your program can handle them. That tests the second function in the above list. Then try sentences to test how all the functions mesh.

You might be wondering how you can try sentences when you haven't yet written the function that handles words beginning with vowels. You don't want to complicate the logic of the program by writing this function yet; doing so would make a bug hard to track down. The idea is to write a stub for this function, as shown here:

```
Function DoVowel(TheWord)
  'Converts a word with an initial vowel
  'into the word in pig latin

  DoVowel = TheWord
End Function
```

Now you can try a sentence such as this:

Can it work?

Your program should display this:

Ancay itay orkway?

At this point, you can be confident of two things. First, the function that handles words with initial consonants is working correctly. Second, the overall logic of your program is working correctly. Now you can write the function that handles words with initial vowels. When you then test the entire program, you'll know that any bugs are located in the new function.

 IP Sometimes it's helpful to have the stub display a message box that identifies the name of the function (in this case, DoVowel). That way, you can be sure that the function is being called when it's supposed to be.

Isolating Logic Errors

Let's assume your testing reveals a logic error. For example, you know the program should take some action 10 times, but instead it wants to go on forever. Obviously, knowing you have a bug isn't enough. You have to isolate it—that is, find the part of the program that's causing the problem. If you've followed the modular approach that I just described, your program is composed of lots of cooperating functions and subprocedures that each do one thing, and your task is a lot easier. Why? Because you end up discovering the function or subprocedure that isn't working right.

Now, let's assume that you've chosen a faulty function or a faulty subprocedure to test. There are only three possibilities:

- What's going in is wrong. A parameter you've passed to the function or subprocedure is confusing it.

- What's going out is wrong. The function or subprocedure is sending incorrect information to another part of the program. For example, the function or subprocedure might be causing an unplanned side effect by changing a script-level variable.

- Some code within the function or subprocedure is wrong. For example, an operation is being performed too many times.

In the first two cases, the problem comes from any or all of the following:

- The value of a parameter when it is passed to the function or subprocedure

- The value that is assigned to a parameter within the function or subprocedure

- The value that is assigned to a script-level variable within the function or subprocedure

How do you decide which situation you're dealing with? Well, it's hard to imagine a short function or subprocedure that you can't analyze on a piece of paper to determine what should happen for various values of test data. Work through the function or subprocedure by "playing computer." (This means that you don't make any assumptions beyond what the computer would know at that point; don't assume variables have certain values unless you can convince yourself that they do.) If you still haven't found the problem, you need to check that the function or subprocedure is doing what it's supposed to do. This can be done using Microsoft Script Debugger, which I'm about to discuss.

On to Actual Debugging

The first part of this chapter described what you have to do, but theoretical knowledge without practical skills won't get a programmer very far. A main point of the rest of this chapter is to describe the *how,* and for VBScript programmers the how is best accomplished by mastering the tools provided by Microsoft Script Debugger (which is included on the companion CD).

If you make a list of what you have to do based on what you just learned, you might come up with this:

■ Stop the execution of a program at the beginning of a specific procedure in order to start checking that procedure. You also need a way to stop a program at a specific line within a procedure.

   You can do either of these tasks in one of two ways. First, you can type a Stop statement (which is nothing more than the keyword Stop) at the beginning of the procedure you want to check. (You can also type a Stop statement within a procedure.) This causes the program to run until the Stop statement is reached, and then Script Debugger is displayed. Second, you can set a *breakpoint* via Script Debugger. A breakpoint is nothing more than the equivalent of a temporary Stop statement.

■ Assign a new value to a parameter or variable and then see the results. At the point in the program when it is stopped, you also need to be able to see the current values of all the variables in the procedure (and of any script-level variables).

   Script Debugger allows you to do this through the magic of its Command window.

■ Run the program one line at a time; in other words, slow execution down to a crawl. By doing this, you will be able to see exactly how your program processes any values you assign to parameters or variables.

   Script Debugger allows you to do this via its Step commands.

That's it—the only thing left is to show you the mechanics.

Starting Script Debugger

Script Debugger is shown in Figure 7-2. Note that Script Debugger includes a full-featured, color-coded HTML editor, in addition to its other features.

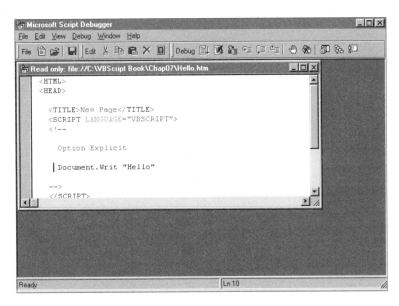

Figure 7-2.   *Script Debugger.*

There are four ways to start Script Debugger:

- ■ With the Web page you want to debug open in Internet Explorer, select Script Debugger from the View menu and then select Open from the cascading menu.

- ■ Use the Stop statement in your VBScript program. Script Debugger will automatically be displayed when the execution of your program reaches the Stop statement.

- ■ Click the Yes button in the dialog box shown in Figure 7-1.

- ■ In Windows Explorer, open the Script Debugger application file (Msscrdbg.exe). Or you can put a shortcut to this file on your desktop, which is a lot easier to get to.

In all but the last case, you will be working with the Web page that is currently displayed in Internet Explorer. In the last case, you can open the source for an existing Web page by selecting Open from Script Debugger's File menu, or you can create a new page from scratch by selecting New from the File menu.

Once Script Debugger is running, you can debug any page that is currently running in Internet Explorer by choosing Running Documents from the View menu. The window shown in Figure 7-3 is displayed.

Figure 7-3.   *The Running Documents window.*

Pick the document you want to debug by following these steps:

1. Open the document tree by clicking the plus sign.

2. Double-click the name of the document.

Before I discuss the mechanics of using Script Debugger, there is one further complication I have to warn you about. When you debug a program that you are running in Internet Explorer, Script Debugger opens the file as "read-only." (You can see this if you look closely at the title bar in Figure 7-2.) Even though you can find out what is wrong, you can't correct the file directly with Script Debugger.

Making the changes requires a somewhat convoluted process, since you cannot simply edit the script that is displayed in the Script Debugger window. When you want to make even the smallest change in a page that is running in Internet Explorer, you have two options.

You can save the Web page with a new name by selecting Save As from Script Debugger's File menu. You can then edit the new file in Script Debugger. After you make your changes, you have to restart the testing procedure by loading the page with its new name back into Internet Explorer, hoping that you won't have to make too many more changes, since each time you'll have to repeat the process of renaming, editing, testing, renaming, and so on.

A second option would be to select Close from the File menu to remove the file from Script Debugger. Then open the file in Notepad by selecting Source from Internet Explorer's View menu. Make the changes, and then start the testing process again.

I prefer the second alternative.

A Debugging Session

I want to lead you through a debugging session step by step. For that, I obviously need a buggy program. Although my example is somewhat simplified, I do want to use a program that could come up in real life. Here's a problem I decided to solve by building a Web page. I am a teacher and I want each student to be able to calculate his or her final grade by entering exam scores on a Web page. Here are the rules I use for determining final grades:

- The final grade is based on three interim exams and a final exam, each of which receives a numeric score.

- The results of the three interim exams and the final exam are totaled. The final exam is counted twice.

- The average of the five scores determines the final grade.

- If the average is 90 or greater, the student gets an "A," 80 or better a "B," and so on.

Here's a first attempt at a program to do this. (You can find this code in the file Grade.htm on the companion CD).

```
<HTML>
<HEAD>

  <TITLE>A grade calculator</TITLE>
  <SCRIPT LANGUAGE="VBSCRIPT">
  <!--

    Option Explicit

    Dim A(4), Average

    For I = 1 To 4
      A(I) = InputBox("What is the student's grade on exam " _
        & I & "?")
    Next

    Average = CalculateAverage(A)
    MsgBox "Your grade is " & CalculateGrade(Average)

'*******************************************************************

    Function CalculateAverage(Grades)
      Dim Total

      For I = 1 = 1 To 4
        Total = Grades(I)
      Next

      CalculateAverage = Total / 4
    End Function

'*******************************************************************

    Function CalculateGrade(Average)

      If Average > 90 Then
        CalculateGrade = "A"
      ElseIf Average > 80  Then
        CalculateGrade = "B"
      ElseIf Average > 70 Then
        CalculateGrade = "C"
      Else
        CalculateGrade = "F"
      End If
```

```
    End Function

    -->
    </SCRIPT>

</HEAD>
<BODY>

</BODY>
</HTML>
```

Let's suppose that I thought writing a program for this problem would be so easy that I opened Notepad, started typing, and moved immediately to the testing process (without first testing each procedure individually).

The Testing Process

Based on the previous scenario, I would open the page in Internet Explorer and the first thing I would see is the dialog box shown in Figure 7-4, telling me that I have an undefined variable. This means that even though I used the Option Explicit statement as I was supposed to, I forgot to declare a variable.

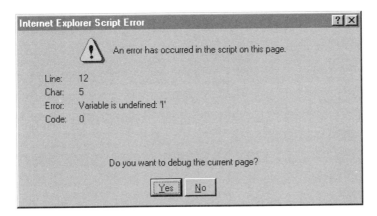

Figure 7-4.   *The first error dialog box.*

I don't need Script Debugger to help me decide what to do, so I would click the No button, select Source from the View menu, and go back to line 12.

Next I would hit myself on the head because I forgot to declare the counting variable named I that I used in the first For-Next loop.

TIP Notepad doesn't have a line counter; you have to count the lines yourself. If you have a favorite editor that does give you line count information, you might want to use that application instead.

This error could be fixed by adding the variable named I to the Dim statement above the loop, saving the file, and then clicking the Refresh button in Internet Explorer. At this point, the first input box would be displayed. I'd start testing the easy cases, for example, where the student receives all 100s or receives all 0s. Entering 100 in all four input boxes would display the message box shown in Figure 7-5.

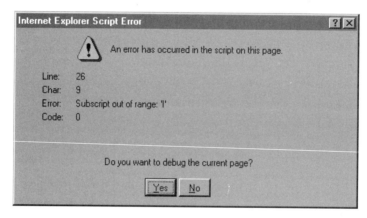

Figure 7-5. *Subscript Out Of Range error dialog box.*

At this point, I'd start the debugger. Clicking the Yes button conveniently places the cursor at (or close to) the offending line. I would then stare at the following code:

```
Function CalculateAverage(Grades)
  Dim Total

  For I = 1 = 1 To 4
    Total = Grades(I)
  Next

  CalculateAverage = Total / 4
End Function
```

I'd made another typo by entering the first line of code instead of the second line:

214

```
For I = 1 = 1 To 4
```

```
For I = 1 To 4
```

I would need to close the debugger, open Notepad, make the change, and save the file. To start the testing process again, I would click the Refresh button in Internet Explorer and enter four 100s as I did the first time. Unfortunately, the message box shown in Figure 7-6 would be the result. A student who gets perfect scores would prefer not to get an F, and I would prefer not to be hanged in effigy, so I would track this bug down quickly.

Figure 7-6.   *The message box the user would see.*

Obviously, there is either something wrong with the function that calculates the average or with the function that uses the average to calculate a letter grade. At this point, I would start to regret not thinking through this program more carefully, exemplifying the first rule of programming:

> *The sooner in the programming process you start writing code,*
> *the longer it is going to take to get it working.*

And, of course, I would have second thoughts about not testing each procedure individually. I decide to continue, knowing I can still use the Stop statement or a breakpoint to test each function individually.

The Stop Statement

There are two ways to stop a program: placing a Stop statement in the program or using a breakpoint. When Internet Explorer reaches a Stop statement, it stops executing the script at that point. The other way is to open the source in Script Debugger, move the cursor to the line where you want to set the breakpoint, and select Toggle Breakpoint from the Debug menu. Unfortunately, clicking the Refresh button in Internet Explorer cancels the breakpoint in Script Debugger. For this reason, I tend to use Stop statements a lot more than breakpoints.

ARNING You must manually remove all Stop statements after you have finished debugging your program.

Now let's assume that I used Notepad to add a Stop statement right after the statements that get the input. Here's what the code would look like:

```
Option Explicit
Dim I, A(4), Average
For I = 1 To 4
  A(I) = InputBox("What is the student's grade on exam " _
    & I & "?")
Next
Stop
⋮
```

I would save the file, click the Refresh button, and enter four 100s again. When Internet Explorer encounters the Stop statement, it automatically opens Script Debugger. You'd see a little yellow arrow at the Stop statement. (See Figure 7-7.)

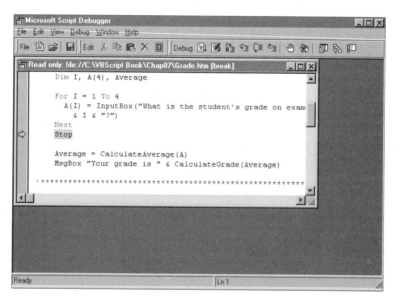

Figure 7-7. *Working with a stopped program.*

Now I'd use the other features of Script Debugger to finish isolating the problem. I'd start with the Command window that lets me look at the values of variables and even change them.

Using the Command Window

When the program stops, select Command window from Script Debugger's View menu. This displays the window shown in Figure 7-8.

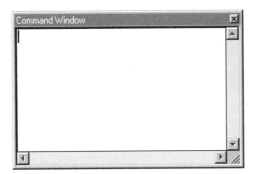

Figure 7-8.   *The Command window.*

The Command window lets you examine and change all the variables that are in the current scope. (This means that you can look at or change script-level variables all the time, but you can look at or change variables inside a procedure only when the program is stopped inside that procedure.) The array named A is a script-level variable, so use the Command window to check whether it contains the correct values. The command that lets you see values is simply a question mark. Type the following command, and then press the Enter key:

```
?A(1)
```

You should see 100 in the Command window. After you check the rest of the array, you know that it correctly contains four 100s. Therefore, the trouble must be in the analysis of the data.

The Command window lets you call functions; all you have to do is enter the required parameters. For example, if you enter the following command you see an "A" show up in the Command window. (See Figure 7-9 on the following page.)

```
?CalculateGrade(100
```

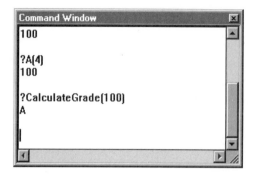

Figure 7-9. *Entering commands in the Command window.*

So far so good. Next you need to try a boundary value, such as 90, for the average. Unfortunately, entering the following command produces a "B" rather than an "A":

```
?CalculateGrade(90)
```

Clearly, the three > symbols in the CalculateGrade function should be changed to >= symbols. After you fix this error and test the function again, you can be confident that the CalculateGrade function is working properly.

The next step is to test the CalculateAverage function. When you do this, keep in mind that the array named A contains four 100s. However, entering the following command produces a value of 25:

```
?CalculateAverage(A)
```

It is clear that there is a problem in the CalculateAverage function.

The Step Commands

The F8 key is the shortcut for the Step Into command.

You are stopped at the line after the data was entered. You want to continue moving through the program line by line. To do this, select Step Into from the Debug menu. The Step Into command tells the debugger to proceed line by line. Each time you select this command, the little yellow arrow that marks your current location moves. For example, if you select Step Into once, you will be on this line:

```
Average = CalculateAverage(A)
```

If you select this command again, you'll go to the first line in the Calculate-Average function (the beginning of the For-Next loop). If you select Step Into two more times, you start the process of adding up the numbers. Use the Command window to check the value of Total on each pass through the loop. This reveals two mistakes in one line. First I wrote this:

```
Total = Grades(I)
```

I should have written this:

```
Total = Total + Grades(I)
```

You need to fix the mistake and restart the testing process. Repeating the above sequence of steps, use the Command window to check the (corrected) value of Total on each pass through the loop. This reveals the second mistake. The grades in the array are strings because they were entered in an input box. The plus sign is joining the strings together instead of adding integers together. You must convert the strings to integers, like this:

```
Total = Total + CInt(Grades(I))
```

Now the Command window tells you that the value of Total is correct on each pass through the loop.

At this point, let's say you believe you've fixed all the bugs in the program, so you decide to retest without going into Script Debugger. You comment out the Stop statement so Script Debugger won't be opened. (You don't delete it yet, since you'll need it if you do find another bug.) Then you find out that the perfect student will get an "A." The solid B student, with four grades of 85, gets a "B." You start to have some hope. Then you test someone who improves dramatically on the final, going from straight 85s to a perfect 100. Since the final counts twice, this student deserves an "A," but the program produces a "B."

You restore the Stop statement and use the Step Into command again. This reveals the last error: the final is *not* being counted twice. Here is the corrected CalculateAverage function:

```
Function CalculateAverage(Grades)
  Dim Total

  For I = 1 To 4
    Total = Total + CInt(Grades(I))
  Next
  Total = Total + CInt(Grades(4))

  CalculateAverage = Total / 5
End Function
```

Since further testing shows the program to be working, you can finally delete the Stop statement.

An alternative to the program you just debugged would be to give students the opportunity to place their grades in text boxes so that they have a chance to double-check their entries. Then they would be able to click on a command button to calculate their final grades. Let's examine that solution, which lets us use a few more debugging techniques.

More on Script Debugger

I hope that I have convinced you how useful Script Debugger can be. There's still a bit more power that you have at your disposal, and this section will show you what else Script Debugger can do.

If you found the Stop statement inconvenient, you have two ways to avoid using it.

- Tell Script Debugger to stop at the first statement in your script.

- Enter a breakpoint in an event procedure of an already loaded script.

To tell the debugger to stop at the first statement in your script, follow these steps:

1. Load the script into Internet Explorer.

2. From the View menu, select Script Debugger.

3. Select Break At Next Statement.

4. From the cascading menu, click the Refresh button.

Telling Script Debugger to stop at the first statement in your script is useful only if you need to start debugging at the first statement in your script or if you can use something other than the Step Into command. (Using just this command, it could take a long time to get to the part of your script that you want to debug.)

For example, it wouldn't be nearly as painful to start at the beginning of your program if you had a way to say, "I know that this procedure is fine; don't bother stepping into it line by line, just do what it says," or "Now that I've checked what I needed to in a procedure, just execute the rest of the statements automatically."

The Shift-F8 key combination is the shortcut for the Step Over command.

Conveniently, Script Debugger has features that match perfectly what you want to do. You tell the debugger to execute all the code in a procedure in one fell swoop by selecting Step Over from the Debug menu when you get to the line that calls the procedure. You tell the debugger to automatically execute the rest of a procedure's statements by selecting Step Out from the Debug menu.

The Ctrl-Shift-F8 key combination is the shortcut for the Step Out command.

To see how to enter a breakpoint in an event procedure of an already loaded script, we'll use a version of the grade calculator in which the final grade calculation is triggered by an event—the user clicking a button. As you can see in Figure 7-10, this version has five labels, five text boxes, and a command button.

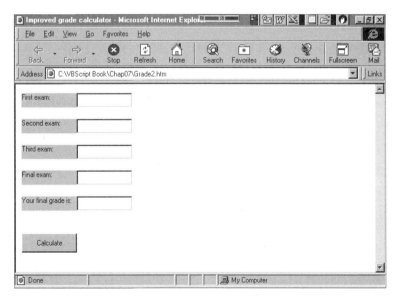

Figure 7-10. *The improved grade calculator.*

Here's the script, which you can find in the file Grade2.htm on the companion CD:

```
Option Explicit

Sub cmdCalculate_Click
  Dim A(4), Average

  A(1) = txtFirstExam.Text
  A(2) = txtSecondExam.Text
  A(3) = txtThirdExam.Text
  A(4) = txtFinalExam.Text

  Average = CalculateAverage(A)
  txtFinalGrade.Text = CalculateGrade(Average)
End Sub

Function CalculateAverage(Grades)
  Dim I, Total

  For I = 1 To 4
    Total = Total + CInt(Grades(I))
  Next
  Total = Total + CInt(Grades(4))

  CalculateAverage = Total / 5   'five grades
End Function

Function CalculateGrade(Average)

  If Average >= 90 Then
    CalculateGrade = "A"
  ElseIf Average >= 80  Then
    CalculateGrade = "B"
  ElseIf Average >= 70 Then
    CalculateGrade = "C"
  Else
    CalculateGrade = "F"
  End If

End Function
```

Nothing happens until the user clicks the button. This is what lets us set a breakpoint successfully. Here's what you need to do:

1. Load the script into Internet Explorer.

2. From the View menu, select Script Debugger.

3. From the cascading menu, select Open.

4. Click anywhere in the first line of the cmdCalculate_Click subprocedure to place the cursor there.

The F9 key is the shortcut for the Toggle Breakpoint command.

5. Place a breakpoint at this line by selecting Toggle Breakpoint from the Debug menu.

Notice the red octagon that the debugger adds at this line. Now the breakpoint is set. If you go back to Internet Explorer, enter the four exam grades and click the Calculate button, Script Debugger will stop at the breakpoint and you can use all the commands you have already seen.

The Ctrl-Shift-F9 key combination is the shortcut for the Clear All Breakpoints command.

You can set multiple breakpoints, all indicated by the red octagons. Each breakpoint can be turned on or off with the Toggle Breakpoint command, or all breakpoints can be removed at once by selecting Clear All Breakpoints from the Debug menu.

 OTE The term *toggle* means to switch back and forth between two states. Therefore, selecting the Toggle Breakpoint command initially turns a breakpoint on. Selecting the same command again, with the cursor on the same line, turns the breakpoint off.

The F5 key is the shortcut for the Run command.

If you have multiple breakpoints and are stopped at one of them, you might want to automatically execute all the code up to the next breakpoint. To do this, select Run from the Debug menu. If you have set only one breakpoint and are stopped there, selecting the Run command executes the rest of the script.

 IP All the commands on the Debug menu have toolbar equivalents.

Error Trapping

Error trapping means telling Internet Explorer not to stop when it encounters an error. This is generally not a good idea. For example, if you are trying to divide by 0 or are trying to get the fifth element in an array with four elements, this is a bug that you should catch and fix. Using error trapping lets you get away with poorly written programs in the sense that your programs will (sort of) run. What they might not do is produce the results your users expect.

Since I feel that error trapping is generally a bad idea and that you should debug your programs first and foremost, why would I end a chapter on debugging by explaining how to do error trapping? The answer is simple: there are errors that have nothing to do with your code; they are caused by things like a bad network connection or a Web site being temporarily down. (In the next chapter, I'll use VBScript to control where Internet Explorer goes and what it does when it gets to a site.) It is for situations like these that you should use error trapping.

The On Error statement, which enables error trapping in VBScript, looks like the following:

```
On Error Resume Next
```

This tells Internet Explorer that if it encounters an error to simply forget about it and move to the next statement.

Having cautioned you against thinking of error trapping as a replacement for debugging your program, I'll explain the actual mechanics of using the On Error statement.

First, this statement works only for the procedure that contains it. This means that you might want to include an On Error statement in each procedure in your program. If you don't do this and an error occurs in a called procedure, Internet Explorer will move to the statement following the *call* (not to the next statement in the called procedure). For example, consider the following outline:

```
Option Explicit
On Error Resume Next

statement1
statement2
MySubprocedure
statement3
statement4

Sub MySubprocedure
  statement5
  statement6
  statement7, which causes an error
  statement8
  statement9
End Sub
```

When the error occurs in statement7, execution proceeds with statement3—not, as you might expect, with statement8. If you want execution to proceed with statement8, you must include an additional On Error statement in MySubprocedure.

As a simpler example, suppose you want to make a calculator that divides the number in one text box by the number in another when the user clicks a button. You write the following sloppy code:

```
Sub cmdDivide_Click
  txtAnswer.Text = txtFirst.Text / txtSecond.Text
End Sub
```

The first time your user tries this after entering 0 in the second text box, Internet Explorer will show him or her a standard error dialog box. You decide that instead of adding the necessary checks to see whether the user's entries make sense you'll use error trapping like this:

```
Sub cmdDivide_Click
  On Error Resume Next
  txtAnswer.Text = txtFirst.Text / txtSecond.Text
End Sub
```

What's the result? Nothing—whatever was in the third text box stays there! This will obviously confuse your users. It is a good idea to inform your users that their work caused an error so that they can report it to the Webmaster. This is done with the Err object.

The Err Object

When Internet Explorer encounters an error, it stores information about the error in the properties of a built-in object named the Err object. The value of the Description property is a string describing the error, and the value of the Number property is an integer representing the error. For example, if a user attempts to divide by 0, the Description property would be set to "Division by zero" and the Number property would be set to 11. The VBScript documentation contains all the VBScript error descriptions with their corresponding error numbers. (Go to the Err Object page, click See Also, and then click Error Messages.)

I strongly suggest that if you do use error trapping in a procedure you always add a fragment similar to the one below at the end of the procedure:

As long as no error occurs, Err.Number = 0.

```
If Err.Number <> 0 Then
    MsgBox "Please tell the owner of this page that the following " _
        & "error occurred: " & vbCrLf & vbCrLf & Err.Description
End If
```

This gives you a fighting chance to know what happened and places you in a position to fix it so that it doesn't happen again.

3

Advanced Topics

The Internet Explorer Object Model

Up to this point, I have used VBScript programming to make a single Web page more interesting. In this chapter, I want to introduce you to a powerful feature of VBScript—the ability to control Microsoft Internet Explorer version 4 itself. This has the potential to make Web pages even more interesting. For example, you can use VBScript to make Internet Explorer go to a new Web page. This new page can be displayed in place of the old page, in a frame that you create on the old page, or even in a whole new browser window. The latter features, as you will soon see, let you show your users the Web equivalent of the television feature named "picture in a picture," where you see a little window, or subpicture, with a show from another channel while you continue to watch your original program on the larger part of the screen.

You can also use VBScript to control exactly what Internet Explorer sends to the server, making Web-based forms faster to submit than when Internet Explorer itself controls this. I'll even show you how to handle cookies with VBScript. (*Cookies* are those often useful, but occasionally invasive, pieces of information that Web servers can leave on your hard disk.)

 OTE The Internet Explorer object model is vast and complicated; I can only cover the most common parts of it here. For more information, see the documentation in the Internet Client SDK, which is included on the companion CD. You also might want to refer to a book on Dynamic HTML, such *Inside Dynamic HTML* by Scott Isaacs (Microsoft Press, 1997).

The Basics of the Internet Explorer Object Model

First I want to make sure that you are comfortable with the term *object model*. Programmers use this term to describe how the various pieces of a program fit together—sort of the equivalent of a family tree where you indicate relationships among family members in a hierarchical fashion. In an object model, the objects are *programmable*—you can set their properties, call specific methods, or write event procedures for them.

 N OTE Properties describe what an object is, methods allow an object to do things, and events are actions that an object can respond to.

Usually there is a topmost object in any object model. In Internet Explorer, this object is named the *window* object, although sometimes it's named the *parent* object. (Another way to understand an object model is to imagine the window object as containing all the other Internet Explorer objects.)

From this point on, the object model gets a little complicated. Figure 8-1 shows a somewhat simplified representation of Internet Explorer's Object model.

While I'll have a lot more to say about the pieces shown in Figure 8-1 (and even more sophisticated versions of this hierarchy later in this chapter), I do hope the names give you a sense of what the objects do. For example, the document object is the actual Web page, and the location object is the URL where the page is located. The key to keep in mind is that all objects in the Internet Explorer object model are like ActiveX controls in the sense that you can change certain properties to customize their behavior and they might have custom events to which you can write specialized event procedures.

T IP ActiveX Control Pad's Script Wizard can be of invaluable help in understanding the basics of the Internet Explorer object model. As you saw in Chapter 2, if you click the plus sign next to the window object, you can see the properties and events of many of the Internet Explorer objects.

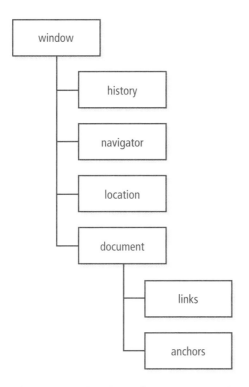

Figure 8-1.   *The topmost levels of the Internet Explorer object model.*

The Window Object

As I discussed in Chapter 2, the two most common events that the window object can respond to are onLoad and onUnload. There are actually seven more events, four of which are described in the following table:

Event	When It Is Triggered
onBlur	The window loses the focus. (The user moves to another window on the desktop.)
onFocus	The window gets the focus. (The user moves to the Internet Explorer window, and its title bar is highlighted.)
onHelp	The user presses the F1 key to access online Help.
onError	An error occurs when loading a document.

For example, you could have a script that included the following:

```
Sub window_onFocus
  MsgBox("Thanks for coming to my page.")
End Sub
```

Whenever the user moves the focus to the Internet Explorer window, he or she will see the message box.

One of the sub-objects of the window object is the *screen* object. The two most useful properties of this object are the *height* and *width* properties because they tell you the dimensions of the user's screen in pixels. (There is also a colorDepth property that tells you how many colors are available on the user's screen.)

 NOTE   The colorDepth property gives the number of bits needed to describe the colors. The actual number of colors available is 2 raised to the number of bits. For example, if colorDepth is 4, the number of colors is 2^4 or 16.

All this can be useful information for a professionally designed Web page. It enables you to design different Web pages depending on whether the user has, say, 640x480 resolution or 1024x768 resolution. For example, why spend the time sending a picture designed for a machine at 1024x768 resolution with 16 million colors if the user has a plain vanilla screen with 16 colors running at 640x480? Send a simpler image instead! It will surely be appreciated.

To do this, you will need to have this information *before* the document loads, so you might write code that starts like this:

```
<SCRIPT LANGUAGE="VBSCRIPT">
<!--

  Option Explicit

  Dim HeightOfScreen, WidthOfScreen, ScreenColors

  HeightOfScreen = window.screen.height
  WidthOfScreen = window.screen.width
  ScreenColors = 2 ^ window.screen.colorDepth
  ⋮

  --!>
</SCRIPT>
```

Please note that you use periods to drill down in the object hierarchy. Eventually, you get to an actual property of an object. The expressions in the above code mean, "Start with the window object, move to its screen sub-object, and finally get the value of the height, width, or colorDepth property of the sub-object."

Some Basic Methods for the Window Object

There are 16 methods for the window object. The following table describes the most important ones:

Method	Description
open	Opens a whole new browser window.
close	Closes the current browser window.
navigate	Goes to another page.
setInterval	Lets you specify a procedure that you want to run periodically while the current page is displayed.
setTimeout	Lets you specify a procedure that you want to run, starting a certain number of milliseconds after the page loads.
clearInterval	Cancels the setInterval method.
clearTimeout	Cancels the setTimeout message.

Using these methods, you can make your Web pages a lot more useful, a lot more dynamic, and a lot more annoying.

The open method

For example, the ability to display a whole new browser window is occasionally very useful, but don't overdo it. Having too many browser windows open at the same time can be really unpleasant on most screens. (And people might not like your displaying images that are not under their control.) For example, the following program opens another browser window with Yahoo's home page in it:

```
Sub window_onLoad
  window.open "http://www.yahoo.com", "Yahoo", "top=0, left=0"
End Sub
```

Notice that I had to use the long form of a Web address with the "http://" that modern browsers like Internet Explorer have made optional.

Nevertheless, as I mentioned, people don't like a Web page that takes control of their browser without giving them a chance to have input. The following version of the above script is much less intrusive:

```
Sub window_onLoad
  Dim YesNo

  YesNo = MsgBox("Shall I open a browser window for searching?", _
    vbYesNo)
  If YesNo = vbYes Then
    window.open "http://www.yahoo.com", "Yahoo", "top=0, left=0"
  End if

End Sub
```

As you can see by running either of the above programs, the last parameter controls how the new window looks when it opens. You can add other items for even finer control. For example, the following code opens the new window in the top left corner but also makes it 100 pixels high and 100 pixels wide.

```
window.open "http://www.yahoo.com", "Yahoo", _
  "top=0, left=0, height=100, width=100"
```

The navigate method
The navigate method lets you specify a new page for the browser to display. For example, you can use the navigate method in a customized home page that exists simply to ask who the user is and goes to one of several specific Web pages based on this information. Here's an example of how to do this:

```
Sub window_onLoad
  Dim YourName

  YourName = InputBox("What is your name?")

  If YourName = "Gary Cornell" Then
  window.navigate "http://www.microsoft.com/vbscript"
  ElseIf YourName = "Bill Clinton" Then
  window.navigate "http://www.whitehouse.gov"
  Else
  window.navigate "http://www.microsoft.com"
  End If

End Sub
```

Timers

Some of the most important methods of the window object have to do with forcing code to run periodically. For example, suppose you want to give somebody only a certain amount of time to read a page because the page is part of an HTML-based tutorial or exam. To do this, use the setTimeout method, which has two required parameters:

```
Window.setTimeout(NameOfProcedureToCall, AfterThisManyMilliSeconds)
```

A line like the following one tells Internet Explorer to call the procedure named ByeBye after one minute has elapsed (60,000 milliseconds = 60 seconds = 1 minute):

```
window.setTimeout("ByeBye", 60000)
```

The following program gives you only a minute to look at the initial page before it goes to Microsoft's home page:

```
Sub window_onLoad
  window.setTimeout "ByeBye", 60000
End Sub

Sub ByeBye
  window.navigate "http://www.microsoft.com"
End Sub
```

If the procedure you are calling requires parameters, you need to specify the parameters in the call to the setTimeout method. Here are some examples of the needed syntax. Suppose you write this:

```
Option Explicit

Dim Gary
Gary = "Gary"

Sub window_onLoad
  window.setTimeout "ByeBye Gary", 60000
End Sub
```

If ByeBye looks like this, you would see a message box with my name before you left the page:

```
Sub ByeBye(Who)
  MsgBox "Goodbye " & Who
  window.navigate "http://www.microsoft.com"
End Sub
```

If the procedure you are calling when the timer times out is a function, be sure you use parentheses inside the quotes to pass parameters:

```
window.setTimeout "ByeByeFunction(Gary)", 60000
```

On the other hand, the setInterval method is used when you want Internet Explorer to wake up a routine periodically—whenever the specified interval has elapsed. The way this works is that when Internet Explorer processes a line like this it will execute the WakeUp procedure every 10 seconds:

```
Window.setInterval "WakeUp", 10000
```

Finally, if you think your script will need to cancel a timing operation that you have started, you should use a slightly different syntax for these methods. Assign the results of the setTimeout or setInterval method to a variable. For example:

```
MyTimeout = window.setTimeout "ByeByeFunction(Gary)", 10000
MyIntervalTimer = window.setInterval "WakeUp", 10000
```

Now, use either one of these:

```
window.clearTimeout MyTimeout
window.clearInterval MyIntervalTimer
```

This tells Internet Explorer to stop keeping track of that particular timer.

Finishing Up with the Window Object

As you saw in Figure 8-1 on page 233, there are few more objects contained in the window object. I'll cover the document object at length in the next section. In this section, I'll explain why you might want to work with the history and navigator objects.

The history object

This object lets you access the History list that Internet Explorer maintains. You can see this History list by clicking the History button on Internet Explorer's toolbar. (Click the button again to hide the History list.)

The history object has one property, *length,* which tells you how many items are stored in the History list, and three methods, which are described in the following table:

Method	What It Does
back	Moves to the previous location in the History list.
forward	Moves to the next location in the History list.
go	Goes to a particular URL in the History list. You specify one of two possible items in parentheses following the keyword go: a string containing the actual URL or the relative position of the URL in the History list. (*Relative position* means that the current page has position 0, the previous page has position –1, the next page has position 1, and so on.)

Suppose, for example, that you want your Web page to allow a user who got to your page by mistake to go back to the previous link. You can use code like this:

```
Sub window_onLoad
  Dim YesNo

  YesNo = MsgBox("Are you here by mistake?", vbYesNo)
  If YesNo = vbYes Then
    window.history.back
  End If

End Sub
```

 TIP Internet Explorer assumes you mean the window object even if you don't explicitly specify it. In the above example, you can write history.back instead of window.history.back.

The navigator object

This object tells you what version of Internet Explorer the visitor to your page is using. Internet Explorer version 4 has many additional features compared to version 3, so you might have to maintain (for a while) two separate pages: one for version 3 users and one for version 4 users. The key property of the navigator object is appVersion, which contains the following string (for Internet Explorer version 4 on Microsoft Windows 95):

```
4.0 (compatible; MSIE 4.0; Windows 95)
```

Of course, it would have been nice if the appVersion property contained a simple number you could check with an If-Then-Else statement, but it doesn't; you have to use Instr, as shown in the following code:

```
Sub window_onLoad

  If Instr(window.navigator.appVersion,"4") Then
    MsgBox("Congratulations for having the latest and greatest.")
    Else
    MsgBox("Don't you want to get Internet Explorer version 4?")
    End If

End Sub
```

The appName property, on the other hand, contains only the string "Microsoft Interner Explorer," so it is less useful. The final property you will use a lot with the navigator object is the cookieEnabled property; I'll cover that in the section on cookies on page 265.

The Document Object

The document object represents the actual Web page. The document object has a few properties that you will work with frequently. More importantly, it contains other objects. For example, it contains all the links on the Web page. As you will soon see, this is very convenient since it enables you to use VBScript to work with all the links on a given Web page.

Document Methods and Properties

You have already seen the fundamental method for working with a document—the write method that lets you display text on the current Web page. There is also an open method that works like the open method for a Window. The more basic properties that you work with are described in the following table:

Property	Description
bgColor	Background color of the page
fgColor	Default color for text
linkColor	Color for links not yet visited
alinkColor	Color for an active link (The mouse is over the link.)

(continued)

continued

Property	Description
vlinkColor	Color for links already visited
title	Title of the page
location	URL of the page
cookie	Cookie stored about the page
lastModified	Date the document was last modified

The lastModified property is convenient but it contains a string, therefore you must use the CDate function to convert it to a date, as in the following example:

```
If CDate(document.lastModified) > #1/1/98# Then
  MsgBox "New page"
Else
  MsgBox "Old page"
End If
```

Many of the Document properties relate to color. You have two choices for specifying colors. The first is to use one of the built-in colors that HTML provides, such as "red" or "blue" (including the surrounding quotes). There are 16 possible colors: aqua, black, blue, fuchsia, gray, green, lime, maroon, navy, olive, purple, red, silver, teal, white, and yellow.

However, there are many machines whose displays allow millions of colors. To take advantage of this feature, you need to use hexadecimal color encoding to specify colors. (Don't worry if the user's machine doesn't have millions of colors available—Internet Explorer will do its best to match the color you want with a color the user has.)

When you use hexadecimal numbers for specifying colors, you use two hex digits for each color so that you can have hues of red, green and blue ranging from 0 to 255.

 OTE Why 255? Well, 255 (FF in hexadecimal) is the most you can get with two hexadecimal digits. It means "15 sixteens and 15 ones," or 255 in decimal.

Colors are described by specifying "*RRGGBB*"; where the intensity of red, green, and blue are each defined by two hexadecimal digits as shown in the table on the following page.

Color Encoding	Result
`document.bgColor = "FF0000"`	Maximum redness
`document.bgColor = "00FF00"`	Maximum greenness
`document.bgColor = "0000FF"`	Maximum blueness

Suppose you want a color that is an equal mixture of all colors with medium brightness. Since 0 is the minimum and 255 is the maximum, you need 123 for each of the red, green, and blue components. Converting 123 to two hexadecimal digits turns out to give 7B. (Why? Because 7B in hexadecimal means "7 sixteens and 11 ones." So, to get an equal mixture of all colors, use this:

```
document.bgColor = "7B7B7B"
```

What Exactly Is Hexadecimal?

Color encoding uses hexadecimal numbers for colors. Hexadecimal means base 16 instead of the base 10 that people normally use. To paraphrase the great songwriter, Tom Lehrer, hexadecimal is just like decimal—if you happen to have 16 fingers rather than 10. The idea is that instead of counting 1, 2, 3...10 (adding a new digit at 10), you count like this:

```
1, 2, 3,...9, A(= 10), B(= 11),...F(= 15), 10(= 16)
```

Now 10 means 16 rather than 10. As another example, 56 in decimal notation means "5 tens and 6 ones." The number A6 in hexadecimal notation means "10 sixteens and 6 ones," or 166 in decimal.

The Objects Inside the Document Object

In the Internet Explorer object model, items with an "s" on the end are usually collections.

Before I go any further, I want to explain a new term that you'll encounter often as you drill down deeper in the Internet Explorer object model— *collection*. As its name suggests, a collection is simply a group of related objects. As you can see in Figure 8-1 on page 233, the document object has a *links* collection that contains all the links on a page so that you can access them easily.

The following table briefly describes the more significant collections contained in the document object.

Object	Description
All	All the HTML tags and elements on the page (often too big to work with effectively)
Anchors	All the anchors in the document
Frames	All the frames in the document
Forms	All the HTML forms on the page
Images	All the images on the page
Links	All the links on the page

An item in a collection is accessed in the same way as an element of an array. For example, the first link in the links collection is accessed like this:

```
document.links(0)
```

The other property you need is the length property, which tells you how many items there are in a collection. For example, the following For-Next loop allows you to get at each link on the current page:

```
For I = 0 To links.length - 1
  'code to work with links(I) goes here
Next
```

First step in using the links collection

For the first step on the road to mastering the power of the links collection, I will show you how to write a script that adds a "picture in a picture" property to a Web page. The result is that a browser window that successively displays each link on the page is placed in the top left corner of the screen.

Let's begin by displaying the small window containing the first link on the current page. Part of the code looks like this:

```
window.open(document.links(0), _
  "NameOfNewWindow", "top=0, left=0, height=175, width=275")
```

Now, how can you work with the window that you just spawned? For example, how can you change it or close it down? The answer is to use the keyword Set. Set lets you keep a *reference* to any VBScript object. For example:

```
Set PicInPicture = window.open(document.links(0), _
  "NameOfNewWindow", "top=0, left=0, height=175, width=275")
```

Then you can use the variable named PicInPicture to refer to the object on the right side of the equal sign. (The reason for the presence of the Set keyword is that VBScript needs to distinguish between making an ordinary assignment and creating a reference to an object.)

Once you have used the Set keyword to create a reference to an object, you can retrieve any property or apply any method available to that object. Simply follow the reference by a dot and the name of the property or method you want. For example, the following line closes the window that the previous code created:

```
PicInPicture.close
```

You'll need to close the window in your example program so that the picture within a picture window closes when the original Web page is unloaded. The window_onUnload procedure looks like this:

```
Sub window_onUnload
  PicInPicture.close
End Sub
```

Here's an approach to a procedure that you can call from window.setInterval:

```
Sub ShowPicInPic

  WhichLink = WhichLink + 1    'WhichLink is script-level variable
  WhichLink = WhichLink Mod document.links.length
  Set PicInPicture = window.open(document.links(WhichLink), _
    "PicInPicture", "top=0, Left=0, height=175, width=275")

End Sub
```

The Mod operator lets you cycle through a specified series of numbers. Using Mod 5, for example, gives you: 0, 1, 2, 3, 4, 0, 1....

Here's the full HTML source (also in the file Links.htm on the companion CD) for a Web page that cycles through the three links on that page:

```
<HTML>
<HEAD>

  <TITLE>Picture within a picture demo</TITLE>
  <SCRIPT LANGUAGE="VBScript">
  <!--

  Option Explicit

  'Script-level variables to keep track of the window
  'we spawned and the link we are currently at
  Dim PicInPicture, WhichLink

  Sub window_onLoad
    Dim ShowIt

    Set PicInPicture = window.open(document.links(WhichLink), _
      "PicInPicture", "top=0, left=0, height=175, width=275")

    ShowIt = window.setInterval("ShowPicInPic", 5000)
  End Sub

  Sub window_onUnLoad
    'use the reference to the spawned window to close it.
    PicInPicture.close
  End Sub

  Sub ShowPicInPic
    WhichLink = WhichLink + 1    'WhichLink is script-level variable
    WhichLink = WhichLink Mod document.links.length
    Set PicInPicture = window.open(document.links(WhichLink), _
      "PicInPicture", "Top=0, left=0, height=175, width=275")
  End Sub

  -->
  </SCRIPT>

</HEAD>
<BODY>

<P>
  <A HREF="http://www.microsoft.com">
    www.microsoft.com
  </A>
</P>
```

(continued)

```
<P>
  <A HREF="http://www.microsoft.com/ie">
    www.microsoft.com/ie
  </A>
</P>

<P>
  <A HREF="http://www.microsoft.com/vbscript">
    www.microsoft.com/vbscript
  </A>
</P>

</BODY>
</HTML>
```

For Each

As you go further with scripting, you will be spending a lot of time manipulating Internet Explorer's built-in collections. One of the most common operations you'll be doing is iterating through various collections. For example, it gets really tiresome to write the following code:

```
For I = 0 To collectionName.length - 1
 'do what needs to be done with collectionName(I).
Next
```

 OTE If you forget that collection items are numbered starting at 0 and you write the following code, your program will crash:

```
For I = 1 To collectionName.length
   'do what needs to be done with collectionName(I)
Next
```

Because of this, VBScript gives you a shortcut to iterate through all the elements in a collection. To use it, declare a variable and write the following code:

```
Dim Thing

For Each Thing In collectionName
  'do what you want with the Thing.
Next
```

For example, the following code displays a message box for each link on the page:

```
Dim TheLink

For Each TheLink In document.links
   MsgBox TheLink
Next
```

That's a lot cleaner than using this code:

```
For I = 0 To document.links.length - 1
   MsgBox document.links(I)
Next
```

Frames

Frames are among the most powerful design features you can add to your Web pages, but don't go overboard. Having 10 frames doing different things on your Web page will surely drive your readers to distraction. The next few sections teach the basics of manipulating frames via VBScript and then show you a much more sophisticated version of the picture in a picture program—a table of contents program that uses three frames, as shown in Figure 8-2. The idea is that as you pass the mouse over a link in the left-hand frame, you'll see the page in the right-hand frame.

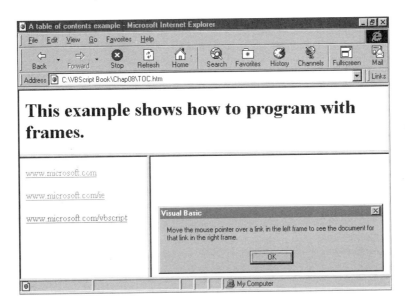

Figure 8-2. *A sophisticated use of frames.*

A Quick Review of Frames

Frames are defined between a pair of tags. In this case, they are the <FRAMESET></FRAMESET> tags. (This pair replaces the <BODY></BODY> pair of tags.) For example, the following text sets up two columns—the left one will always be 40 percent of the width of the browser, and the right one will always be 60 percent of the width of the browser:

```
<FRAMESET COLS="40%, 60%">
  <FRAME SRC="Left.htm">
  <FRAME SRC="Right.htm">
</FRAMESET>
```

HTML lets you use an asterisk to indicate the remainder. For example, instead of the first line in the above code, you can use the following line:

```
<FRAMESET COLS="40%, *">
```

 OTE It is possible to use pixels to specify the width of a frameset, but that is not a good idea unless you know how large the user's screen is.

You should give each frame a name. It will help you when you write code that works with the frames. For example:

```
<FRAMESET COLS="40%, 60%">
  <FRAME SRC="Left.htm" NAME="LeftFrame">
  <FRAME SRC="Right.htm" NAME="RightFrame">
</FRAMESET>
```

Notice that each frame gets its own document. That's why a closer approximation to the full Internet Explorer object model is shown in Figure 8-3:

You can nest frames. This lets you have both row frames and column frames, row frames within a column frame, and so on. For example, our table of contents program has three frames:

- A row frame containing text that explains the example

- A left column frame that shows all the links on the page

- A wide right column for displaying the document selected by moving the mouse pointer over one of the links in the left column frame.

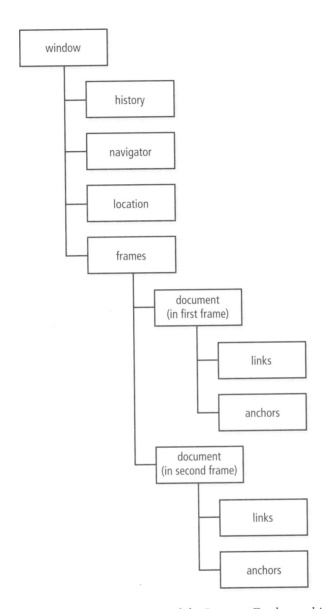

Figure 8-3.   *A more complete version of the Internet Explorer object model.*

The HTML for these four frames is on the following page.

```
<FRAMESET ROWS="25%, *">
  <FRAME NAME="TopFrame">

  <FRAMESET COLS="25%, *">

    <FRAMESET ROWS="70%, *">
      <FRAME NAME="LeftForLinks">
      <FRAME NAME="LeftForPicInPic">
    </FRAMESET>

    <FRAME NAME="RightForDoc">
  </FRAMESET>
</FRAMESET>
```

Programming with Frames

Programming with frames is not much different than programming with any other Internet Explorer object. As I stated earlier, give each frame a name when you define it. You can then access the document object of a frame like this:

```
frames.NameOfFrame.document
```

 IP   The Set keyword can make code that uses frames (or any other Internet Explorer objects) much cleaner. Once you write the following line, you can use the variable LeftDoc in your code instead of the longer Frames.LeftFrame.Document.

```
Set LeftDoc = frames.LeftFrame.document
```

Security issues in frame programming

Before I give you an example of programming using frames, I have to make a confession. Originally, I intended to write a version of the picture in a picture program that worked automatically. The program was supposed to discover the links in one window and display the associated Web pages in another. Well, I discovered that the newer, stricter security model in Internet Explorer version 4 wouldn't let me do it—a document in one frame can use no information contained in the document in another frame.

The idea is that a script should not be allowed to "harvest" information from a secure site just because it happens to be currently displayed in a frame in your browser. Without getting into the full details of my failed attempt, I do want to show you the key lines that caused an "Access is denied" error message. (See Figure 8-4.)

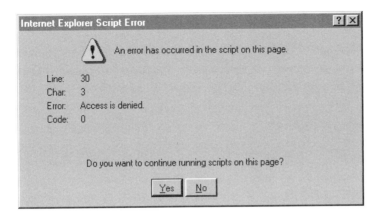

Figure 8-4. *The Access Is Denied error message.*

I had two frames named, naturally enough, RightForDoc and LeftForLinks. Here's the offending statement:

```
frames.RightForDoc.document.Location.href = _
    frames.LeftForLinks.document.links(WhichLink)
```

As you can see, the problem is that I was trying to access information in the LeftForLinks frame for use in the RightForDoc frame. This is prohibited by the strict security that Internet Explorer version 4 enforces.

A table of contents example

Although you can't make it happen automatically, you can certainly program a Web page so that clicking a link in a table of contents frame displays a new document in a separate frame. This is not prohibited by the security model since you are not trying to harvest information from the document in the separate frame but simply using information already available in the table of contents frame.

There are two ways to do this:

■ A way that uses the TARGET attribute of the anchor tag and involves only HTML

■ A way that uses VBScript to detect when a person has clicked a link

VBScript, however, can do far more than the TARGET attribute can do—it can even detect if the user simply passes the mouse pointer *over* a link. So, let's imagine for a moment that sometime in the not too distant future, Internet connections are so fast that getting a Web page is essentially instantaneous. Adding an instant preview feature to a Web page that would be activated when the user passed the mouse over a link would then be a great feature to have. In the next example, I'll show you how to write a VBScript program that will preview a page in the right-hand frame whenever a user passes the mouse pointer over a link in the left-hand frame.

The key to writing this is to remember that any anchor can respond to three events: the onClick event (just like the Click event that you already know); the onMousedown event, which is triggered when the user presses the mouse button but doesn't release it; and onMouseover, which is triggered when the user passes the mouse over a link. The latter event is the one we will be playing with.

 IP   You can change the status bar of the window to give the user a clue about the link. Simply have a line like this in the onMouseover event for that link:

```
window.status = "Descriptive Text"
```

The best way to associate an event procedure with an object is to give that object a name. For example, the following tag results in these three possible event procedures:

Tag	Event Procedures

`<A HREF="http://www.microsoft.com"`
`  NAME="MSLink">`
	`MSLink_onMouseover`
	`MSLink_onMousedown`
	`MSLink_onClick`

The HTML source for the main Web page of the example (also in the file TOC.htm on the companion CD) is pretty simple—it sets up the frames in the correct way and names them appropriately:

```
<HTML>
<HEAD>

  <TITLE>A table of contents example</TITLE>
  <SCRIPT LANGUAGE="VBSCRIPT">
  <!--

  Sub window_onLoad
    frames.TopFrame.document.write _
      "<H1>This example shows how to program with frames.</H1>"
```

```
    MsgBox "Move the mouse pointer over a link in the left frame " _
      & "to see the document for that link in the right frame."
  End Sub

  -->
  </SCRIPT>

</HEAD>

<FRAMESET ROWS="35%, *">
  <FRAME NAME="TopFrame">

  <FRAMESET COLS="35%, *">
    <FRAME NAME="LeftForLinks" SRC="TOC_SRC.htm">
    <FRAME NAME="RightForDoc">
  </FRAMESET>

</FRAMESET>

</HTML>
```

All the real work is done in the file named TOC_SRC.htm (which is also included on the companion CD). This file contains the onMouseover event procedures, which send information to the right-hand frame of the main Web page. In order for this to work, you need a way to refer to the window object that the frame sits in. You can do this by using the reserved word "Parent." For example, look at the following key line in the MSLink_onMouseover event procedure:

```
parent.frames.RightForDoc.location.href = MSLink.href
```

This line tells Internet Explorer to find the window object containing the current frame and then look for a particular frame in its frames collection. Here's the full HTML source from the TOC_SRC.htm file that is referred to in the TOC.htm file:

```
<HTML>
<HEAD>

  <SCRIPT LANGUAGE="VBSCRIPT">
  <!--

    Sub MSLink_onMouseover
      parent.frames.RightForDoc.location.href = MSLink
    End Sub
```

(continued)

251

```
      Sub IELink_onMouseover
        parent.frames.RightForDoc.location.href = IELink
      End Sub

      Sub VBScriptLink_onMouseover
        parent.frames.RightForDoc.location.href = VBScriptLink
      End Sub

    -->
    </SCRIPT>

  </HEAD>
  <BODY>

    <P>
      <A HREF="http://www.microsoft.com" NAME="MSLink">
        www.microsoft.com
      </A>
    </P>

    <P>
      <A HREF="http://www.microsoft.com/ie" NAME="IELink">
        www.microsoft.com/ie
      </A>
    </P>

    <P>
      <A HREF="http://www.microsoft.com/vbscript" NAME="VBScriptLink">
        www.microsoft.com/vbscript
      </A>
    </P>

  </BODY>
  </HTML>
```

Intrinsic HTML Controls

Up to this point, I have used ActiveX controls for my examples—the main reason being that ActiveX controls provide lots of options for components on a Web page, so learning how to use them is very important. On the other hand, if you want to write Web pages that are usable by *all* versions of Internet Explorer on *all* possible platforms, you can't assume that there will be a specific ActiveX control available on every user's machine. (The Microsoft Forms 2.0 ActiveX controls are always available on machines running Windows 95 or Microsoft Windows NT, however.) For these situations, you need to use a "lowest common denominator approach" when creating your Web pages. This requires turning to the intrinsic HTML controls that are part of the Internet Explorer object model, even though the design of your Web pages will be more limited if you use these controls instead of ActiveX controls. Most of the intrinsic HTML controls work in a manner similar to their ActiveX counterparts. For example, there is an intrinsic HTML button control for which you can write a Click event procedure, just as you can for a command button ActiveX control.

The following table gives brief descriptions of the most important intrinsic HTML controls.

Intrinsic HTML Control	Description
button	Equivalent to a command button ActiveX control
text	A one line area for user entry of text
textarea	A multiline area for user entry of text
password	A text control that displays asterisks instead of echoing what the user enters
radio	A group of controls that show multiple options, allowing the user to select *one* of them
checkbox	A control that lets the user select one or more possibilities from a group of options
select	Used for a list of possibilities (resembles a list box ActiveX control)
reset	A button that lets you restore the controls on an HTML form to their initial values
submit	A button that sends information to the server when the user clicks it
hidden	Used to store information that the user isn't supposed to see

The ActiveX equivalent of a radio control is an OptionButton control.

NOTE The password control is actually a mixed blessing. Although it hides what the user enters, you can't check the password in your VBScript code. This is because most people know enough to select Source from the View menu, and once they do, they would be able to see any code that checks the password. If you use a password intrinsic control, you'll have to send the information to the server to be checked there.

Using the Intrinsic HTML Control

One nice plus of using an intrinsic HTML control is that you don't need to use a CLSID; instead, you simply write some pure HTML code.

The Intrinsic Button Control

Here's an example of the HTML tag for an intrinsic button control with a caption of Click Me:

```
<INPUT TYPE=button NAME=Button1 VALUE="Click Me">
```

The VALUE attribute specifies the caption, but the NAME attribute is what you use in your VBScript code. For example, the onClick event procedure for the button I just defined looks like this:

```
Sub Button1_onClick
  'code goes here
End Sub
```

Notice how similar this is to the way you write an event procedure for a command button ActiveX control. The only difference is that you use "onClick" rather than "Click".

Intrinsic Text Controls

You place an intrinsic text control on your Web page in much the same way as an intrinsic button control. The optional VALUE attribute specifies the initial text, and the optional SIZE attribute specifies roughly how many characters wide the control should be. Here's an example of the HTML tag for an intrinsic text control:

```
<INPUT TYPE=text NAME=Text1 VALUE="Initial text" SIZE=25>
```

As with many of the intrinsic HTML controls, the methods and events of a text control are related. For example, there is a focus method that shifts the focus to the control, a blur method that shifts the focus away from the control, and a select method that selects all the text in the control. For example:

```
Text1.focus    'shifts the focus to the Text1 control
Text1.blur     'shifts the focus to the next available item
Text1.select   'selects all the text in the Text1 control
```

But you can also write onFocus, onBlur, and onSelect event procedures for an intrinsic text control that will be executed when the user shifts the focus to the control, shifts the focus away from the control, or selects the text in the control, respectively. For example, the following code reports the current contents of the Text1 control when the user shifts the focus somewhere else:

```
Sub Text1_onBlur
   MsgBox "You typed " & Text1.value
End Sub
```

The textarea control

The multiline textarea control uses a slightly different format in its HTML tag. Here's an example of what you need to use:

```
<TEXTAREA NAME=TextArea1 ROWS=5 COLS=25></TEXTAREA>
```

This sets up a text area with room for five lines of 25 characters per line. Notice that unlike the previous two controls, the textarea control needs a closing </TEXTAREA> tag. The NAME attribute is again crucial for coding, and you can opt to include a VALUE attribute identical to that for a text control. The textarea control allows the user to press the Enter key (to start a new line) when entering text in the control; the contents of the control will then contain a string with the equivalent of the vbCrLf constant in each place the Enter key was pressed. Otherwise, the properties, methods, and events of a textarea control are the same as those for a text control.

Check Boxes and Radio Buttons

A check box requires the user to make a yes/no decision for a single option. A group of radio buttons, on the other hand, requires the user to make one choice from a set of options. For example, imagine that you want to create a Web page for buying a computer. Whether a Zip drive is to be included is a yes/no decision, so you would use a check box for this. The monitor size, on the other hand, is a choice that must be made from a set of options. The user needs to select from a 15-inch monitor, a 17-inch monitor, a 19-inch monitor, and so on. (This assumes that you are requiring a monitor to be included as part of the computer package.) Figure 8-5 on the following page shows what a check box and a group of radio buttons look like on a Web page.

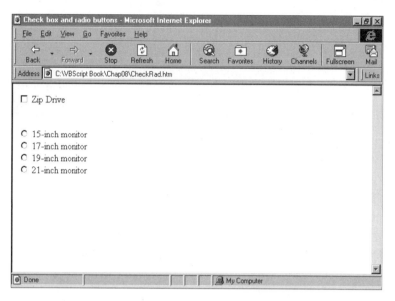

Figure 8-5.   *A check box and a group of radio buttons.*

Check boxes

The HTML code for an intrinsic checkbox control is a little trickier than
the code for an intrinsic text control because you need to include the text
that will appear next to the check box itself. You place this text following
the INPUT tag, as shown in this example:

```
<INPUT TYPE=checkbox NAME=ZipDrive>
  Zip Drive<BR>
```

Each time the user checks or unchecks the box, the onClick event is
triggered. You use an If-Then statement in the onClick event procedure
to determine whether the box is checked, as shown here:

```
Sub ZipDrive_onClick

  If ZipDrive.checked Then
    NumberOfDisks = InputBox("How many Zip disks would you like?")
  End If

End Sub
```

Radio buttons

Radio buttons are a little trickier than check boxes since you have to determine which of the buttons is currently selected. Before I show you how to

do that, here are the HTML tags for a group of radio buttons that allow the user to select a monitor size:

```
<INPUT TYPE=radio NAME=MonitorType>
  15-inch monitor<BR>
<INPUT TYPE=radio NAME=MonitorType>
  17-inch monitor<BR>
<INPUT TYPE=radio NAME=MonitorType>
  19-inch monitor<BR>
<INPUT TYPE=radio NAME=MonitorType>
  21-inch monitor<BR>
```

Notice how all the radio buttons in this example have the same NAME attribute. This is how Internet Explorer knows that they should be treated as one group of radio buttons. (You can have multiple groups of radio buttons on a single Web page.) Usually you don't worry about the onClick event for a radio button; instead you have a separate command button that checks which of the radio buttons is selected. There are two things to keep in mind when you write the code for this command button. First, information about the group of radio buttons is stored in an array. Second, the checked property is True only for the particular radio button that the user selected.

For example, here's some code you can use to analyze what the user selected after he or she confirms the choice by clicking a button named MonitorChoice:

```
Sub MonitorChoice_onClick

  If MonitorType(0).checked Then
    MsgBox "Don't you think a 15-inch monitor is too small nowadays?"
  ElseIf MonitorType(1).checked Then
    MsgBox "Good choice, but the 19-inch monitor is a great value."
  ElseIf MonitorType(2).checked Then
    MsgBox "The 19-inch monitor gives great performance and value!"
  ElseIf MonitorType(3).checked Then
    MsgBox "You're lucky, I wish I had a 21-inch monitor!"
  Else
    MsgBox "Please select a monitor."
  End If

End Sub
```

You can also assign a value to each radio button. This lets you assign a number or a word, as you can see in the following example:

```
<INPUT TYPE=radio NAME=MonitorType VALUE=15>
```

You can then pick up the value with an expression like this:

```
MonitorType(0).value
```

The other property that you'll use a lot is the length property, which indicates how many items are in the group of radio buttons. Finally, radio buttons can respond to an onClick event, although using one is unusual.

The Intrinsic Select Control

The select control is among the most useful of the intrinsic HTML controls because it lets you build a list of possibilities at the time the document is loading. (Using Dynamic HTML, it is possible to change the contents of the resulting list box after the page is loaded.) The select control, like the textarea control, has a closing as well as an opening tag. For example, the HTML code for a select control that allows the user to choose the abbreviation for a state in the northeastern United States might start like this:

```
<SELECT NAME=NorthEasternStates SIZE=3>
  <OPTION>CT
  <OPTION>NJ
  <OPTION>NY
</SELECT>
```

The SIZE attribute determines how many items the user can see at one time. If there are more items in the list than you specify with this attribute, Internet Explorer will automatically add scroll bars.

Once you have displayed the select control and the user has interacted with it, there are two important results you'll want to know:

- The position of the selected item in the list
- The actual value of the item the user selected

The first result is the value of the selectedIndex property. The second result can be found by indexing into the array held in the options property. For example, let's suppose there's a command button named SelectState. Here's the code that determines which item is currently selected after the user clicks the SelectState command button:

```
Sub SelectState_onClick
  Dim ItemNumber, ItemText

  ItemNumber = NorthEasternStates.selectedIndex
  ItemText = NorthEasternStates.options(ItemNumber).Text
  MsgBox "You selected item number " & ItemNumber & vbCrLf _
    & "The state you chose is " & ItemText
End Sub
```

Another way to find out which item was selected is to use the selected property. This is especially useful when you have set the MULTIPLE attribute of the select control to True, which allows the user to select multiple items. To make multiple selections, the user simply has to click while holding down the Ctrl key. The code then typically takes the following form:

```
If NameOfSelectControl.Options(I).selected Then
  ⋮
```

As an example of using this, suppose we want to allow the user to select multiple items for a sandwich being ordered via the net. Here's the HTML source for this example, which you can also find in the file Select.htm on the companion CD:

Another possibility would be to use several check boxes, but a select control can take up much less space on the page since it can add scroll bars if needed.

```
<HTML>
<HEAD>

  <TITLE>Multiple selection example</TITLE>
  <SCRIPT LANGUAGE="VBSCRIPT">
  <!--

    Sub SelectYourExtras_onClick
      Dim I, Items
      Items = vbCrLf
```

(continued)

```
      For I = 0 To Extras.options.length - 1
        If Extras.options(I).selected Then
          Items = Items & vbCrLf & Extras.options(I).text
        End If
      Next

      MsgBox "Your sandwich will have: " & Items
    End Sub

  -->
  </SCRIPT>

</HEAD>
<BODY>

<SELECT NAME=Extras SIZE=4 MULTIPLE>
  <OPTION>Cheese
  <OPTION>Mayonnaise
  <OPTION>Mustard
  <OPTION>Oil
  <OPTION>Onions
  <OPTION>Pepper
  <OPTION>Tomato
  <OPTION>Vinegar
</SELECT>

<BR><BR><BR>

<INPUT TYPE=button NAME=SelectYourExtras VALUE="Submit your order">

</BODY>
</HTML>
```

Forms

An HTML form is any part of your Web page that has its source enclosed by the <FORM></FORM> pair of tags. (You can have multiple forms on a single Web page.) A form contains intrinsic HTML controls and possibly ActiveX controls. You can specify the program to be executed on the server when the user finishes entering information on the form, and you can also specify how that information will be sent to the server. Forms are intimately tied to server-side programming, so I will cover this important topic here only briefly. (In particular, you can't run any form examples on your own machine unless you have Windows NT running Internet Information Server, since you would need to set up programs on a server in order to process the data sent by the form.)

OTE   The contents of any ActiveX control must be mirrored in a hidden in-trinsic HTML control in order to be properly sent to the server when the user submits the form.

However, you can instruct the server to do the following processes by using the <FORM></FORM> pair of tags:

- Package the information sent by the user. (The information is usually sent as a string, which might be encoded.)

- Run a particular program, known as an *active server page,* on the server once the information is sent to it.

OTE   *Programming Active Server Pages* by Scot Hillier and Daniel Mezick (Microsoft Press, 1997) is a great book about active server pages.

For example, this code tells the server to process the data using an active server page named AnAspFile.asp:

```
<FORM NAME=Form1 METHOD=POST
  ACTION="http://TheServerName/FolderWithAspFiles/AnAspFile.asp">
```

Traditionally, when the user clicks a submit button inside the form, all the information is packaged by the browser and sent to the server to be processed by the program indicated in the ACTION attribute. This is not the best way to proceed—it doesn't give you a chance to do the client-side validation that is one of the main advantages of using VBScript. Therefore, it's better to write an onSubmit event procedure for the form in order to check the user's entries.

For example, consider a form that you might use to verify an address, as shown in Figure 8-6 on the following page. You want to submit the data only if all the fields have been filled in.

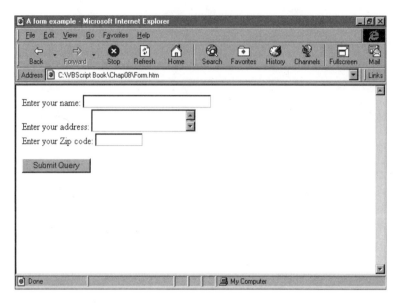

Figure 8-6.   *An address form.*

The trick here is to write the onSubmit event procedure as a function that returns True if you want to submit the data and returns False if you don't. This means you can use code like this for a form named AddressForm:

```
Function AddressForm_onSubmit
  Dim BadData

  BadData = False

  If AddressForm.YourName.value = "" Then BadData = True
  If AddressForm.YourAddress.value = "" Then BadData = True
  If Len(AddressForm.YourZipCode.value) <> 5 And _
    Len(AddressForm.YourZipCode.value)<> 10 Then
    BadData = True

  'Decide whether to send the data,
  'depending on the value of BadData
  If BadData Then
    MsgBox "Bad data"
    AddressForm_onSubmit = False
  Else
    MsgBox "Good data"
    AddressForm_onSubmit = True
  End If

End Function
```

Here's some HTML code you can use to test this. (You can't test the actual submission process without a server to run the ACTION request.) The full HTML source is in the file Form.htm on the companion CD.

```
<BODY>

<FORM NAME=AddressForm>
  Enter your name:
  <INPUT TYPE=text NAME=YourName SIZE=30>
  <BR>
  Enter your address:
  <TEXTAREA NAME=YourAddress ROW=2 COL=30></TEXTAREA>
  <BR>
  Enter your zip code:
  <INPUT TYPE=text NAME=YourZipCode SIZE=10>
  <BR><BR>
  <INPUT TYPE=submit>
</FORM>

</BODY>
```

Cookies

Cookies are the only acceptable way for a Web site to leave information on your computer—and their use is quite controversial. So what is a cookie? It's simply a piece of information, such as the user's color preferences for that Web site or the user's name and password. But the point is that cookies are stored on the *user's* hard disk. Cookies are often a great convenience; they can save the user the trouble of retyping information. This said, cookies remain controversial because many people think they are intrusive—and these people will use Internet Explorer's security options to prevent your Web pages from depositing a cookie on their systems!

 OTE To run a VBScript code that uses cookies, the Web page containing the code must be downloaded from a server. This means you must have Microsoft Personal Web Server installed on your machine, or you must download the page from a separate Web server.

Using cookies in VBScript code is simple. The cookie property of the document object lets you create attributes much like the ones used in HTML tags, as shown in the example on the following page.

```
Sub window_onLoad
  Dim NameCookie, PasswordCookie, ExpirationDateCookie

  NameCookie = "USERNAME=gcornell"
  document.cookie = NameCookie

  PasswordCookie = "PASSWORD=NoneOfYourBusiness"
  document.cookie = document.cookie & ";" & PasswordCookie

  ExpirationDateCookie = "EXPIRES=" & (Now + 365)
  document.cookie = document.cookie & ";" & ExpirationDateCookie

End Sub
```

When your user loads a Web page that executes the above lines and his or her security level permits it, Internet Explorer will create a new text file in the user's Windows\Cookies folder with this information. The file will be named *UserName@WebSite*.txt (where *UserName* is the user's name and *WebSite* is the address of the Web page). For example, the full pathname of one of my cookie files is: "C:\Windows\Cookies\gary cornell@microsoft.txt." One year from now, the file will cease to be accessible to that Web page.

 OTE If you omit the string with the expiration date from the cookie file, Internet Explorer will store the cookie information only for the current session. This is useful for things like a shopping session on a Web site.

If you think there might be a cookie for the current Web page on the user's system, you'll want to analyze its contents. (Internet Explorer's security model lets a Web page analyze only its own cookie.) For example, the code for your Web page might start out like this:

```
Sub window_onLoad

  If document.cookie = "" Then
    MakeCookie      'make the cookie for a first-time user
  Else
    AnalyzeCookie   'go to the analyze cookie procedure
  End If

  'code for anything else you want to do in the onLoad procedure
  ⋮
End Sub
```

To understand the kind of code you'll need to analyze an existing cookie, you must understand how the document.cookie string stores its information. It's a string like this, in which the individual attributes are separated by semicolons:

```
USERNAME=gcornell;PASSWORD=NoneOfYourBusiness;…
```

Thus, you use VBScript's built-in Split function with a semicolon as the delimiter in order to store the individual pieces in an array for further analysis. The subprocedure might take the following form:

```
Sub AnalyzeCookie
  Dim ThePieces
  ThePieces = Split(document.cookie, ";")
  'Do what you want with each piece.
  ⋮
End Sub
```

The MakeCookie procedure works as you have already seen, except that in practice you should use the On Error statement at the beginning of the procedure. This statement is necessary because users might have set their security levels so as to not allow you to place any cookies on their machines.

Introduction to Dynamic HTML

An element is any programmable object in an HTML document.

This chapter introduces you to an exciting new level of Web page development—*Dynamic HTML*. Dynamic HTML lets you control (via programming) essentially every visible element on your Web page, including text and images. For example, up to this point, you haven't been able to change any displayed text after the page has finished loading because the Document.Write statement puts the text on the page *before* the page is loaded. Dynamic HTML, on the other hand, lets you make changes *after* the page has loaded onto the user's machine. Using the ability of Microsoft Internet Explorer version 4 to retain an image of the page that can be modified and regenerated, Dynamic HTML allows changes to be made by using the computing power of the user's machine—rather than by building a new page on the server and then sending it over the net.

Do you want an item always to be *exactly* in the middle of the page, no matter how large or small the page is, no matter what the resolution capabilities of the user's machine are? Dynamic HTML can do this as well, and with greater precision, than you could ever hope to achieve with simple <BR> and <C> tags.

Finally, Dynamic HTML lets you use *style sheets* to describe the different elements on your Web pages. By defining standards for text, such as a standard size and font for a particular heading level, you can make global changes simply by changing the predefined style. For example, you can change all your <H1> heads by changing the <H1> style; you don't have to do it by hand for each <H1> head.

OTE An analogous use of styles was one of the main reasons why early versions of Microsoft Word were so much more powerful than other word processors of the time. Microsoft Word was one of the first word processors to use styles to define what paragraphs should look like.

While I will cover the basic use of styles in this chapter, I won't go into style sheets. For more information on this advanced topic, I recommend *Inside Dynamic HTML* by Scott Isaacs (Microsoft Press, 1997).

Event Procedures

In the last chapter, I wrote an onMouseover event procedure for a link so that a document would be displayed in a separate frame whenever a user moved the mouse pointer over that link. This was possible because Internet Explorer version 3 introduced the onMouseover event for a link. Now that Internet Explorer version 4 has introduced Dynamic HTML, *every* visible object surrounded by tags will trigger an onMouseover event when the user moves the mouse pointer over that object.

OTE Of course, the onMouseover event is not the only event. There are onMouseout, onClick, onKeypress, and lots more. (See the "Events" section beginning on page 282 for more on the rich supply of events that Dynamic HTML supports.)

In Dynamic HTML, you use the ID attribute rather than the Name attribute.

You can therefore write VBScript code (in the form of an event procedure) to control what happens when the user moves the mouse pointer over any object. For example, suppose you want some action to occur whenever the mouse pointer passes over a certain <H1> head. In order for this to happen, you need to expand the heading level tag so that it includes a name you can refer to in your event procedure:

```
<H1 ID=Test>Move the mouse pointer over me!</H1>
```

Now you can write an onMouseover event procedure for the head named Test, as shown in this example:

```
Sub Test_onMouseover
  MsgBox "Welcome to Dynamic HTML!"
End Sub
```

Here's the entire program, which you can find in the file First.htm on the companion CD:

```
<HTML>
<HEAD>

  <TITLE>A first Dynamic HTML Demo</Title>
  <SCRIPT LANGUAGE="VBSCRIPT">
  <!--

    Option Explicit

    Sub Test_onMouseover
      MsgBox "Welcome to Dynamic HTML!"
    End Sub

  -->
  </SCRIPT>

</HEAD>
<BODY>

  <H1>This is a plain old H1 head.</H1>

  <BR><BR><BR>

  <H1 ID=Test>
    This is a dynamic H1 head.
    Move the mouse over me to see what happens.
  </H1>

</BODY>
</HTML>
```

Figure 9-1 on the following page shows what happens when you move the mouse pointer over the dynamic H1 head in this sample.

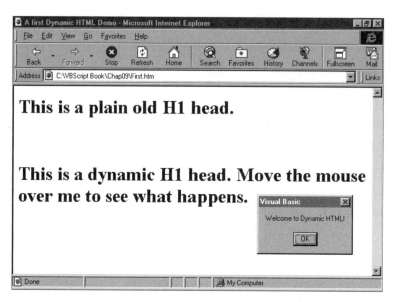

Figure 9-1.   *A first Dynamic HTML demo.*

Using the InnerText Property

Dynamic HTML defines a property named *innerText* for every element.
This property contains the text surrounded by the pair of tags for the element in question. In the previous demo, for example, Test.innerText contains the text, "This is a dynamic H1 head. Move the mouse over me to see
what happens."

The great thing about Dynamic HTML is that when you change the inner-
Text property of an element, the text on the page changes automatically.
There's no more worrying about using Document.Write before the page
finishes loading. For example, suppose that you want to modify the previous Web page so that if the user clicks a dynamic H1 head, more text is
displayed. Here's the kind of code you would need to add:

```
Sub Test_onClick
  Test.innerText = Test.innerText _
    & " You clicked me. Don't do it again, " _
    & "or the text will look really silly."
End Sub
```

Notice that this takes the previous text in the heading (the previous value of Test.innerText) and appends the new string. This is why clicking twice displays the text shown in Figure 9-2.

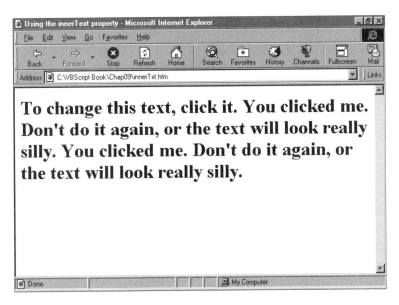

To change this text, click it. You clicked me. Don't do it again, or the text will look really silly. You clicked me. Don't do it again, or the text will look really silly.

Figure 9-2.   *The result of not obeying directions.*

Here's the full HTML source, which you can also find in the file innerTxt.htm on the companion CD:

```
<HTML>
<HEAD>

  <TITLE>Using the innerText property</Title>
  <SCRIPT LANGUAGE="VBSCRIPT">
  <!--

    Option Explicit

    Sub Test_onClick
      Test.innerText = Test.innerText _
        & " You clicked me. Don't do it again, " _
        & "or the text will look really silly."
    End Sub

  -->
  </SCRIPT>
```

(continued)

```
</HEAD>
<BODY>

  <H1 ID=Test>To change this text, click it.</H1>

</BODY>
</HTML>
```

In addition, there's an *outerText* property that returns the whole tag—including the inner text. By changing this property, you can change the level of a head, turn a head into a paragraph or a link, and so on. For example, the following code changes the head named Test to regular text when the user clicks it:

```
Sub Test_onClick
  Test.outerText = "I used to be a head, but not anymore."
End Sub
```

Here's the full HTML source for this example, which you can also find in the file outerTxt.htm on the companion CD:

```
<HTML>
<HEAD>

  <TITLE>Using the outerText property</Title>
  <SCRIPT LANGUAGE="VBSCRIPT">
  <!--

    Option Explicit

    Sub Test_onClick
      Test.outerText = "I used to be a head, but not anymore."
    End Sub

  -->
  </SCRIPT>

</HEAD>
<BODY>

  <H1 ID=Test>
    To change this head to regular text, click it.
  </H1>

</BODY>
</HTML>
```

Styles

The last section showed you the power you get by using just two new properties (innerText and outerText) of the many new properties that the various HTML objects have in Dynamic HTML. Now I'll explain another powerful property available in Dynamic HTML—the *style* property. This property allows you to change characteristics like font, font size, text color, and even whether the object is visible at all. To set an object's initial style (when the page loads), you need to use the STYLE attribute, as shown in this example:

```
<P ID=StyledText STYLE="color:red">This is red text.</P>
```

To change the characteristics of the StyledText paragraph after the page has loaded, you change the paragraph's style property by using a line like this:

```
StyledText.style.color = "black"
```

Here's the full HTML source of an example of this (also in the file Style.htm on the companion CD):

```
<HTML>
<HEAD>

  <TITLE>An example of styles</Title>
  <SCRIPT LANGUAGE="VBSCRIPT">
  <!--

    Option Explicit

    Sub StyledText_onClick
      StyledText.style.color="black"
    End Sub

  -->
  </SCRIPT>

</HEAD>
<BODY>

<P ID=StyledText STYLE="color:red">
  This is red text. Click me, and I'll become black text.
</P>

</BODY>
</HTML>
```

Here's another example. The display property of the style property determines whether the information is visible. There are two values:

- "none" (The information is hidden.)

- "" (The information is visible.)

The following example (also in the file Display.htm on the companion CD) makes some text visible after the user clicks anywhere on the page. This is done by giving the <BODY> tag an ID and then writing an onClick event procedure for the body:

```
<HTML>
<HEAD>

  <TITLE>An example of the display property</Title>
  <SCRIPT LANGUAGE="VBSCRIPT">
  <!--

    Option Explicit

    Sub TheBody_onClick
      StyledText.style.display = ""
    End Sub

  -->
  </SCRIPT>

</HEAD>
<BODY ID=TheBody>

  <H1>Click anywhere on the page to see the hidden text.</H1>

  <P ID=StyledText STYLE="display:none">This is the secret text.</P>

</BODY>
</HTML>
```

One of the most useful applications of this feature in dynamic HTML is to have hidden text reveal itself when the user moves the mouse pointer over a particular place on a Web page. The key to this, as you have probably already figured out, is to change the display property of the hidden text by using the onMouseover event procedure of the object in that particular place.

Some Common Styles

I hope by now I have convinced you how beneficial it can be to change the style property—and that the code that does this won't be difficult to write. The main problem with styles is that there are just so many options! To be honest, I can't possibly cover them all in this chapter, but I will describe the most common ones.

 OTE   Keep in mind that styles can be combined into a style sheet. You can then change styles for the entire Web page all at once. See the book *Inside Dynamic HTML* that I mentioned previously for more on style sheets.

Here are short descriptions of the three font properties you will use:

Font-family   This property specifies the kind of font to use for the text. Some examples are:

```
<P ID=StyledText STYLE="font-family:Arial">
<P ID=StyledText STYLE="font-family:Times">
```

Here is what the Arial font and the Times font look like:

This is set in Arial. Notice that Arial lacks the little projections at the ends of the letters. These are called *serifs*, so Arial is a *sans serif* font. (*Sans* is French for "without.")

This is set in Times. Notice how Times does have the serifs on the letters. Times is a serif font.

Instead of naming a particular font, you can specify either serif or sans serif. Then you simply trust Internet Explorer to use the standard font for that style on the user's machine. (This will be Arial for sans serif fonts and Times for serif fonts on most machines.) Using the font-family property is straightforward except for a complication that will always occur for any style property name that contains a hyphen. When you use VBScript to control such a property, you need to remove the hyphen. For example, your code might look like this:

```
StyledText.fontFamily = "Times"
```

Font-style   This property sets the style of the font. You have three choices: normal, italic, or oblique. For example:

```
<P ID=StyledText STYLE="font-family:Times; font-style:italic">
```

Notice that I used the semicolon to put more than one style property in this tag. Again, since the font-style property name contains a hyphen, you need to use the term fontStyle in your VBScript code.

Font-size   As you might expect, this property specifies the size of the font. The two most common measurements used for font sizes are *points* (abbreviated *pt*) and *pixels*.

The following code puts the paragraph into 12-point Arial type:

```
<P ID=StyledText STYLE="font-family:Arial; font-size:12pt">
```

Pixels is abbreviated *px,* as in the following example:

```
<P ID=StyledText STYLE="font-family:Arial; font-size:24px">
```

Remember to use the term fontSize in your VBScript code.

Suppose you want to write a script that increases the size of the text each time the user clicks it. The trick is that the fontSize property returns a string like "8pt" or "20px." You need to extract the number so you can add 1 to it. To do this, use the Left function to remove the last two characters, and convert the result to an integer. Add 1 to the integer, convert it back to a string, and append either "pt" or "px." Here's the code that does this for the case when the text is in points:

```
Temp = StyledText.style.fontSize
Temp = Left(Temp, Len(Temp) - 2)
Size = CInt(Temp) + 1
Temp = CStr(Size) & "pt"
StyledText.style.fontSize = Temp
```

Here's a program (also in the file fontSize.htm on the companion CD) that incorporates this code, with the added feature that the whole process starts over when you get to 24-point type:

```
<HTML>
<HEAD>

  <TITLE>Using the fontSize property</Title>
  <SCRIPT LANGUAGE="VBSCRIPT">
  <!--

    Option Explicit

    Sub StyledText_onClick
      Dim Temp, Size

      Temp = StyledText.style.fontSize
      Temp = Left(Temp, Len(Temp) - 2)
      Size = CInt(Temp) + 1
      If Size > 24 Then Size = 8
      Temp = CStr(Size) & "pt"
      StyledText.style.fontSize = Temp
    End Sub

  -->
  </SCRIPT>

</HEAD>
<BODY>

  <P ID=StyledText STYLE="font-size:8pt">
    Click me to see my size increase.
  </P>

</BODY>
</HTML>
```

NOTE You can also specify the font size in inches (with the abbreviation "in"), in centimeters (with the abbreviation "cm"), and as a percentage of the base size that Internet Explorer is currently using. For example, to make text twice as big as the base size, use this:

```
StyledText.style.fontSize = "200%"
```

277

Text alignment properties

In traditional HTML, you have no way to change margins or to align text, other than centering it. Now with Dynamic HTML, not only can you control these features at the time you design your Web page, you can also change them via code after the page loads. The following table describes the most common alignment properties:

Alignment Property	Description
margin-left	Sets the left margin using either points (pt), pixels (px), inches, (in), or centimeters (cm).
margin-right	Sets the right margin using points (pt), pixels (px), inches (in), or centimeters (cm).
margin-top	Sets the top margin using points (pt), pixels (px), inches (in), or centimeters (cm).
text-indent	Sets how much the text should be indented from the margin. You can *outdent* text by specifying negative values, which give you text outside the current margin. The units you can use are points (pt), pixels (px), inches (in), or centimeters (cm).
text-align	Aligns the text. The three possibilities are left, right, and center.

The VBScript code for this doesn't require any new techniques. (Just remember to remove the hyphen for the name of the property.) For example, the following modification of our size-increasing code (also in the file Margin.htm on the companion CD) causes the left margin to increase by one point each time you click the text.

```
Sub StyledText_onClick
  Dim Temp

  Temp = StyledText.style.marginLeft
  Temp = Left(Temp, Len(Temp) - 2)
  Temp = CInt(Temp) + 1
  Temp = CStr(Temp) & "pt"
  StyledText.style.marginLeft = Temp
End Sub
```

A Size-Changing Function

Before I go on, it should be pretty obvious that you will often be using this kind of code to rebuild the size for a style property. So it makes sense to make a function out of it. Let's design a function that works with a string in which the last two characters are the unit and all the characters before the unit are the number that represents the size. The function should have a second parameter for the size increase (or decrease) you want to make. Here's one possible version:

```
Function ChangeSize(OldSize, Increment)

  Dim Temp, Number

  Temp = Left(OldSize, Len(OldSize) - 2)
  Number = CInt(Temp) + Increment
  Temp = CStr(Number) & Right(OldSize, 2)

  ChangeSize = Temp
End Function
```

It would be easy to modify this code to create a function that allows percentage changes. I'll leave that one to you.

Positioning Objects

Probably the most exciting feature that was added with Dynamic HTML is the ability to place any part of your Web page at a specific place and then change these positions dynamically via your VBScript code. This ability applies to any element you put on your page; you can make images, text, ActiveX controls, or other elements appear exactly where you want them to appear. More precisely, you can individually control:

- The horizontal position of an object (the *x-coordinate*).

- The vertical position of an object (the *y-coordinate*).

- How objects overlap and which one is on top when they do overlap (the *z-order*). (I won't cover techniques for manipulating the z-order, however.)

You can use *absolute positioning* or *relative positioning* to place an element on your Web page. An example of absolute positioning is "Put this image 1 inch from the top of the document window." Relative positioning uses percentages instead of units of measurement. For example, "Place this element by going down 30 percent of the height of the page."

Here's an example of an HTML tag that uses absolute positioning to place an image 1 inch down and indent it one-half inch from the top of the document. (I'll explain all the various style parameters that go into this tag in a moment.)

```
<IMG ID=MyImage
  STYLE="position:absolute;top:1in;left=.5in" SRC=AGif.gif>
```

The next example places the top of the image 10 percent of the way down and the left edge of the image 50 percent of the way across it.

```
<IMG ID=MyImage
  STYLE="position: relative;top:10%;left=50%" SRC=AGif.gif>
```

To see how these two methods differ, open Position.htm on the companion CD and try resizing your browser window.

Relative positioning is generally the better way to go. If you use relative positioning, you get a consistent look and feel, regardless of how users resize their browser windows or what their screen resolutions are. If you use absolute positioning, you can run into problems trying to account for different sizes of browser windows or when the user resizes the window.

The most important of the positioning properties are those that control the left and top positions of an element, but you aren't restricted to using only these properties. There are two additional variants of each of these tags, so there are a total of six properties in all. The additional variants are described in the following table:

Property	Description
PixelLeft	Returns or sets the position in pixels, so no string manipulations are needed to work with the value
PosLeft	Returns the value of the Left property in the current units as a number, so no string manipulations are needed to work with this
PixelHeight	Returns or sets the height of the item in pixels, so no string manipulations are needed to work with the value
PosHeight	Returns the value of the Height property in the current units as a number, so no string manipulations are needed to work with this

Let's suppose you want to write a program that animates a logo by moving it across the page. The idea would be to change the Left position of the image until it gets to the side of the page and then start it over again at the left edge. In this case, you clearly want to move a few pixels at a time so you would use the PixelLeft property. To make the animation possible, you would change the position in a routine specified using the SetInterval method. (You saw this method in the last chapter.) Finally, you need a way of knowing where the right edge of the browser window is or, in other words, how wide the document window is in pixels. This turns out to be the value of:

```
Document.Body.OffsetWidth
```

Here's the HTML page (also in the file Animate.htm on the companion CD):

```
<HTML>
<HEAD>
  <TITLE>Animation</Title>
  <SCRIPT LANGUAGE = VBScript>
  <!--

    Option Explicit

    Dim TheTimer
```

(continued)

```
Sub Window_Onload()
  TheTimer = Window.SetInterval("Animate", 100)
End Sub

Sub Animate()
  If Picture.Style.PixelLeft >= _
     Document.Body.OffsetWidth Then
     Picture.Style.PixelLeft = 0
     msgbox Picture.Style.PixelLeft
  Else
     Picture.Style.PixelLeft = Picture.Style.PixelLeft + 10
  End If
End Sub
-->
</SCRIPT>

</HEAD>
<BODY>

  <IMG ID=Picture
    STYLE="position:relative;top:0;left:0"
    SRC="Agif1.jpg">

</BODY>
</HTML>
```

 IP Notice that I specify a left value of 0 in my STYLE attribute within my <IMG> tag. Generally speaking, you should always supply initial values for the attributes you want to modify via a script; otherwise, Internet Explorer might not let you change them.

Events

An element is any object that you can modify via a script.

The other pillar on which dynamic HTML stands is the rich supply of events that you can script. Before I go further into this, I want to make sure that you are comfortable with the term *element* that I have used occasionally so far in this book. An element is any object that you can modify via a script. For example, all the information between an opening tag and a closing tag is an element. The document itself is an element, as is the mother element—the Window object. All the elements on your Web page will respond to the events described in the following two tables—most should already be familiar to you:

Mouse Events	User Action
onMouseover	Moving the mouse pointer over the element
onMouseout	Moving the mouse out of the element
onMousedown	Pressing any of the mouse buttons inside the element
onMouseup	Releasing any of the mouse buttons while the mouse pointer is in the element
onMousemove	Moving the mouse pointer within the element
onClick	Clicking the left mouse button on the element
onDblclick	Double-clicking the left mouse button on the element

This table describes the key events:

Keyboard Event	User Action
onKeypress	Pressing and releasing a key (full down-and-up cycle) or triggering multiple events of this type if the key is held down
onKeydown	Pressing a key triggers only one event no matter how long the key is held down
onKeyup	Releasing a key

There are actually 39 events that the browser will report to you for possible scripting. Obviously, specific types of elements will respond to different subsets of these 39; however, all elements can be scripted for the events listed in the preceding tables, so I'll use only those events in the remaining examples.

 OTE   You might see the event names written in all lowercase letters, for example "onmousedown". This is the style used in both JavaScript and JScript, because those languages are case sensitive. Since VBScript is not case sensitive, VBScript programmers tend to use mixed case capitalization.

Handling Events

You have already seen the most common and easiest to understand way of writing code to handle an event. Create a procedure that has the following form:

```
Sub ObjectID_EventName( )
```

The following example would let you write code that is triggered by someone clicking on an item whose ID is Picture:

```
Sub Picture_OnClick
```

This is the model that Visual Basic uses to link event-handling procedures to particular objects.

However, the event-handling model in Internet Explorer is even richer than the model in Visual Basic; Internet Explorer's more varied methods for linking event-handling procedures to objects allows you to tell the browser to associate the same event handler with multiple objects. Here's an example of the HTML code you would need to write in order to run the same event procedure when the user clicks any of three separate paragraphs:

```
<P ID=First OnClick="ParagraphClicked"
  STYLE="font-family:Times">
  This is the first paragraph.
</P>
<P ID=Second OnClick="ParagraphClicked"
  STYLE="font-family:Times">
  This is the second paragraph.
</P>
<P ID=Third OnClick="ParagraphClicked"
  STYLE="font-family:Times">
  This is the third paragraph.
</P>
```

The Window.Event Object

This object is the key to event handling in Dynamic HTML. In fact, all the information about any event that happens in Internet Explorer is stored in the Window.Event object. Since it has 21 possible pieces of information stored in it, I won't be able to go over all of them in this introductory book. However, I do want to introduce you to some of the most important of them with some sample code.

The SrcElement property

Once you associate the same event with many different elements, you need a way to know which element triggered the action. This is given by the following line of VBScript code:

```
Window.Event.SrcElement
```

 ARNING You can't use the keyword Event alone. Event is a reserved word in VBScript.

In the line of code above, I used the SrcElement property of the Window.Event object. This property, as its name suggests, returns the source of the event, which is the object that triggered the event. A line of code like the following one can serve as an invaluable last ditch debugging tool to check which element triggered the event because it pops up a message box with the element's ID:

```
MsgBox Window.Event.SrcElement.ID
```

As another example of using the Window.Event.SrcElement property, the following HTML page changes the font in the paragraph you click on to Arial—no matter which of the three paragraphs you click on. It changes the correct paragraph because of the following code:

```
Window.Event.SrcElement.Style.FontFamily="Arial"
```

You can translate this line as: "Find the source of the event, then find its Style property, then find its font and change that font to Arial." Here's the HTML page (which is also in the file Multiple.htm on the companion CD:

```
<HTML>
<HEAD>

  <TITLE>Associating event handlers with multiple objects</TITLE>
  <SCRIPT LANGUAGE = VBScript>
  <!--

    Option Explicit
```

(continued)

```
      Sub ParagraphClicked()
        Window.Event.SrcElement.Style.FontFamily="Arial"
      End Sub

    -->
    </SCRIPT>

</HEAD>
<BODY>

<P ID=First OnClick="ParagraphClicked"
  STYLE="font-family:Times">
  This is the first paragraph.
</P>
<P ID=Second OnClick="ParagraphClicked"
  STYLE="font-family:Times">
  This is the second paragraph.
</P>
<P ID=Third OnClick="ParagraphClicked"
  STYLE="font-family:Times">
  This is the third paragraph.
</P>

</BODY>
</HTML>
```

Before moving on to the other properties of the Window.Event object, I want to stress that SrcElement is definitely the most important of these properties. This is because once you have the object that triggered the event, you are in the best position to react to it.

Simplifying Your Event-Handling Code

You will see a line like this at the beginning of many sophisticated event handlers in VBScript:

```
Set Source = Window.Event.SrcElement
```

The Set statement gives you a reference to the object that was the source of the event. Once you have such a reference, you can make the event-handling analysis code shorter and clearer. (And, as I mentioned before, it is very helpful when debugging to have a reference to the source of an event.)

Other properties of the Window.Event object

The following table gives short descriptions of the other important properties of the Window.Event object—with the exception of CancelButton, which I'll discuss in the section titled "Event Bubbling and Canceling Events" on page 290.

Property	Description
AltKey	Returns true if the Alt key was down when the event occurred
CtrlKey	Returns true if the Ctrl key was down when the event occurred
ShiftKey	Returns true if the Shift key was down when the event occurred.
Button	Tells you which mouse button (if any) was down when the event occurred, as follows: 0 = no button 1 = Left button 2 = Right button 4 = Middle button
ScreenX, ScreenY	Returns the location of the mouse pointer in relation to the whole screen
X, Y	Returns the location of the mouse pointer in relation to the usable area of the browser (the part of the browser that displays the page itself, excluding things like toolbars, scrollbars, and the title bar)
KeyCode	Returns the ASCII code of the key that was pressed

Let's start with an example that uses the KeyCode property. The onKeypress event triggers this example.

 OTE There are also onKeydown and onKeyup events, which give you finer control. As their names suggest, these events are triggered by the mere act of pressing or releasing a key. The onKeypress event, though, is triggered by the combination of pressing and releasing. It works best for processing user input of actual characters.

As an example of the onKeypress event, I will show you a script that produces a warning message if a user tries to press any key other than a digit (0-9). Setting the Event object's returnValue property to False causes the key press to be ignored. The main part of the code is shown here:

```
Sub TheText_OnKeyPress()
  Dim TheSource
  Set TheSource = Window.Event
  If TheSource.KeyCode < Asc(0) Or _
     TheSource.KeyCode > Asc(9) Then
     MsgBox "Bad key"
     TheSource.returnValue = False
  End If
End Sub
```

Here's the HTML (which can also be found in the file KeyPress.htm on the companion CD):

```
<HTML>
<HEAD>

  <TITLE>Handling the onKeypress event</Title>
  <SCRIPT LANGUAGE = VBScript>
  <!--

    Option Explicit

    Sub TheText_OnKeyPress()
      Dim TheSource

      Set TheSource = Window.Event
      If TheSource.KeyCode < Asc(0) Or _
         TheSource.KeyCode > Asc(9) Then
        MsgBox "Bad key"
        TheSource.returnValue = false
      End If
    End Sub

  -->
  </SCRIPT>

</HEAD>
<BODY>

<H1>
  This page will warn you if you enter anything else
  but a digit in the text box below.
</H1>
```

```
<BR><BR>

<INPUT ID = TheText TYPE=Text>

</BODY>
</HTML>
```

Using another example, suppose you want to turn off the message if a user held down the Shift key while entering the nondigit character. You would change the code to:

```
Sub TheText_OnKeyPress()
  Dim TheSource
  Set TheSource = Window.Event
  If TheSource.ShiftKey Then
    ' do nothing, shift key was down
  ElseIf  TheSource.KeyCode < Asc(0) Or _
          TheSource.KeyCode > Asc(9) Then
    MsgBox "Bad key"
    The Source.returnValue = false
  End If
End Sub
```

Mouse Events

To demonstrate the mouse events, I want to show you a program that reports in a text area the current position of the mouse pointer on the Web page. The secret to this is to write code—in the Document_OnMouseMove procedure—that uses the Window.Event.X and Window.Event.Y properties. Here's the main routine—notice how I reset the Value property of the TextArea object in the code:

```
Sub Document_OnMouseMove()
   Dim Temp, TheSource
   Set TheSource = Window.Event
   Temp = "The X position of the mouse is " & TheSource.X
   Temp = Temp & ". The Y position is " & TheSource.Y & "."
   TheText.Value = Temp
End Sub
```

Here's the complete HTML (which is also in the file MousePos.htm on the companion CD):

```
<HTML>
<HEAD>

  <TITLE>Handling the onMounsemove event</Title>
  <SCRIPT LANGUAGE = VBScript>
  <!--
```
(continued)

```
    Option Explicit

    Sub Document_OnMouseMove()
      Dim Temp, TheSource

      Set TheSource = Window.Event
      Temp = "The X position of the mouse is " & TheSource.X
      Temp = Temp & ". The Y position is " & TheSource.Y & "."
      TheText.Value = Temp
    End Sub

  -->
  </SCRIPT>

</HEAD>
<BODY>

<H1>
  This page will always tell you in the text box below where
  the mouse pointer is. Move the mouse around and see.
</H1>

<BR><BR>

<TextArea ID = TheText Rows=4 COL=40>
</TextArea>

</BODY>
</HTML>
```

Event Bubbling and Canceling Events

The last topic I want to cover is a technical complexity in the way Internet Explorer handles events. When you click in an object like a text box, the event is also reported as a click in all the objects containing the text box. For example, the Document object that contains the text box will also get a report of that click. Try the following script (included in the file EventBub.htm on the companion CD):

```
<HTML>
<HEAD>

  <TITLE>Event bubbling</Title>
  <SCRIPT LANGUAGE = VBScript>
  <!--

    Option Explicit
```

```
      Sub Document_OnClick()
        MsgBox "You clicked in the document."
      End Sub

      Sub TheText_OnClick()
        MsgBox "You clicked in the text box."
      End Sub

    -->
    </SCRIPT>

</HEAD>
<BODY>

<H1>
  This page will tell you where you clicked.
</H1>

<BR><BR>

<TextArea ID = TheText Rows=4 COL=40>
</TextArea>

</BODY>
</HTML>
```

If you open this page and then click inside the text area, you will see both messages. Now, in a way this makes sense; the text area is, after all, inside the document, so when you click in the text area you really are also clicking in the document at the same time. But what if you want to respond to a click only when it occurs *outside* the text area?

In general, the Internet Explorer event reporting mechanism sends events up the chain of containers. In the preceding example, the text area is contained in the Window object, so the event is also reported to the Window object. However, if you had opened the page in a frame inside another frame, the chain of containers would look like this:

Text Area -> Document -> First Frame -> Second Frame -> Window

The click event would then be reported to all five levels—or more if you had even more containers.

Of course, Internet Explorer is sensible about the order in which it triggers events; it starts from the lowest level and then moves, or *bubbles,* up the various levels for the object's containers until it gets to the Window object, which contains everything. Clearly, it would be nice to have a way of capturing the event so that it stops at a particular level in the chain that you determine. You can do this by setting the CancelBubble property of the Window.Event object to True in the container at which you want to stop the bubbling from continuing.

The following code is a version of the previous page that doesn't trigger the Document_OnClick event when you click in the text area but will report it if you click anywhere else in the document, because of this line of code in the TheText_OnClick event procedure:

```
Window.Event.CancelBubble = True
```

Here's the complete HTML (also included in the file Cancel.htm on the companion CD):

```
<HTML>
<HEAD>

  <TITLE>Canceling Event bubbling</Title>
  <SCRIPT LANGUAGE = VBScript>
  <!--

    Option Explicit

    Sub Document_OnClick()
      MsgBox "You clicked in the document."
    End Sub

    Sub TheText_OnClick()
      MsgBox "You clicked in the text box."
      Window.Event.CancelBubble = True
    End Sub

  -->
  </SCRIPT>

</HEAD>
<BODY>

<H1>
  This page will tell you where you clicked but will
    report the answer only once!
</H1>
```

```
<BR><BR>

<TextArea ID = TheText Rows=4 COL=40>
</TextArea>

</BODY>
</HTML>
```

Scriptlets

I want to end this chapter (and this book) by introducing you to one of the most exciting new technologies that is a result of Dynamic HTML. This is the ability to use HTML pages that you created using Dynamic HTML just like you use ActiveX controls—as reusable objects. *Scriptlets* are incredibly interesting and very useful because:

- They are small, so they don't take much time to download.

- They are as secure as Dynamic HTML itself.

- They will run in potentially even more places than ActiveX controls will run.

- They are a neat and elegant idea.

A Scriptlet is embedded in your Web page using the <OBJECT> tag, as in the following example code:

```
<OBJECT Width = 400 Height = 100 ID=AnimationScriptlet
  TYPE="text/x-scriptlet" DATA="ScriptIt.htm">
</OBJECT>
```

Notice that you don't need a CLASSID like you would for an ActiveX control—although you are still using the <OBJECT> tag. You simply include a special TYPE="text/x-scriptlet" attribute and specify the name of the HTML file that defines the Scriptlet using the DATA attribute.

Now—about the Scriptlet itself. Any dynamic HTML page will work fine as a base on which to build your Scriptlet. For example, the animation page you saw earlier is by itself a perfectly good Scriptlet. You probably want to do more, such as assign your Scriptlets custom properties and custom methods (and even custom events) that you can control. So first add a custom property to the Animation Dynamic HTML page (Animate.htm on the companion CD). The easiest kind of Scriptlet property (one for setting a simple value) can be built into a Scriptlet by declaring a variable in the Scriptlet file like this:

```
Public_AnimationSpeed = 50
```

 ARNING Don't use the Option Explicit statement in a Scriptlet, or your custom properties and methods won't work.

This becomes a Scriptlet property named AnimationSpeed. (The Public_ drops out for the name of the property when you access it via a script in another HTML page.) This property starts out with a default value of 50, but you can change it via VBScript using the Scriptlet's ID as in the following code:

```
IDOfScriptlet.AnimationSpeed = 100
```

Next I'll demonstrate a method named Start that actually tells the Scriptlet to start the animation. Methods you want your Scriptlet to expose to the world are simply script functions or subroutines defined in the Scriptlet file with the keyword "Public_" before them. The name that follows Public_ becomes the name of the method you call to use the Scriptlet; Public_ drops out from the name. For example, the following code shows how you can rewrite the Animation Dynamic HTML page to include a method named Start that you can use to control the Scriptlet:

```
Sub Public_Start()
  Dim TheTimer
  TheTimer = Window.SetInterval("Animate",
    Public_AnimationSpeed)
End Sub
```

Notice how I used the variable that is holding the AnimationSpeed property to set the timer interval in this Start method. Here I must use "Public_" before the property name because I'm accessing the custom property from within the Scriptlet.

That's it—you're done. You have created a Scriptlet that animates a single graphics image. Of course, the source for this file is hardwired into the Scriptlet—why not modify the Scriptlet to add a property that lets you set the filename? I'll leave that enhancement up to you; here's a version of the Scriptlet that lets you start the animation and also lets you set the speed of the animation (also in the file Scriptlt.htm on the companion CD):

```
<HTML>
<HEAD>
  <TITLE>Animation</Title>
  <SCRIPT LANGUAGE = VBScript>
  <!--
    Public_AnimationSpeed = 50

    Sub Public_Start()
      TheTimer = Window.SetInterval("Animate", _
        Public_AnimationSpeed)
    End Sub

    Sub Animate()
      If Picture.Style.PixelLeft >= _
        Document.Body.OffsetWidth Then
        Picture.Style.PixelLeft = 0
      Else
        Picture.Style.PixelLeft = Picture.Style.PixelLeft + 10
      End If
    End Sub
  -->
  </SCRIPT>

</HEAD>
<BODY>

  <IMG ID=Picture
    STYLE="position:relative;top:0;left:0"
    SRC="Agif1.jpg">

</BODY>
</HTML>
```

Notice that when you use a Scriptlet as part of another Web page, the title of the page doesn't show up—even if you have one.

Next I'll discuss the HTML pages that use the Animation Scriptlet. The crucial lines are the ones that set the animation speed and the ones that start the animation. For simplicity, I'll put the code for this in the Window_OnLoad procedure along with an InputBox that prompts the user for the animation speed. Then I'll write some code that checks whether the entry in the InputBox is a number and makes it positive if it is negative. If you don't enter a valid number, I simply use the default value for the speed that is already embedded in the Scriptlet (50). Here's what that code for this event procedure looks like:

```
Sub Window_Onload()
  Speed = InputBox("Please enter the animation speed.")
  If IsNumeric(Speed) Then
    Speed = Abs(Speed)
    AnimationScriptlet.AnimationSpeed = Speed
  End If
  AnimationScriptlet.Start
End Sub
```

In the actual HTML that uses this Scriptlet, I made one change in the Window_OnLoad event. I used Dynamic HTML yet one more time to make the Scriptlet as wide and as high as the page using the following lines:

```
AnimationScriptlet.Width = Document.Body.OffsetWidth
AnimationScriptlet.Height = Document.Body.OffsetHeight
```

Here is the full HTML page (also located in the file UseScrlt.htm on the companion CD):

```
<HTML>
<HEAD>

  <TITLE>Using Scriptlets</Title>
  <SCRIPT LANGUAGE = VBScript>
  <!--

    Option Explicit

    Dim Speed

    Sub Window_Onload()
      AnimationScriptlet.Width = Document.Body.OffsetWidth
      AnimationScriptlet.Height = Document.Body.OffsetHeight

      Speed = InputBox("Please enter the animation speed.")

      If IsNumeric(Speed) Then
        Speed = Abs(Speed)
        AnimationScriptlet.AnimationSpeed = Speed
      End If

      AnimationScriptlet.Start
```

```
    End Sub

    -->
    </SCRIPT>

</HEAD>
<BODY>

<OBJECT Height = 100 ID=AnimationScriptlet
   TYPE="text/x-scriptlet" DATA="Scriptlt.htm">
</OBJECT>

</BODY>
</HTML>
```

Obviously, there is a lot more to Scriptlets—in particular creating custom events or more sophisticated properties that are not so easily represented by public variables. Scriptlets are such a new technology that there's not a lot of information available about them yet. I hope these few pages whetted your appetite to go further. Your best source of information at the current time is probably the Microsoft Web site at http://www.microsoft.com/msdn/sdk/inetsdk/help/scriptlets/scrlt.htm.

 OTE   To visit this page, you will have to register for Microsoft's "Developer Network Online." This is a free service.

In any case, I suggest trying this URL first and then using the search feature of Microsoft's Web site to find more references to Scriptlets.

VBScript Versus Visual Basic

The following table lists features of VBScript (Microsoft Internet Explorer 4) that are not found in current versions of Microsoft Visual Basic (Visual Basic and Visual Basic for Applications).

Category	Feature/Keyboard
Formatting strings	FormatCurrency
	FormatDateTime
	FormatNumber
	FormatPercent
	MonthName
	WeekdayName
Intrinsic constants	vbGeneralDate
	vbLongDate
	vbLongTime
	vbShortDate
	vbLongDate
	vbTristateFalse
	vbTristateMixed
	vbTristateTrue
	vbTristateUseDefault
Rounding	Round

(continued)

continued

Category	Feature/Keyboard
Strings	Filter
	InstrRev
	Join
	Replace
	Split
	StrReverse
Script Engine Identification	ScriptEngine
	ScriptEngineBuildVersion
	ScriptEngineMajorVersion
	ScriptEngineMinorVersion

The following table lists features in Visual Basic and Visual Basic for Applications that are not found in VBScript (Internet Explorer 4).

Category	Omitted Feature/Keyword
Array Handling	Option Base
	Declaring arrays with lower bound <> 0
Collection	Add, Count, Item, Remove
	Access to collections using ! character (e.g., MyCollection!Foo)
Conditional Compilation	#Const
	#If ... Then ... #Else
Control Flow	DoEvents
	GoSub ... Return, GoTo
	On Error GoTo
	On ... GoSub, On ... GoTo
	Line numbers, Line labels
	With ... End With
Conversion	CVar, CVDate
	Str, Val
Data Types	All intrinsic data types except Variant
	Type ... End Type
Date/Time	Date statement, Time statement
	Timer

(continued)

continued

Category	Omitted Feature/Keyword
DDE	LinkExecute, LinkPoke, LinkRequest, LinkSend
Debugging	Debug.Print End, Stop
Declaration	Declare (for declaring DLLs) New Optional ParamArray Property Get, Property Let, Property Set Static
Error Handling	Erl Error On Error … Resume Resume, Resume Next
File Input/Output	All traditional Basic file I/O
Financial	All financial functions
Object Manipulation	TypeOf
Objects	Clipboard Collection
Operators	Like
Options	Def*type* Option Base Option Compare Option Private Module
Select Case	Anything except tests for equality
Strings	Fixed-length strings LSet, RSet Mid Statement StrConv

Reserved Words

Alphabetical Keyword List

+ (Addition Operator)

– (Negation, Subtraction Operator)

& (Concatenation Operator)

/ (Division Operator)

= (Equals Operator)

<> (Not Equals Operator)

< (Less Than Operator)

> (Greater Than Operator)

<= (Less Than Or Equal To Operator)

>= (Greater Than Or Equal To Operator)

^ (Exponentiation Operator)

\ (Integer Division Operator)

* (Multiplication Operator)

Abs Function

Add Method

AddFolders Method

And Operator

Array Function

Asc Function

AtEndOfLine Property

AtEndOfStream Property

Atn Function

Attributes Property

AvailableSpace Property

BuildPath Method

Call Statement

CBool Function

CByte Function

CCur Function

CDate Function

CDbl Function

Chr Function

CInt Function

Clear Method

CLng Function

Close Method

Column Property

CompareMode Property

Const Statement

Copy Method

CopyFile Method

CopyFolder Method

Cos Function

Count Property

CreateFolder Method

CreateObject Function

CreateTextFile Method

CSng Function

CStr Function

Date Function

DateAdd Function

DateCreated Property

DateDiff Function

DateLastAccessed Property

DateLastModified Property

DatePart Function

DateSerial Function

DateValue Function

Day Function

Delete Method

DeleteFile Method

DeleteFolder Method

Description Property

Dictionary Object

Dim Statement

Do ... Loop Statement

Drive Object

Drive Property

DriveExists Method

DriveLetter Property

Drives Collection

Drives Property

DriveType Property

Each (For Each ... Next Statement)

Else (If ... Then ... Else Statement)

Empty

Eqv Operator

Erase Statement

Err Object

Exists Method

Exit Statement

Exp Function

Explicit (Option Explicit Statement)

False

FileExists Method

File Object

Files Collection

Files Property

FileSystem Property

FileSystemObject Object

Filter Function

Fix Function

Folder Object

FolderExists Method

Folders Collection

For ... Next Statement

For Each ... Next Statement

FormatCurrency Function

FormatDateTime Function

FormatNumber Function

FormatPercent Function

FreeSpace Property

Function Statement

GetAbsolutePathName Method

GetBaseName Method

GetDrive Method

GetDriveName Method

GetExtensionName Method

GetFile Method

GetFileName Method

GetFolder Method

GetObject Function

GetParentFolderName Method

GetSpecialFolder Method

GetTempName Method

HelpContext Property

HelpFile Property

Hex Function

Hour Function

If … Then … Else Statement

Imp Operator

InputBox Function

InStr Function

InStrRev Function

Int Function

Is Operator

IsArray Function

IsDate Function

IsEmpty Function

IsNull Function

IsNumeric Function

IsObject Function

IsReady Property

IsRootFolder Property

Item Property

Items Method

Join Function

Key Property

Keys Method

LBound Function

LCase Function

Left Function

Len Function

Line Property

LoadPicture Function

Log Function

Loop (Do … Loop Statement)

LTrim Function

Mid Function

Minute Function

Mod Operator

Month Function

MonthName Function

Move Method

MoveFile Method

MoveFolder Method

MsgBox Function

Name Property

Next (For … Next Statement)

Not Operator

Nothing

Now Function

Null

Number Property

Oct Function

On Error Statement

OpenAsTextStream Method

OpenTextFile Method

Option Explicit Statement

Or Operator

ParentFolder Property

Path Property

Private Statement

Public Statement

Raise Method

Randomize Statement

Read Method

ReadAll Method

ReadLine Method

ReDim Statement

Rem Statement

Remove Method

RemoveAll Method

Replace Function

RGB Function

Right Function

Rnd Function

RootFolder Property

Round Function

RTrim Function

ScriptEngine Function

ScriptEngineBuildVersion Function

ScriptEngineMajorVersion Function

ScriptEngineMinorVersion Function

Second Function

Select Case Statement

SerialNumber Property

Set Statement

Sgn Function

ShareName Property

ShortName Property

ShortPath Property

Sin Function

Size Property

Skip Method

SkipLine Method

Source Property

Space Function

Split Function

Sqr Function

StrComp Function

String Function

StrReverse Function

Sub Statement

SubFolders Property

Tan Function

TextStream Object

Then (If ... Then ... Else Statement)

Time Function

TimeSerial Function

TimeValue Function

TotalSize Property

Trim Function

True

Type Property

TypeName Function

UBound Function

UCase Function

VarType Function

VolumeName Property

Weekday Function

WeekdayName Function

Wend (While ... Wend Statement)

While ... Wend Statement

Write Method

WriteBlankLines Method

WriteLine Method

Xor Operator

Year Function

FAQ (Frequently Asked Questions)

Here's my take on the most frequently asked questions about VBScript. You have already seen a lot of this information in this book; the purpose of this appendix is to collect it all in a convenient place for future reference.

 OTE   Microsoft's own FAQ that I used as a basis for this appendix can be found at *www.microsoft.com/vbscript*

1. **What is VBScript?**

   VBScript's official name is Microsoft Visual Basic Scripting Edition. It's a subset of the Visual Basic for Applications (VBA) language, although it has a few new features that haven't yet made their way into VBA. You can find it both in browsers and in third-party products. It can even be used to program Microsoft Windows 95 and Microsoft Windows NT by using the Microsoft Windows Scripting Host (currently available at *www.microsoft.com/management/ wsh.htm*). VBScript is designed to work with ActiveX controls or other components that use either ActiveX technologies or Dynamic HTML, including Scriptlets.

2. **How do I get VBScript?**

VBScript is part of Internet Explorer version 4 or later for the Windows platform. (This means millions of people have VBScript and don't even know it!)

3. **Where can I find further information about VBScript after I finish this book?**

You should make it a habit to visit the VBScript site on the World Wide Web at *www.microsoft.com/vbscript*. This site has a list of non-Microsoft sites that you might find useful. I find that *www.inquiry.com* has lots of useful information. Yahoo! (*www.yahoo.com*) is also a good place to search for information about VBScript sites. There is a set of newsgroups that Microsoft maintains on VBScript where you can go to ask (or answer) specific questions. (To find out how to access these newsgroups, click on the Resources link at *www.microsoft.com/ vbscript*. Although these newsgroups are maintained by Microsoft, most of the answers are posted by people from outside Microsoft.)

4. **How does VBScript compare to JavaScript and Java?**

JavaScript is a language designed by Netscape Communications for programming Web pages. Thus, VBScript and JavaScript are designed to do the same sorts of things. In my opinion, JavaScript has a much steeper learning curve than VBScript since JavaScript uses syntax similar to the cryptic C programming language. Java, on the other hand, is a powerful language from Sun Microsystems that has little, if anything, to do with JavaScript. Java is a general-purpose programming language that requires a lot of study to master, and of course, as a full-featured general-purpose programming language, it can do far more than activate Web pages.

5. **What platforms will support VBScript inside a browser?**

Eventually, every platform that has a version of Internet Explorer will probably support VBScript. Check out the VBScript Web site (*www.microsoft.com/vbscript*) for updates.

6. **Can VBScript be used outside a browser?**

   Yes. Although it requires some knowledge of sophisticated programming to add VBScript to an application, once that is done by the application's vendor, you will be able to use VBScript to control that product. Many companies have announced that they will be adding VBScript to their products and—most exciting of all—Microsoft has announced that you can use VBScript to control Windows 95 and Windows NT itself. (Currently, the program you need to do so can be downloaded from *www.microsoft.com/management/wsh.htm*.) Many other companies have announced that they will be adding VBScript to their products. (VBScript is freely licensable. Obviously, you must include the appropriate trademark and copyright information, but you can use and distribute VBScript free of any royalties.)

7. **You said VBScript can use objects that other people have already created, but what sort of objects?**

   VBScript itself also comes with a few objects, such as message boxes, that you can use. The other objects that you typically control via VBScript are:

   - ActiveX controls (See Chapter 2.)

   - Objects provided by Internet Explorer (See Chapter 8.)

   - Scriptlets (See Chapter 9.)

   - Java programs (or applets)

   (Although I didn't talk about controlling applets in this book, you control them using VBScript in the same way you control an ActiveX control or a Scriptlet—by giving them a name and invoking their methods or properties. See Chapters 2 and 9 for more on these techniques.)

8. **I tried the Document.Write method, but why isn't it working for me?**

   This problem is most commonly caused by your placing the code with the Document.Write statement in the wrong section of the HTML page. Code that will affect the page must be placed before the <BODY> section.

9. **How do I use a label to identify a text box? I never can get them to line up properly.**

This is best done with more advanced methods for positioning controls on a Web page (See Chapter 9.)

10. **I got an error message when I used *View Source*. I made the changes, went back to Internet Explorer, and nothing happened. I got the same error message. Why?**

You have to save the changed source file from Notepad and then re-fresh the Web page.

11. **I added a picture to an ActiveX control. Why is my <OBJECT> tag now filled with nonsense?**

If the "nonsense" follows the DATA attribute and looks something like this, it's not nonsense at all; it's a coded version of the image you are using:

```
DATA="DATA:application/x-
oleobject;BASE64,QDIF12nOzRGndwDdARQ8VwACEACgAAAA//
8AAOwJAABOAwAAsIFn2krCzxG1
hACqAKcdGmx0AAAwAwAAR01GOD1hUAAgANX/AP////9mM8zMzMxmM8wzM5mZ
mZkzM5kzAGZmZmYzADMzMzMAAAAAAP//zP//mf//Zv//M///AP/M///MzP/M
mf/MZv/MM//MAP+Z//+ZzP+Zmf+ZZv+ZM/+ZAP9m//9mzP9mmf9mZv9mAP8z
//8zzP8zmf8zZv8zM/8zAP8A//8AzP8Amf8AZv8AM/8AAMz//8z/zMz/mcz/
Zsz/M8z/AMzM/8zMM8zMzMZszMM8zMAMyZ/8yZzZsMM8zMAMyZ/8yZZzAAAAAAAAAAAAAAAACwAAAAA
KYaJ5sYoE9IzYonrweGZK4CA4YUdbRwHyCVZZKWdJ4a0wwkY7TEw11BJ9AQX
Yf0AdABnPVGJ11plvaX11/wEAQA7AAIMAPAAAAAAgMAAAAAAA==
">
```

12. **I am a little confused about the difference between variables inside procedures and functions and script-level variables. Can you explain this a little bit more?**

A variable inside a procedure or function has a limited life span. VBScript creates it while it is processing the code inside the procedure or function but then throws it away when the procedure or function finishes executing. You can't see the variable after the procedure ends, and the variable's value will have vanished. (That's why they are called *local* variables.)

A script-level variable, on the other hand, is one that is used (hope-fully after first using a Dim statement) *outside* any procedure or function. Such variables can be seen by all code in the page. (They are sometimes called *global variables* for this reason.) Because they can be seen everywhere, changes you make to script-level variables anywhere persist. This can be useful, but the cost is that bugs often result from using script-level variables inappropriately.

13. **I need to keep track of the number of times a function or a procedure is used (such as a button counter). How can I do this?**

    In VBScript, the only way to do this is to use a script-level variable.

14. **Can I have a local variable (a variable inside a procedure or function) with the same name as a script-level variable?**

    Yes, but this is a very bad practice. The local variable hides (*shadows*) the script-level variable so that you can't see the current value of the script-level variable.

15. **Can I include more than one library of useful functions and procedures in my script?**

    Yes, just give the location of each of them inside separate lines like this:

    ```
    <SCRIPT LANGUAGE=VBScript SRC=LocationAndNameOfFile1>
    </SCRIPT>
    <SCRIPT LANGUAGE=VBScript SRC=LocationAndNameOfFile2>
    </SCRIPT>
    ```

16. **I am a little confused about the structure of a VBScript page. There are helper functions I create, there are the procedures I write to handle events for the ActiveX controls, and so on. Can you give me a framework that I can use for placing these kinds of procedures appropriately in all my pages?**

    "All" is always tricky, but here's the framework I use:

    ```
    <HTML>
    <HEAD>
    <TITLE>The Title of the page>
    <SCRIPT>Tags with name of .vbs files with useful procedures
    and functions already written</SCRIPT>

    <SCRIPT>Tag that starts your script
    ```

    (continued)

```
Dim statements for script-level variables

Any statements for script-level variables
Any statements you want VBScript to execute independently of
any events

Event procedures and any helper functions and
subprocedures
</SCRIPT>End of your script

</HEAD>
<BODY>Start of the actual HTML
HTML for your Web page
<OBJECT>tags for the ActiveX controls
</BODY>
</HTML>
```

Index

About the Author

Gary Cornell received his Ph.D. from Brown University and teaches at the University of Connecticut. He has written or cowritten more than twenty books that teach various aspects of programming to both beginning and experienced programmers. Among other awards for his writing on programming, he won a "Reader's Choice" award from the *Visual Basic Programmer's Journal* in 1996 for his introductory book on Visual Basic, which is now in its fifth edition.

The manuscript for this book was prepared and submitted to Microsoft Press in electronic form. Text files were prepared using Microsoft Word 97 for Windows 95. Pages were composed by Microsoft Press using Adobe PageMaker 6.51 for Windows, with text in Melior and display type in Frutiger Condensed. Composed pages were delivered to the printer as electronic prepress files.

Cover Designer
Gregory Erickson

Cover Illustrator
Phil Howe

Interior Graphic Designer
Kim Eggleston

Interior Graphic Artist
Michael Victor

Principal Compositor
Paul Vautier

Principal Proofreader/Copy Editor
Teri Kieffer

Indexer
Shane-Armstrong Information Systems

Register Today!

Return this
Learn Microsoft®Visual Basic®
Scripting Edition Now
registration card for
a Microsoft Press® catalog

U.S. and Canada addresses only. Fill in information below and mail postage-free. Please mail only the bottom half of this page.

1-57231-347-1   *LEARN MICROSOFT® VISUAL BASIC®*   *Owner Registration Card*
                      SCRIPTING EDITION NOW

NAME

INSTITUTION OR COMPANY NAME

ADDRESS

CITY   STATE   ZIP

Microsoft *Press*
Quality Computer Books

**For a free catalog of
Microsoft Press® products, call
1-800-MSPRESS**